THE HIDDEN INNS OF
WALES

By Peter Long

© Travel Publishing Ltd.

Regional Hidden Places

Cambs & Lincolnshire
Chilterns
Cornwall
Derbyshire
Devon
Dorset, Hants & Isle of Wight
East Anglia
Gloucs, Wiltshire & Somerset
Heart of England
Hereford, Worcs & Shropshire
Highlands & Islands
Kent
Lake District & Cumbria
Lancashire & Cheshire
Lincolnshire & Nottinghamshire
Northumberland & Durham
Sussex
Thames Valley
Yorkshire

National Hidden Places

England
Ireland
Scotland
Wales

Hidden Inns

East Anglia
Heart of England
Lancashire & Cheshire
North of England
South
South East
South and Central Scotland
Wales
Welsh Borders
West Country
Yorkshire
Wales

Country Living
Rural Guides

East Anglia
Heart of England
Ireland
North East of England
North West of England
Scotland
South
South East
Wales
West Country

Published by: Travel Publishing Ltd, 7a Apollo House, Calleva Park, Aldermaston, Berks, RG7 8TN

ISBN 1·902·00790·5

© Travel Publishing Ltd

First published 2000, second edition 2003,

Printing by: Ashford Colour Press, Gosport

Maps by: © Maps in Minutes ™ (2003)
© Crown Copyright, Ordnance Survey 2003

Editor: Peter Long

Cover Design: Lines & Words, Aldermaston

Cover Photograph: The Castle Inn, Pengenffordd,
nr Talgarth, Powys

Text Photographs: © www.britainonview.com

FOREWORD

The *Hidden Inns* series originates from the enthusiastic suggestions of readers of the popular *Hidden Places* guides. They want to be directed to traditional inns "off the beaten track" with atmosphere and character which are so much a part of our British heritage. But they also want information on the many places of interest and activities to be found in the vicinity of the inn.

The inns or pubs reviewed in the *Hidden Inns* may have been coaching inns but have invariably been a part of the history of the village or town in which they are located. All the inns included in this guide serve food and drink and some offer the visitor overnight accommodation. A full page is devoted to each inn which contains a coloured photograph, full name, address and telephone number, directions on how to get there, a full description of the inn and its facilities and a wide range of useful information such as opening hours, food served, accommodation provided, credit cards taken and details of entertainment. *Hidden Inns* guides however are not simply pub guides. They provide the reader with helpful information on the many places of interest to visit and activities to pursue in the area in which the inn is based. This ensures that your visit to the area will not only allow you to enjoy the atmosphere of the inn but also to take in the beautiful countryside which surrounds it.

The *Hidden Inns* guides have been expertly designed for ease of use and this guide is the first to be printed in full colour. *The Hidden Inns of Wales* is divided into five chapters each of which is laid out in the same way. To identify your preferred geographical region refer to the contents page overleaf. To find a pub or inn and details of facilities they offer simply use the index to the rear of the guide or locator map at the beginning of each chapter which refers you, via a page number reference, to a full page dedicated to the specific establishment. To find a place of interest, again use the index to the rear of the book or list found at the beginning of each chapter which will guide you to a descriptive summary of the area that includes details of each place of interest.

We do hope that you will get plenty of enjoyment from visiting the inns, pubs and places of interest contained in this guide. We are always interested in what our readers think of the inns or places covered (or not covered) in our guides so please do not hesitate to write to us. This is a vital way of helping us ensure that we maintain a high standard of entry and that we are providing the right sort of information for our readers. Finally if you are planning to visit any other corner of the British Isles we would like to refer you to the list of Travel Publishing guides to be found at the rear of the book.

Travel Publishing

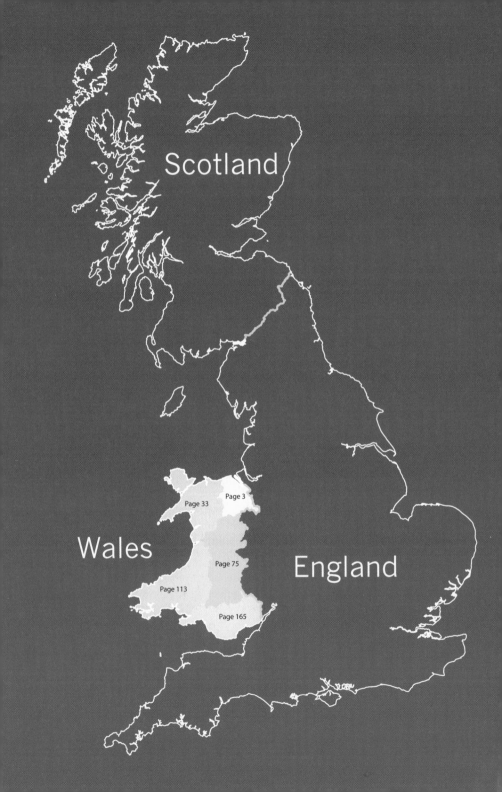

CONTENTS

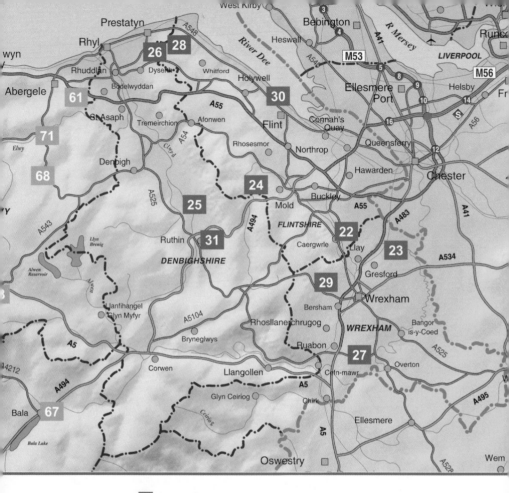

Please note all cross references refer to page numbers

NORTH WALES BORDERLANDS

This area of Wales, the North Wales Borderlands, can easily be overlooked by visitors to the country as they speed westwards, but it is mistake not to stop and explore the towns, villages and countryside, as they are rich in history and scenic beauty. Each of the different areas has its own special character and scenery: the Clwydian Hills, a 22-mile designated Area of Outstanding Natural Beauty; the Dee estuary; the broad, gentle sweep of the Vale of Clwyd with historic towns like Ruthin, St Asaph and Denbigh; Wrexham, the largest town in North Wales, and its surrounds; The Maelor, where the Cheshire Plains transform into the Welsh Hills; Chirk and the beautiful Ceiriog Valley. The Romans certainly forayed into the area from their major town of Chester and there is also evidence of Celtic settlements.

However, it was during the 13th century that Edward I, after his successful campaign against the Welsh, set about building his ambitious Iron Ring of huge fortresses along the Dee estuary and the North Wales coast. Each was built a day's march from the last and the first stronghold was begun at Flint in 1277. Though the great fortresses are now in ruins, the remains of this massive project - the largest seen in Europe - are still very much in evidence today. The most impressive survivor of these marcher fortresses is Chirk Castle, a rectangular building with a massive drum tower at each corner. Visitors can see the dismal dungeons and the elegant state rooms, which contain some fine Adam-style

PLACES OF INTEREST

Afonwen 7	Hawarden 11
Bangor-is-y	Holywell 11
·coed 7	Llanfihangel Glyn
Bersham 7	Myfyr 12
Bodelwyddan 7	Llangollen 12
Bryneglwys 7	Mold 14
Caergwrle 8	Overton 16
Cefn-mawr 8	Rhosesmor 16
Chirk 8	Rhuddlan 16
Corwen 9	Ruthin 17
Denbigh 9	St Asaph 18
Dyserth 10	Tremeirchion 20
Flint 10	Whitford 20
Glyn Ceiriog 10	Wrexham 20
Gresford 11	

furniture, tapestries and portraits, and the grounds are also well worth a visit. The National Trust maintains this imposing csatle and is responsible for one of the most fascinating houses in Briatin. This is Erdigg, a late-17th century mansion with stunning stats rooms, restored outbuildings, a large walled garden and a country park. The land around the Dee estuary is home to a great number of waders and wildfowl which feed on the mudflats left by the retreating tides.

Between the estuary and the Clwydian Range lie small, compact villages as well as the market towns of Holywell and Mold. Holywell is home to one of the so-called Seven Wonders of Wales (see below). This is St Winifride's Well, which has been a place of pilgrimage since the 7th century and was so famous that it was known as the Lourdes of Wales. The well is enclosed by a chapel that was built by Margaret Beaufort, the mother of Henry VII. Mold, the capital of Flintshire, has a museum where a room is dedicated to the memory of Daniel Owen, who wrote in Welsh about ordinary life and who has been called the Welsh Dickens. The painter Richard Wilson spent his childhood and his last years in Mold and is buried in the parish

Vale Crucis Abbey

churchyard. The Clwydian Range, a grassy line of hills above the Vale of Clwyd, offers fabulous views and exhilarating walks; it is one of the five designated Areas of Outstanding Natural Beauty in Wales. Further south lie Llangollen and the Dee Valley. Llangollen is a delightful old town in a picturesque riverside setting which is not only a charming place to visit but is also the home of the annual International Music Eisteddfod (not the same as the National Eisteddfod). An eisteddfod was, originally, a meeting of bards where prizes were awarded for poetry reading

Alwen Reservoir, Clwyd

and singing and, while local events still draw people from all over the country, the event at Llangollen has a true international flavour with such eminent figures as Luciano Pavarotti having graced its stage. Though this northern gateway to the country is not a particularly large area, it boasts all but one of the Seven Wonders of Wales, wonders which while not quite as spectacular as the more familiar Seven Wonders of the World are nonetheless all interesting in their own right and well worth a visit. They are listed in the famous 19th century rhyme:

Pistyll Rhaeadr and Wrexham Steeple,
Snowdon's Mountain without its people,
Overton Yew Trees, St Winefride's Well,
Llangollen Bridge and Gresford Bells.

Llangollen Canal

The Borderlands offer an impressive variety of attractions, from castles and country houses to churches and museums, country parks and farm parks, lakes and canals, and leisure pursuits from walking, cycling and riding to birdwatching, superb fishing for salmon and trout on the Rivers Dee and Clwyd, sea fishing in the Dee estuary and trout or coarse fishing at numerous lake fisheries. And in the region there are more than 20 golf courses. The course at Chirk, established as recently as 1991, has the distinction of boasting the longest hole in Britain, at 664 yards. The club at Mold offers picturesque vistas of the Clwydian countryside, and Holywell Colf Club is also located in one of the most pleasant areas of the region. Festivals and other special events are staged throughout the year, and visitors to the area are welcome to attend many rehearsals as well as performances by the renowned Welsh choirs - a unique and moving occasion that will long be remembered as part of the Welsh experience.

AFONWEN

A small village in the Clwydian Range, Afonwen is home to one of the largest craft and antique centres in north Wales. **Afonwen Craft and Antique Centre** not only has a whole host of crafts, accessories and gifts for sale, including furniture, crystal, china and silver, but exhibitions and demonstrations are held here on a regular basis.

BANGOR-IS-Y-COED

Bangor-is-y-coed, also known as Bangor-on-Dee, is in the area known as the Maelor, where the Cheshire Plains turn into the Welsh Hills. The village is well known to race-goers as it is home to a picturesque **Racecourse**, situated on the banks of the River Dee, that holds meetings during the National Hunt season. The village itself has a charming 17th century bridge said to have been built by Inigo Jones. There are also claims that the Romans settled here but it is more likely that they were in Holt as, at the pottery works, there is firmer evidence of their presence in the area.

BERSHAM

Lying in part of the **Clywedog Valley and Trail** that skirts around the south and west of Wrexham and includes several places of industrial interest, this village was established around 1670 and was the home of the Davis brothers. The fine workmanship of these two famous iron masters can be seen in the beautiful gates at Chirk Park and at St Giles'

Church in Wrexham. The master and owner of **Bersham Ironworks** from 1762, John 'Iron Mad' Wilkinson, was himself famous for the cannons he bored for use in the American War of Independence and for the cylinders he produced at the ironworks for James Watt's steam engines.

BODELWYDDAN

The village church, known as the **Marble Church**, was built in 1856-60 by Lady Willoughby de Broke as a memorial to her husband. The landmark white spire is of local limestone while, inside, there is an arcade of marble, with 14 different types of marble used.

Opposite the eye-catching church stands **Bodelwyddan Castle**, a Victorian country house and estate which occupies the site of a 15th century house. The castle is the Welsh home of the National Portrait Gallery, and as well as the wonderful collection of Victorian portraits on display, visitors can also see beautiful furniture on loan from the Victorian and Albert Museum and sculptures from the Royal Academy.

BRYNEGLWYS

Standing on the slopes of Llantysilio Mountain, the large 15th century Church of St Tysilio, in the heart of the village has a connection with the family who helped to found Yale University in the United States. Close to the village lies **Plas-Yn-Yale**, the former home of the Yale family and the birthplace of Elihu Yale's father. Elihu himself was born in 1647 in Boston, Massachusetts, and went on to become a governor of India before coming to England. Known for his philanthropy, Elihu was approached by an American College who, after receiving generous help, named their new college in Newhaven after him.

In 1745, 24 years after his death, the whole establishment was named Yale University. Elihu Yale is buried in the Church of St Giles in Wrexham.

CAERGWRLE

Once occupied by the Romans as an outpost station for nearby Chester, **Caergwrle Castle**, which stands on a high ridge, probably started life as a Bronze Age hill fort. It was Dafydd, brother of Llewelyn the Last, who constructed the fortification more or less in its present form and it was from here, in 1282, that Dafydd launched his last, and fatal, Welsh attack on English Edward I.

CEFN-MAWR

Towering some 126 feet above the River Dee and carrying the Llangollen branch of the Shropshire Union Canal, **Pontcysyllte Aqueduct** is a magnificent construction some 1,007 feet in length. Built in 1805 by

Thomas Telford, this cast iron trough supported by 18 stone pillars was much scorned by people at the time although today it is greatly admired and is still used regularly by pleasure boats.

CHIRK

This attractive border town's origins lie in the 11th century castle of which, unfortunately, little remains except a small motte close to the town's 15th century church. Today, Chirk is perhaps better known for the National Trust owned **Chirk Castle** which lies a mile outside the town and is the most impressive survivor of the marcher fortresses built by Edward I. Just south of the town are two splendid constructions that span the Ceiriog valley: the first, an aqueduct built in 1801 by Thomas Telford, carries the Llangollen branch of the Shropshire Union Canal, while the other one is a viaduct built in 1848 to carry the new Chester to Shrewsbury railway line over the River Ceiriog.

Shropshire Union Canal

CORWEN

This market town, in a pleasant setting between the Berwyn Mountains and the River Dee, has for many years been known as the Crossroads of North Wales and was once the headquarters of Owain Glyndwr, who gathered his forces here before entering into his various campaigns. The 13th century church at Corwen has an incised dagger in a lintel of the doorway that is known as **Glyndwr's Sword**. The mark was reputedly made by Glyndwr when he threw a dagger from the hill above the church in a fit of rage against the townsfolk. However, the dagger mark actually dates from the 7th to 9th centuries and there is another such mark on a 12th century cross outside the southwest corner of the church. It was in the Owain Glyndwr Hotel in 1789 in Corwen that a local man, Thomas Jones, organised a bardic festival that laid the foundations for the modern eisteddfod.

DENBIGH

Recorded as a small border town in the 11th century, Denbigh grew to become a residence for Welsh princes and a leading centre of Welsh power. Today, it still retains a charm that is enhanced by buildings dating from the 16th century onwards; most of the centre is now a conservation area. The old town is concentrated around the castle that was built on the site of a Roman settlement and commands good views over the Vale of Clwyd.

Denbigh Castle was one of the biggest and most imposing fortifications in Wales and its ruins are still an impressive sight as they crown the top of a steep hill above the town. A large stretch of the **Town Walls** still exists and can be walked today, providing a splendid historic view of the town, particularly the section that includes Countess Tower and the Goblin Tower.

Gradually Denbigh developed around its market place and town square, and by the time of the first Elizabethan era it was one of the largest and richest towns in North Wales, and also a centre of culture. Of particular interest is **Back Row**, where part of Denbigh's original medieval street pattern still exists and where several 15th century buildings, including the Golden Lion Inn, still give a flavour of those times.

One of the few towns in Wales approved of by Dr Samuel Johnson during his travels through the Principality, Denbigh was the birthplace of Henry Morton Stanley, the man who found the explorer David Livingstone and addressed him with the immortal words "Dr Livingstone, I presume".

Three miles south of Denbigh, on the A525 Ruthin road, stands the Church of St Dyfnog, whose chief treasure is a marvellous "Tree of Jesse" window (the Tree of Jesse, most often seen depicted in church windows, details the family tree of Christ down from Jesse, the father of King David). This superb window, made in 1553, was saved from destruction during the Civil War by being buried in a dug-out chest, which can also be seen in the church.

DYSERTH

Lying in the foothills of the Clwydian Range, below Craig Fawr's slopes, this village, in the scenic Vale of Clwyd, boasts a 60 foot waterfall as well as a charming parish church which dates from the 13th century.

Just to the west of the village lies **Bodrhyddan Hall**, the 17th century manor house of the Conwy family, who have had their home here since the early 15th century. The house contains much to interest the visitor, including panels that came from the chapel of a ship of the Spanish Armada that foundered off the coast of Anglesey; Hepplewhite chairs; suits of armour and ancient weapons, and a family portrait by Sir Joshua Reynolds. The **Gardens** here too are of interest, the main feature being a box-edged Victorian parterre designed by William Andrews Nesfield, father of the famous William Eden Nesfield, who remodelled the house in 1875.

FLINT

A small town that was once the port for Chester, Flint can boast two historical firsts: it was the first associated borough in Wales to receive a charter (in 1284) and it was also the site of the first of Edward I's Iron Ring fortresses. Dotted along the North Wales coast, a day's march apart, Edward I's ring of massive fortresses represented Europe's most ambitious and concentrated medieval building project. Started after the Treaty of Aberconwy in 1277 and completed in 1284 by James of St George, **Flint Castle**, now in ruins, stands on a low rock overlooking the coastal marshes of the Dee estuary towards the Wirral peninsula. Originally surrounded by a water-filled moat, the remains of the Great Tower, or Donjon, are an impressive sight. Set apart from the main part of the castle, this tower, which is unique among British castles, was intended as a last retreat and, to this end, it was fully self-sufficient, even having its own well.

GLYN CEIRIOG

This former slate mining village is home to the **Chwarel Wynne Mine Museum** which, as well as telling the story of the slate industry that used to support the village, gives visitors a guided tour of the caverns. There is also a nature trail around the surrounding countryside. A narrow gauge tramway, the Glyn Valley Railway, once linked the Shropshire Union Canal at Gledrid with the quarries and mines at Glyn Ceiriog. Opened in 1873 and originally horse-drawn, it was later converted to steam and diverted through Chirk Castle estate to meet the Great Western Railway at Chirk station. It carried slate, silica, chinastone and dolerite downstream and returned with coal, flour and other commodities. It also carried passengers, and though it closed in 1935, the bed of the tramway can still be seen here and there, and the Glyn Valley Tramway

Group was founded in 1974 to conserve evidence of the GVR. The Group has little museums in the Glyn Valley Hotel at Glyn Ceiriog and the former waiting room at Pontafog station, and is currently seeking funds to establish a GVR Museum and Visitor Centre in the old locomotive shed and yard at Glyn Ceiriog.

The village lies in the secluded Vale of Ceiriog and, just to the west, is the beautiful **Ceiriog Forest** which offers surprisingly pastoral views and vistas along with forest walks and trails.

GRESFORD

This former coal mining town was the site of a mine explosion in 1934 that killed 266 men. The colliery closed in 1973 but the wheel remains in memory of those who lost their lives in this terrible disaster. The town's **All Saints' Church** is one of the finest in Wales and it is also home to the famous **Gresford Bells**, one of the Seven Wonders of Wales, which are still rung every Tuesday evening and on Sundays.

HAWARDEN

Mentioned in the Domesday Book, this small village close to the English border has two castles: one a ruin dating from the 13th century and another that was once the home of the Victorian Prime Minister, William Gladstone.
Hawarden Castle, Gladstone's home for some 60 years after his marriage to the daughter of Sir Stephen Glynne in 1839, was started in 1750 and enlarged and castellated by Sir Stephen in 1809. The

remains, chiefly the circular keep and the hall, of the older castle still stand in **Castle Park**.

The parish church, as well as having stained glass windows by Burne-Jones, also houses the **Gladstone Memorial Chapel**, where marble effigies of the distinguished statesman and his wife, who are buried in Westminster Abbey, can be seen. The village's connections with Gladstone continue to this day as the former Prime Minister donated his collection of books to the famous **St Deinol's Residential Library**, which lies adjacent to the church.

HOLYWELL

In the town lies one of the Seven Wonders of Wales, **St Winefride's Well**, which was once a place of pilgrimage and, at one time, was referred to as 'The Lourdes of Wales'. According to tradition, Winefride, the niece of St Beuno, was beheaded by Prince Caradoc after refusing his advances. It is claimed that a spring gushed from the place where her head fell and that she returned to life after her head had been replaced by her uncle. Thought to have healing qualities, the well has been visited by pilgrims since the 7th century and still is, particularly on St Winefride's Day, the nearest Saturday to 22 June. **St Winefride's Chapel** was built by Margaret Beaufort (the mother of Henry VII) in around 1500 to enclose three sides of the well. Linking Holywell with the ruins of Basingwerk Abbey is the **Greenfield Valley Heritage Park**, a 70-

acre area of pleasant woodland and lakeside walks with a wealth of monuments and agricultural and industrial history. The trail through the park leads down towards the coast and to the ruins of **Basingwerk Abbey**, built by Cistercian monks in 1132. The abbey survived until the Dissolution of the Monasteries in the 16th century by Henry VIII. In a tranquil setting that contrasts with the busy roads not far away, this magnificent ruin contains an arch that is a fine example of Norman ecclesiastical architecture.

LLANFIHANGEL GLYN MYFYR

This sleepy village lies in the fertile vale through which the River Alwen runs. Just to the north lies the **Clocaenog Forest**, Wales' second largest commercial plantation, which covers much of the southern moorland between the vales of Clwyd and Conwy. On the edge of the forest lies **Llyn Brenig**, a massive man-made reservoir that was completed in 1976 to accompany the smaller **Llyn**

Alwen, which dates from the early 1900s. Close to the dam, and reached along the B4501, is a Visitor Centre which explains the local history and ecology of this tranquil Welsh valley as well as acting as a starting point for lakeside walks. By the lake, depending on the time of year, butterflies such as Orange Tip and Tortoiseshell can be seen and, along with the water sports on the lake, fishing is also available.

LLANGOLLEN

This busy and picturesque town draws visitors from all over the world who come here not only to enjoy Llangollen's beautiful riverside position but also for the annual **International Musical Eisteddfod** which has been held here since 1947. For six days every July musicians, choirs, folk singers and dancers from all over the world, and many performing in their national costumes, converge on the town to take part in this wonderful cultural event that is centred around the **Royal International Pavilion**. This event should not be confused with the **National Eisteddfod**, the annual Welsh language cultural festival whose venue alternates between the north and south of the country. The first recorded eisteddfod was held at Cardigan Castle in 1176, and the modern eisteddfod began as a competition

Llangollen Eisteddfod

between bards at the Owain Glyndwr hotel in Corwen in 1789; it became a truly national event at Llangollen in 1858, when thousands of people came to Llangollen from all over the country. Throughout the rest of the year there are many other attractions in Llangollen to keep visitors satisfied. In particular, close to the river, is the **Lower Dee Exhibition Centre**, which incorporates three attractions in one place. The **Doctor Who Exhibition** is the world's largest collection of memorabilia dedicated to the cult television programme, while the **International Model Railway World** is the world's largest permanent exhibition of model railways. Finally, visitors young and old will find the **Dapol Toy Factory**, where many of the models for the other two exhibitions on the site are made, a fascinating place to wander around.

Plas Newydd

In the 19th century, Llangollen was famous as the home for 50 years of the Ladies of Llangollen: Lady Eleanor Butler and Miss Sarah Ponsonby. These two eccentric Irish women ran away from their families in Ireland and set up home together in 1780 in a cottage above the town. As well as devoting their lives to "friendship, celibacy and the knitting of blue stockings", the ladies also undertook a great deal of improvements and alterations that turned a small, unpretentious cottage into the splendid house - **Plas Newydd** - that is seen today. The marvellous 'gothicisation' of the house was completed in 1814 and some of the elaborate oak panels and the glorious stained glass windows were donated to the couple by their famous visitors, who included Sir Walter Scott, William Wordsworth, the Duke of Gloucester and the Duke of Wellington. The ladies were both buried in the churchyard of St Collen, sharing a grave with their friend and housekeeper Mary Caryll.

In the town centre, spanning the River Dee, is an eye-catching **Bridge** dating from 1347 which was originally constructed by John Trevor, who went on to become the Bishop of St Asaph. One of the Seven Wonders of Wales, this four-arched bridge has been rebuilt and widened in places over the years and is still used by today's traffic. On the northside of the river is **Llangollen Station**, home of the Llangollen Railway Society. Since taking over the disused line in 1975, the Society has restored the railway track and journeys along the banks of the River Dee can be taken on this delightful steam railway. The station houses a museum with a collection of engines, coaches and rail memorabilia. Also along the banks of the Dee lies **Llangollen Wharf**, from where pleasure cruises have started since 1884. Some trips are horse-drawn, while others cross the Pontcysylte aqueduct in the narrow boat *Thomas Telford*.

On the banks of another waterway, the **Llangollen Canal**, a branch of the Shropshire Union Canal, is the **Llangollen Canal Exhibition Centre** and just a short walk further on are the dramatic remains of the Iron Age fort **Castell Dinas Bran**. The main route north out of Llangollen passes the impressive ruins of **Valle Crucis Abbey**. A little further northwards along this road lies the spectacular **Horseshoe Pass** which affords remarkable views of the surrounding countryside. From the top of the pass can be seen the Vale of Clwyd and the ridge of Eglwyseg Rocks where Offa's Dyke path runs.

MOLD

The small county town of Flintshire, Mold is proud to claim the novelist and local tailor Daniel Owen as one of its own. Writing only in Welsh, it was Owen's honest accounts of ordinary life which were to not only make him one of the greatest 19th century novelists but also gained him the title the 'Welsh Dickens'. His statue stands outside the town library which is also the home of Mold's **Museum**, where a room is dedicated to Owen's memory. Another son of Mold was Richard Wilson, an 18th century landscape painter who spent his childhood in the town and who, after studying abroad, returned to his native Wales to concentrate on the dramatic scenes of mountainous Welsh countryside which became his trademark. Wilson's memorial can be found near the north entrance to the parish church.

Dating from the 15th century and built to celebrate Henry VII's victory at Bosworth, **St Mary's Church** has some interesting stained glass windows as well as some fine architectural ornamentation. A light and airy building, this church was constructed on the site of an earlier church whose original oak roof, carved with Tudor roses, has been retained in part. The church stands at the foot of **Bailey Hill**,

Castell Dinas Bran

the site of a Norman motte and bailey fortification which was built at this strategic point overlooking the River Alyn by Robert de Montalt. First captured by the Welsh in 1157 and then again by Llywelyn the Great in 1199, ownership of the castle passed through many hands and today, not surprisingly, little remains of the fortress; its site is now marked by a bowling green. The town owes its name to de Montalt, who gave Mold its English name which, like the Welsh (Yr Wyddgrug), means 'The Mound'.

On the outskirts of Mold lies **Clwyd Theatre Cymru**, which offers a wide range of entertainment for the culturally hungry including theatre, music and frequent exhibitions of art, sculpture and photography. It has a bar, coffee shop, bookshop, free covered parking and disabled access. The composer Felix Mendelssohn was said to have been inspired by the town's surroundings when writing his opus *Rivulet* and the nearby limestone crags provide panoramic views over the surrounding countryside.

One such scenic area lies four miles from Mold on the A494 - **Loggerheads Country Park**, which is situated on the edge of the Clwydian Range. Classified as an Area of Outstanding Natural Beauty, this large park is an ideal environment for all the family, especially younger members, as there are various trails which are each about one and a half miles long. The trails all start near the late-18th century mill building that used water from the River Alyn to drive a water wheel and two sets of stones to grind corn from the local farms.

Around 200 years ago, Loggerheads was part of the lead mining industry, which was founded in this area of ore-bearing limestone, and many relics of those days remain and can still be seen within the quiet woodland. There is a fine selection of local arts, crafts and souvenirs on display in the Craft Shop at the **Loggerheads Countryside Centre**, where there is also a tea room.

The smooth browned slopes of the **Clwydian Range** ascend from the broad and fertile planes of the Vale of Clwyd and **Moel Famau** (The Mother of Mountains), which at 1,820 feet is the range's highest peak. It is well worth the climb to the summit as not only are there the remains of a **Jubliee Tower**,

Moel Famau, Clwydian Range

started in 1810 to commemorate George III's Golden Jubilee (blown down in a storm in 1852) but the panoramic views are breathtaking. Westwards lies the Vale of Clwyd with the river stretching down to the Irish Sea and, to the east, the land rolls gently down to the Dee estuary.

OVERTON

This substantial border village is home to another of the Seven Wonders of Wales - the **Overton Yew Trees**, 21 trees that stand in the churchyard of the village Church of St Mary. Dating from medieval times, these tall, dark and handsome trees have a preservation order placed upon them. Within the church itself there are some interesting artefacts from the 13th century.

RHOSESMOR

Moel Y Gaer, near this small village, was considered to be a fine example of an Iron Age hill fort until archaeological digs unearthed evidence that suggested this site had been inhabited from as far back as 3500 BC.

To the west of the Rhosesmor lie the remains of a short section of **Wat's Dyke**, a much shorter dyke than Offa's which is thought to have been built by the Mercian King Aethelbald in the 8th century. Just under 40 miles long, the dyke ran southwards from the Dee estuary to Oswestry.

RHUDDLAN

The site of an early Norman stronghold known as **Twt Hill**, which today is marked by a prominent earthen mound, Rhuddlan is now overshadowed by its impressive castle ruins. One of the Iron Ring of fortresses built by Edward I, **Rhuddlan Castle**, as one of the most massive and impenetrable of his defences, was the king's headquarters during his campaign and it was from here that Edward issued the Statute of Rhuddlan (in March 1284) that united the Principality of Wales with the Kingdom of England. He also gave the town a Royal Charter when his sovereignty was confirmed. The statute, which lasted until the Act of Union in 1536, was enacted on the site now occupied by Parliament House and there is a commemoration tablet on the wall which is said to be from the original building. Although the castle, like many, was partially destroyed during the Civil War, the town is still sometimes

Rhuddlan Castle

referred to as the 'Cradle of Wales'.

While the castle in its heyday was a magnificent example of medieval defensive building, the most impressive engineering feat in the area was the canalisation of the River Clwyd to give the castle access, by ship, to the sea some three miles away. The remains of the dockgate, **Gillot's Tower**, can still be seen - this was built by James of St George, who was also responsible for the interesting concentric plan of the castle which allowed archers, stationed on both the inner and outer walls, to fire their arrows simultaneously.

RUTHIN

This old market town lies in the Vale of Clwyd, more or less surrounded by a ring of hills, with a layout that appears to have changed little from medieval days. In fact, a description of Ruthin made in Elizabethan times, where it is described as "the grandest market town in all the Vale, full of inhabitants and well replenished with buildings", is as true today as it was then. **St Peter's Square** is a good place from which to view the town; it was here, in 1679, that the town's last execution took place, when a Catholic priest was hung, drawn and quartered. Situated behind a magnificent set of 18th century wrought iron gates stands the town's splendid **St Peter's Church**. Founded in the late 13th century as a collegiate church,

its notable features include an early 16th century oak roof that consists of 408 carved panels while behind the church there are some beautiful buildings in the collegiate close - 14th century cloisters, the Old Grammar School of 1284 and 16th century almshouses - that are reminiscent of Anthony Trollope's *Barchester Towers*.

St Peter's Square itself is edged with many lovely buildings, including the particularly eye-catching 15th century Myddleton Arms with its unusual Dutch style of architecture and its seven dormer windows that have been dubbed the 'eyes of Ruthin'. At one time there were around 60 inns and pubs in Ruthin - one for every 10 men in the town - and nine of these were to be found around the square. On the south side of St Peter's Square stands the impressive wattle and daub **Old Courthouse**, which dates from 1401 and was a temporary resting place for prisoners, who were kept in the cells below the magnificent beamed court room. On Clwyd Street, a major new attraction opened in May 2002. This is

Ruthin

Ruthin Gaol, through whose gates thousands of prisoners - men, women and children, the guilty and the innocent - passed between 1654 and 1916. Visitors (all volunteers these days!) can see how prisoners lived their daily lives: what they ate, how they worked, the punishments they suffered. The cells, including the punishment, "dark" and condemned cell, can be explored, and there are hands-on activities for children. In Castle Street can be found one the oldest town houses in North Wales. **Nant Clwyd House** is a fine example of Elizabethan architecture although the present 16th century building shows traces of an earlier house. During the reign of Elizabeth I it was the home of Dr Gabriel Goodman, an influential man who was the Dean of Westminster for 40 years. Ruthin is also renowned for **Maen Huail**, a stone that stands in the market place and which, according to legend, marks the place where Huail was beheaded by King Arthur because of rivalry in love.

Ruthin Castle, begun in 1277 by Edward I, was the home of Lord de Grey of Ruthin who, having proclaimed Owain Glyndwr a traitor to Henry IV, was given a large area of land originally held by the Welshman. After Glyndwr crowned himself Prince of Wales, de Grey was the first to suffer when Ruthin was attacked in 1400. Though the town was all but destroyed, the castle held out and survived the onslaught. During the Civil War, the castle again came under siege, this time surviving for 11 weeks in

Ruthin Castle

1646 before eventually falling to General Mytton, who had the building destroyed. Partially restored and then owned by the Cornwallis-West family, Ruthin Castle played host, before and during World War I, to many famous and influential Edwardians including the Prince of Wales (later Edward VII), the actress Mrs Patrick Campbell and Lady Randolph Churchill, the mother of Winston Churchill. Today, the castle, with its charming grounds and roaming peacocks, is a hotel that specialises in medieval banquets.

ST ASAPH

This small town, on a ridge between the River Clwyd and Elwy, ranks as a city because of its cathedral. Standing on a hill and constructed on the site of a Norman building, **St Asaph's Cathedral** is not only the country's smallest cathedral but it has also had to endure a particularly stormy past. It was founded in AD 560 by St Kentigern, who left his small church in 573 in the hands of his favourite pupil, Asaph, while he returned to Scotland. The cathedral was sacked by Henry III's forces in 1245 and then destroyed during Edward I's conquest of Wales just some 37 years later. Edward wished to rebuild at nearby Rhuddlan but Bishop Anian II insisted that the new cathedral remain at St Asaph and so the building still standing today was begun by Anian and completed by his two successors.

In 1402 the woodwork was burnt during Owain Glyndwr's rebellion (it was subsequently restored by Bishop Redman) and by the 17th century the matters were so desperate that many of the possessions were sold and the Bishop's Palace became a tavern! However, St Asaph's Cathedral has survived and today it holds several treasures including a first edition of the William Morgan Welsh Bible (dating from 1588) that was used at the Investiture of Charles the Prince of Wales in 1969.

Bishop of St Asaph from 1601 to 1604, William Morgan began his mammoth task of translating the Bible into Welsh while he was a rector and, during his ministry over the parish of Llanrhaeadr ym Mochnant, his congregation grew so upset with his neglect of his pastoral duties for his translation work that he had to be escorted by armed guards to the church. Not only was the finished work of importance to the Welsh churches, each one of which received a copy, but it also set a standard for the

Welsh language, which, without being codified, could have been lost forever. A special monument, the **Translator's Memorial**, commemorates and names those who, under Morgan's guidance, assisted him in translating the Bible. Major restoration work on the Cathedral was entrusted to Sir George Gilbert Scott, who also worked on the restoration of the cathedrals at Bangor and St David's as well as building many churches and houses throughout the United Kingdom. (The Scott dynasty takes a bit of sorting out: Sir George Gilbert Scott (1811-1878), the most prolific builder and restorer, had two architect sons, George Gilbert Scott Jr (1839-1897) and John Oldrid Scott (1842-1913). John Oldrid's son Sir Giles Gilbert Scott (1880-1960) was responsible for Liverpool Cathedral.)

In the centre of St Asaph is **Elwy Bridge**, which is believed to date from the 17th century although it was the fine renovation work by Joseph Turner in 1777 that allows it to carry today's heavy traffic. The River Elwy is linked with a particularly fishy tale about Bishop Asaph, after whom the town is named. One day, Queen Nest, the wife of Maelgwn Gwynedd, King of North Wales, lost a precious ring - the ancient and sacred ring of the Queens of the North - while bathing in the river. Upset and fearing her husband's anger, the Queen went to St Asaph to ask for his help in retrieving the ring. Comforting the lady, St Asaph invited the royal couple to dine with him the following evening where he told Maelgwn about the loss of the ring. The king's terrible rage could only just be contained by St Asaph and he suggested they begin their meal. As the king cut into the locally-caught salmon on his plate, lo and behold, the sacred ring fell from the flesh of the fish!

TREMEIRCHION

This small village is home to several buildings of interest. The 13th century village church houses a 14th century tomb-niche containing the effigy of a vested priest while, in the chancel, a tablet commemorates Hester Lynch Piozzi who is better known as Dr Johnston's Mrs Trale. In 1774, Mrs Trale inherited a house in Tremeirchion she had known in her childhood and which, unfortunately, was dilapidated and in need of great repair. Following her marriage to the Italian musician, Gabriel Piozzi, the couple rebuilt the house living there happily until Piozzi's death.

In 1567, Sir Richard Clough, a wealthy merchant, built a house, Bachegraig, near the village. Though the house is now demolished, the gatehouse still stands and its unusual architectural style so shocked the local inhabitants that they thought the devil must have been the architect and had also supplied the bricks. The local story has it that the devil baked the bricks in the fires of hell and, to this day, a nearby stream is known as Nant y Cythraul or the Devil's Brook.

WHITFORD

Close to the village can be found a curious monument, **Maen Achwyfaen** (The Stone of Lamentation). This Celtic cross, sculptured in a wheel shape, is said to have been erected in about 1000AD and is the tallest such cross in Britain; the person or event which it commemorates is unknown. The renowned 18th century travel writer, Thomas Pennant, is buried in the graveyard adjacent to the grand 19th century church.

WREXHAM

This once small market town, which is considered to be the unofficial capital of North Wales, is now a busy place with plenty to offer the visitor. Growing and prospering around the commercial importance of its brick and tile manufacturing, brewing, steel and coal, Wrexham still holds a variety of markets today. An interesting experience for city dwellers is the cattle market held on Saturdays where farmers from the surrounding area come to socialise and oversee transactions and where visitors to the market can wander around soaking up the rural atmosphere.

For those wishing to find out more about the town and its social, industrial and local history then **Wrexham Museum**, housed in the County Buildings that were originally constructed as the militia barracks in 1857, is a very good place to start. The discovery of a skeleton nearby - it became known as Brymbo Man - traces the town's history back as far as the Bronze Age while the Romans are also known to have settled in the Wrexham area. Both Roundhead and Cavalier troops were garrisoned in the town during the Civil War and, in more peaceful times, in the late 19th century, Britain's first lager brewery was built in Wrexham in 1882.

The suburb of Acton was the birthplace of Judge Jeffreys, the notoriously harsh lawman who was nicknamed 'Bloody' for his lack of compassion and his belief in swift justice.

Perhaps Wrexham's best known building, and one that's a particular favourite of American tourists, is the **Church of St Giles** that dominates the town's skyline. It is famous for being the burial place of Elihu Yale, the benefactor of Yale University, who was laid to rest here on his death in 1721. Yale's tomb was restored in 1968 by members of Yale University to mark the 250th anniversary of the benefaction and it can be found in the churchyard to the west of the tower. While the churchyard

certainly holds interest, the church itself is also well worth taking the time to look over; its 136 foot pinnacle tower is one of the Seven Wonders of Wales. Begun in 1506 and much restored, this Gothic tower still carries some of the original medieval carvings and, in particular, those of St Giles, which are recognisable by his attributes of an arrow and a deer.

Just to the south of Wrexham and found in a glorious 2,000-acre estate and **Country Park**, is the National Trust's **Erddig**, one of the most fascinating houses in Britain. An extraordinarily detailed exhibition of family memorabilia collected by the servants is on show, and in the stunning state rooms are 18th and 19th century furniture and furnishings, including some exquisite Chinese wallpaper. The outbuildings have been restored, and the grounds contain a superb walled garden that is home to the National Ivy Collection. Along with Erddig, which lies within the **Clywedog Valley and Trail**, is **King's Mill**, a restored mill that dates from 1769 although an older mill has been on the site since 1315.

THE BRIDGE

HARWARDEN ROAD, CAERGWRLE, NR WREXHAM, CLWYD LL12 9DT
TEL: 01978 760977

North Wales Borderlands

Directions: The village lies on the A541 about 3 miles north of Wrexham.

In the small village of Caergwrle, a short drive north from the centre of Wrexham, stands **The Bridge**. The village of Caergwrie has a long and varied history, part of which includes being a spa town, and the ruins of the baths can be seen to this day. Caergwrie also boasts a castle, still standing and open to the public. The Bridge was built in 1745 and for over 250 years has been at the centre of local activity with a wonderfully welcoming atmosphere in the two bars. Long a favourite with the locals, The Bridge has excellent tenants in Sylvia and Phil Weaver, who have a warm and genuine welcome for all their customers, whether familiar faces or first-timers.

The inn is open from 4.00 on Tuesdays and all day the rest of the week for the service of drinks. Two real ales – Burtonwood Bitter and a regularly changing guest – are always on tap, and other favourite tipples include Burtonwood Top Hat and Smooth, and an abundance of lagers both draught and bottled. The décor follows a medieval theme with coats of arms dotted among the exposed beams and polished brasses, while an old stone fireplace adds a warming touch in cooler weather. Food is served in a separate dining area from 12 till 8 (on Sunday from 12 to 3, no food Tuesday) and booking is necessary for the traditional Sunday roast. The main menu and specials board offer a well-chosen selection of familiar dishes.

🕐 12-11, from 4 on Tuesday

🍴 A la carte

🅿 Car park

❓ Caergwrle Castle 1 mile, Wrexham 4 miles, Hawarden Castle 5 miles, Loggerheads Country Park 6 miles

THE BUTCHERS ARMS

CHESTER ROAD, ROSSETT, CLWYD LL12 0HW
TEL: 01244 570233

Directions: The inn is on the B5445 Chester road, a short distance from the centre of Rossett, between Wrexham and Chester.

The Butchers Arms is a good-looking redbrick building on Chester Road in Rossett, just a short distance from the English border and an easy drive up to Chester. The tenants here are John and Sue Richmond-Potter, who were in charge between 1983 and 1991 and who returned in September 2002; that means they know their clientele and they know the area. The pub is open all day every day for serving drinks, with Burtonwood Bitter and a rotating guest heading the list of ales. Burtonwood Smooth is another popular choice to enjoy in the bar or outside when the sun shines: a couple of French style picnic tables are set out in front of the pub and there's off road parking and patio seating at the side and rear.

The bar is traditionally appointed, with pleasant lighting, a wood panelled counter and pictures and photographs of local spots. Food is served from 12 to 2.30 and from 6.30 to 10.30 and can be enjoyed anywhere on the premises – there are plenty of tables and chairs throughout. The menu itself will come as something of a surprise – and a very pleasant one. The printed list and the specials board offer a tempting selection of dishes from Italy and the Mediterranean. Children are very welcome at The Butchers Arms, which is a very agreeable place to pause on a journey or to seek out for its excellent hospitality. Wrexham to the south has plenty to offer the visitor, including bustling markets, while Chester, across the border to the north, is one of the most fascinating and historic cities in the United Kingdom.

- 🕐 12-11
- 🍴 A la carte · Italian + Med cooking
- 🅿 Off road parking
- ❓ Wrexham 4 miles, Chester 5 miles

THE CROWN INN

CILCAIN ROAD, PANT-Y-MWYN, NR MOLD, FLINTSHIRE CH7 5EH
TEL: 01352 740347

> **Directions:** From Mold, take the A541 Denbigh road. After ¼ mile, turn left at the road signposted Gwernaffield and Pant-y-Mwyn. The inn is in Pant-y-Mwyn on the left.

When Keith, who has had over 40 years experience in the trade, arrived at **The Crown Inn** at the end of 2002 he also brought with him his loyal, friendly and efficient staff. He immediately set about putting the place back firmly on its feet, and there's already a homely, hospitable feel in the bar, assisted by a cheerful fire that blazes a welcome. At least one real ale is always on tap, along with a good selection of draught and bottle beers, lager, cider and stout. Perhaps the most important change Keith has brought about is making food available; customers can choose from a printed menu or a specials board, and food is served throughout the day.

There are non-smoking areas in the dining room, and children are very welcome. Building up an appetite and a thirst should not be a problem hereabouts, as this is great walking country. The Clwydian Range provides both exercise and breathtaking views, and just south of the village is Loggerheads Country Park, with discovery trails, varied natural habitats and a visitor centre. The busy market town of Mold is less than 2 miles away. Wits need to be sharpened and memories stirred into action every other Sunday at The Crown, when the pub quiz starts at 8.30. In his short time at the helm Keith has already made great strides here, and he will doubtless soon build up a clientele of both local customers and tourists.

- 🕐 Open all day summer and weekends; open evenings in winter
- 🍴 Pub meals
- £ All the major cards
- Ⓟ Car park
- ♫ Quiz every other Sunday
- ❓ Mold 2 miles, Loggerheads Country Park 2 miles

THE DROVERS ARMS

RHEWL, NEAR RUTHIN, DENBIGHSHIRE LL15 2UD
TEL: 01824 703163

> **Directions:** The inn is on the A525 Ruthin-Denbigh road about 1½ miles from Ruthin town centre.

On the A525 Ruthin-Denbigh road, about 1½ miles from Ruthin town centre, the **Drovers Arms (Freehouse)** is a very attractive 17th century cream and green inn, slate-roofed, with hanging baskets, picnic tables on a front patio, and a beer garden at the side. Inside, the scene is every bit as appealing, with beams, open fires and brick-fronted bar counter where real ales (resident and guest) are among the good range of draught and bottled beers dispensed. The inn is also an excellent place for a snack or a meal, with an extensive Monday to Saturday lunchtime selection chalked up on the board, a traditional choice for Sunday lunch and a wide-ranging evening home cooked Pub food menu.

The inn is in the capable and experienced hands of Allen Given and

Amanda Nancarrow, who have a friendly greeting for all customers, who include regulars from the neighbouring towns and villages, motorists, cyclists and ramblers. Pool and dominoes are the favourite games with the locals, there's a popular quiz every Sunday night and a lively karaoke session on a Friday every six weeks. The top football matches are shown on satellite tv. The banks of the River Clwydog and the surrounding countryside provide very pleasant walks and walkers are welcome to use the large car park and facilities. The old market town of Ruthin, surrounded by hills in the Vale of Clwyd, is well worth spending time to explore. It is certainly one of the most interesting towns in North Wales, with a large number of interesting buildings spanning Medieval, Tudor, Georgian, Regency and Victorian architecture all in evidence.

- 🕐 12-11 (winter 12-3 & 5-11); Fri & Sat 12-11, Sun 12-10.30
- 🍴 A la carte
- £ Mastercard, Visa
- 🅿 Car parking
- ♪ Quiz Sunday, karaoke every 6 weeks, dominoes, darts
- @ www.thedroversarms.co.uk
- ❓ Ruthin 1½ miles, Denbigh 5 miles

THE EAGLE & CHILD INN

GWAENYSGOR, NR RHYL, FLINTSHIRE LL18 6EP
TEL/FAX: 01745 856391

> **Directions:** The village of Gwaenysgor is situated 1 mile off the A5151, 2 miles northeast of Dyserth.

Built as a farmhouse in the early part of the 19th century, but an inn for more than 100 years, **The Eagle and Child** takes its name from the crest of the Stanley family, sometime Lords of the Manor. A Free House, with a fine range of real ales and other beers and lagers, the inn is also well known for its excellent food. Clinton Borders, who owns and runs the inn with his wife Sue, prides himself with the homecooked food he serves, and he keeps his customers happy and well fed with his menu of classic dishes, the printed list being supplemented by daily specials chalked up in the bar by a fine sculpture of an eagle and child. Mushroom stroganoff could be one of four vegetarian dishes always available, and to round off the meal there's a tempting choice of sweets. Sandwiches and filled jacket potatoes provide quicker snacks. Food is served every lunchtime and evening, and booking is strongly advised at all times.

Horse brasses and sporting pictures add to the traditional look in the bar and dining area. Flower tubs and hanging baskets provide a riot of colour at the front of the inn while at the back is a large patio area with tables and chairs, looking onto a well kept, award winning garden. Throughout the Spring and Summer the garden is alive with the glorious colours and scent of the many plants and shrubs that grow in the neat and interesting flower beds. A perfest place to sit and enjoy a drink in the sunshine. There are some splendid walks in the vicinity of the inn, including Craig Fawr, a limestone hill with nature trails and a myriad of wildlife.

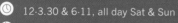

- 🕐 12-3.30 & 6-11, all day Sat & Sun
- 🍴 A la carte
- £ Mastercard, Visa, Electron, Switch, Solo
- ? Offa's Dyke 1 mile, Prestatyn 1 mile, Craig Fawr 2 miles, Bodrhyddan Hall 2 miles

THE MILL INN

MILL LANE, TREVOR ISA, CEFN MAWR, NR WREXHAM,
DENBIGHSHIRE LL14 3NL
TEL: 01978 821799

Directions: The inn stands in the hamlet of Trevor Isa, close to Cefn Mawr, off the A539 Ruabon-Llangollen road.

The Mill Inn is a neat little white painted building in the hamlet of Trevor Isa, which is located off the A539 Ruabon-Llangollen road. In the 17th century, it is already recorded as a favourite gathering place for the local community, which was largely involved in the lead mining industry. The front of the pub is adorned in spring and summer with attractive hanging baskets, and the sides and back of the building are almost hemmed in by pretty trees and shrubs. Since 2000 this delightful inn has been owned and run by Colin Frankel, who has recently expanded its scope by making bar food available. The Mill is open all day every day for drinks – the house real ales are Old Speckled Hen and Tetleys, with an extra option in the summer and at Christmas, there is also Tetleys Smooth, Castlemaine XXXX, Ansells Mild, Hydes Black, Carlsberg and Carlsberg Export, so

beer and lager drinkers are never short of choice.

Pool, darts, crib and dominoes are also available, and twice a month on a Friday night live entertainment is laid on. Lead mining is of course no longer the mainstay of the local community, but many traces of the workings still remain, and another reminder of the region's industrial past is Llangollen Canal, a branch of the Shropshire Union Canal. One of the area's leading landmarks is Thomas Telford's Pontcysyllte Aqueduct, which carries the canal high above the River Dee. Offa's Dyke Path runs nearby, a popular choice with both serious and casual walkers, and among many other attractions in the vicinity of the inn are the ruins of 13th century Valle Crucis Cistercian Abbey.

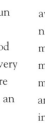

- 11am-11pm every day
- Bar meals
- Live music twice a month on a Friday
- Chirk Castle and gardens 3 miles, Pontcysyllte Aqueduct ¼ mile.

THE RED LION COUNTRY INN

LLANASA, NR HOLYWELL, FLINTSHIRE CH8 9NE
TEL: 01745 854291 FAX: 01745 888605

Directions: From J16 on the M56 take the A5117, A550 and A494 to Ewloe. Turn right on to the A55 towards the North Wales coast. Continue through Pantasaph then turn right on to A5151. At Trelawnyd turn right and follow the signs to Llanasa; the Red Lion is in the centre of the village.

In the heart of a picturesque conservation village in the gentle rolling countryside of the Clwydian Range, **The Red Lion Inn** (Y Llew Coch) is a delightful old building dating from the 17th century. Before becoming the splendid inn it is today, it was once a police station complete with holding cells. As pretty as a picture, particularly in summer when festooned with colourful hanging baskets, the inn is a wonderful central meeting place for the village as well as a fine place for visitors. The interior is just as well cared for as the outside, and with open fires, beamed ceilings and exposed stone walls, there is abundant old-world character.

The landlords, John and Mary Law, came here in October 1999 and are ably assisted by their two daughters, Jane and Vicky, their son Ian, Jane's husband Gareth and Ian's wife Joanne. They all work very well as a team, and their efforts are rewarded with a growing reputation for hospitality, a fine range of drinks (including several real ales) and above all the top-quality food prepared by Jane and Ian. The choice of dishes cooked in the modern British style is varied and very tempting, and booking is essential, particularly at the weekend. The Red Lion has recently added another string to its bow with the coming on stream of five superbly appointed en suite double rooms, including a bridal suite with a four-poster bed. It has thus become a comfortable, convivial base for touring this part of North Wales.

- 🕐 12-11, Sun to 10.30
- 🍽 A la carte, table d'hote, bar snacks
- £ Mastercard, Visa
- 🛏 En suite bedrooms
- Ⓟ Car park
- 🎵 Live entertainment 1st Friday each month; regular pianist
- ❓ Beaches 2 miles, Prestatyn 4 miles, Rhyl 6 miles, Bodrhyddan Hall 4 miles; walking, cycling, riding, fishing, golf, birdwatching

TYN-Y-CAPEL INN

CHURCH ROAD, MINERA, NR WREXHAM LL11 3DA

TEL: 01978 757502   FAX: 01978 755166

North Wales Borderlands

Directions: Minera lies on the B5430 just off the A525 about 4 miles west of Wrexham

---

On a historic route once used by drovers and monks, **Tyn-y-Capel Inn** dates back in parts over 400 years. Other parts are much more recent, but the whole place has a warm, welcoming appeal and the picturesque setting is another plus, overlooking the countryside where there are still traces of the lead mines that once supported the local community. Owner Dylan Roberts is intimately involved with the running of the pub, and he's also the chef; he worked here as head chef for a year before taking over the free house in August 2001, since when as owner chef he has enhanced the inn's reputation as a place to seek out for its cuisine and for its well kept ales. Three real ales are always on tap – Tetley, Old Speckled Hen and a rotating guest – and there's an excellent selection

of other beers, both draught and bottled.

Dylan's splendid dishes are served in the 40-cover non-smoking restaurant Wednesday to Saturday evenings (6-9) and Wednesday to Sunday lunch (12-2.30), and booking is strongly recommended on Friday and Saturday evenings and Sunday lunch. Some of the dishes on the main menu are well loved classics such as shepherd's pie, while many are temptingly just that bit different – chicken liver, whisky and allspice pâté; swordfish with an oriental stir-fry; steak with a Roquefort glaze. Desserts like apple and redcurrant crumble, treacle baked bananas or chocolate, hazelnut and honey cheesecake are definitely not to be resisted. A late night bar snack menu offers smaller portions of similar dishes. An excellent wine list complements the fine food. Children are welcome until 7.30.

- 🕐 2-3 & 6-11. Closed Mon & Tues lunchtimes except Bank Holidays
- 🍴 A la carte + evening snacks
- 💷 All the major cards
- 🅿 Car park
- 🎵 Quiz Sunday, live music Saturday, occasional themed food evenings
- ❓ Clywedog Valley and Trail, Nant Mill Countryside Centre 1 mile, Wrexham 4 miles; nature trails, hiking, climbing.

THE WHITE HORSE INN

HIGH STREET, BAGILLT, FLINTSHIRE CH6 6AP

TEL: 01352 733283

Directions: The village of Bagillt is 4 miles northwest of Flint, just off the main A548; the inn is in the centre of the village.

Owners since the late 1980s, Roger and Elizabeth Wilson have made a great success of the **White Horse Inn**, a 200-year-old hostelry in the middle of the village of Bagillt. One of the main reasons for this success is the consistent high quality of the food served in the Stables Restaurant, where the menu offers a splendid choice of dishes catering for appetites both large and small. The home-made steak & ale pie is an all-time favourite, and among other popular choices are steaks, a bonanza mixed grill, curries, quiche, salads and a seafood platter. Vegetarians have a choice of at least six main courses, and home-made fruit pie rounds off a meal in fine style.

Children are welcome, and one of the eating areas is designated non-smoking. Food is served Tuesday to Saturday

🕐 Open every evening and all day Sat & Sun

🍴 A la carte + snacks

Ⓟ 2 car parks

🎵 Pub games

❓ Flint 2 miles, Holywell 2 miles

evenings and Sunday lunch; booking is necessary at the weekend. The White Horse is a smart, well-furnished pub with bags of atmosphere and a relaxed, convivial feel. All the classic pub games are played, with darts, pool and dominoes all having an avid following. The owners maintain commendably high standards here and are never tempted to rest on their laurels: the latest development is the construction of an extension that will house the lounge bar. The pub has two spacious car parks.

Bagillt stands on the Dee Estuary, just off the A548 coast road. A short drive north is Holywell, a place of pilgrimage since the 7th century; in the other is Flint, once the port for Chester, and site of one of King Edward I's Iron Ring Fortresses.

WYNNSTAY ARMS HOTEL

WELL STREET, RUTHIN, DENBIGHSHIRE LL15 1AN
TEL: 01824 703147 FAX: 01824 705884

Directions: The hotel is centrally located in the town of Ruthin, which lies on the A525 7 miles southeast of Denbigh.

Dating back to the mid-18th century, and an inn since 1836, the **Wynnstay Arms Hotel** has in its time seen service as council offices and a butcher's shop. Occupying a prime corner site, the black and white building is a notable landmark in the centre of town, and the interior is a pleasing combination of original features and more contemporary decor. In the bar, two rotating real ales are on tap, along with a full range of beers, lagers, cider and stout. The printed menu and specials board provide plenty of variety in the 35-cover non-smoking restaurant, where the home-cooked specials are the lunchtime favourites and the charcoal grills are very popular choices in the evening.

- 🕐 12-11
- 🍴 A la carte
- £ All except Diners
- 🛏 6 en suite rooms
- Ⓟ Rear car park
- 🎵 Quiz Tuesday, live music Saturday
- ❓ The sights of Ruthin; Moel Famau in the Clwydian Range 3 miles, Denbigh 7 miles

Between January and Easter the restaurant is closed Monday to Wednesday evenings except for bookings. For guests staying overnight six well-fitted bedrooms are available throughout the year; children and dogs are welcome, and the tariff includes a hearty breakfast. Tuesday is quiz night at the Wynnstay Arms, and there's live entertainment on Saturday, starting at about 8 o'clock. The hotel has some parking spaces at the rear, and there's a large public car park opposite. Martin Desmond is the tenant, Paul Auld the licensee. The old market town of Ruthin is well worth a leisurely visit, the main places of interest including the Old Courthouse, the Gaol, the Elizabethan Nant Clwyd House and the splendid St Peter's Church.

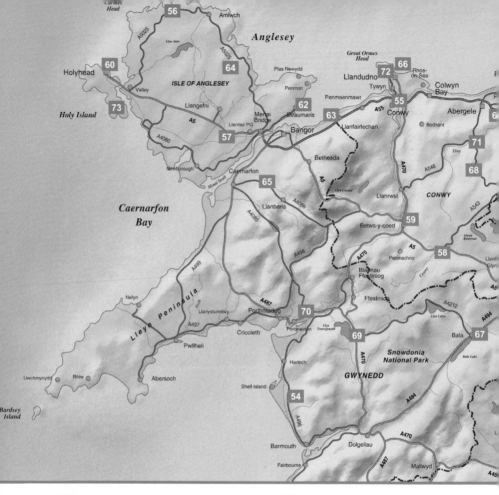

Please note all cross references refer to page numbers

NORTH WEST WALES

The coast of North Wales is a perennially popular stretch of British coastline that draws visitors in their thousands to its holiday resorts. This very traditional region, where Welsh is often still spoken on a daily basis, has many treasures, both man-made and natural, to discover. The coastline, from Prestatyn to Bangor was, before the coming of the railways, littered with small fishing villages. During the 19th century, as the hours of millworkers from the industrial towns of Lancashire and others working in the factories of the Midlands were reduced, the concept of an annual holiday, albeit in some cases just the odd day beside the sea, became widespread. Served by the newly built railway network, the fishing villages expanded to accommodate the visitors. Not only were boarding houses and hotels built for the society visitors coming to take the sea air, but amusements and entertainment became a regular feature. Llandudno, always considered a "cut above", still retains much of its Victorian and Edwardian charm, while other resorts, such as Rhyl, have endeavoured to counter the unsettled British summer weather by the creation of indoor complexes.

This area is not without its history. Prestatyn, to the east, lies at one end of Offa's Dyke. Built more as a line of

Conwy Valley, nr Tal-y-Cafn

demarcation rather than a fortification, the dyke runs from the coast southwards to Chepstow. Still substantially marking the border, many sections of the ancient earthwork are visible and can be seen from the waymarked footpath that runs the length of the dyke. It was also along the coast that Edward I built his Iron Ring of castles and, while many are in ruins, two, in particular, are exceptional. Conwy Castle, now a World Heritage Site, is not only massive but was built in such a position that the surrounding land provides suitable protection from attack. Caernarfon Castle, as much a royal residence as a fortress, was the place where Edward created the first Prince of Wales when he crowned his own son. Centuries later, in 1969, it was in the grounds of the splendid castle ruins that Queen Elizabeth invested the same title on her eldest son, Prince Charles.

Caernarfon and Bangor lie at opposite ends of the Menai Strait, the channel of water that separates mainland Wales from the Isle of Anglesey. It was not until the 19th century that a bridge was constructed across the strait, and Thomas Telford's magnificent Menai Suspension Bridge of the 1820s was joined, some 30 years later, by Stephenson's Britannia Bridge. Two great monuments to 19th century engineering, the bridges still carry traffic, both road and rail, today. The Isle of Anglesey, with its rolling hills, fertile farmland and miles of wild and craggy coastline, has attracted settlers from the Stone Age onward and is littered with evidence of Neolithic, Bronze Age and Iron Age people. Anglesey has its impressive castle, Beaumaris, built by Edward I to repel invasion from its neighbours. Today's invaders are largely tourists and holidaymakers, attracted by the elegant seaside resorts, the fishing, the sailing and the walking.

To the south of Anglesey lies the Llyn Peninsula, which forms the great

Dolbadarn Castle

curve of Caernarfon Bay. This is one of the most secluded and most beautiful parts of Wales, and over 100 miles of its shoreline is designated an Area of Outstanding Natural Beauty. During the Middle Ages, Bardsey Island, lying off the western tip of the peninsula, was a place of pilgrimage, and the ancient route to Aberdaron, from where the pilgrims sailed to their destination, can still in parts be followed. Reminders of the area's early Christian past can be found throughout Llyn, along with more ancient monuments such as hill forts. This region, like the northern coast and the Isle of Anglesey, has been a favourite holiday destination since the coming of the railways in the mid-19th century.

The attractive Victorian resorts along the southern shore of the peninsula are sheltered and provide plenty of scope for sailing, swimming and fishing. The birthplace of one of the country's greatest statesmen, David Lloyd George, is a popular place to visit, but the whole region is filled with splendid attractions to see and exciting things to do. Perhaps the most visited of all is

the fantasy village of Portmeirion, built from the 1920s to the 1970s by Sir Clough Williams-Ellis.

There are three National Parks in Wales, and Snowdonia, at some 840 square miles, is the largest and certainly the most

Sunrise from Snowdon

dramatic scenically. Set up in 1951, and embracing a number of mountain and hill ranges, Snowdonia also extends southwards into the heart of Wales and incorporates stretches of the coastline and Cadair Idris. There are several routes up to the summit of Snowdon beginning

Trearddur Bay

at various points around its base. Some call for more energy than others, but the least arduous ascent is by the Snowdon Mountain Railway that runs from Llanberis. At, and around, nearby Betws-y-Coed, the walking is gentler and includes surviving tracts of the vast forests that once covered much of Wales. From the earliest times, this region was mined for its minerals. Gold was known here long before the Romans arrived, and as recently as the 19th century there were mini-gold rushes in a belt that stretched from Bontddu along the line of the River Mawddach. Copper, lead and slate were also mined up until the start of the 20th century, and the scars left by those industries can still be seen today. Several of the mines have found new roles as visitor attractions, along with the little railways that once carried the minerals from the mines and quarries to the coast. In the middle of the 19th century, the coastal villages and towns, many of them obscure, quiet fishing communities, were put on the map and changed radically in character with the arrival of the main railway network. As the fashion for sea air grew and communications were made easier, they became popular seaside resorts, and today many of them still retain Victorian and Edwardian buildings constructed to cater for holidaymakers. The scenery throughout the region is truly inspirational, and few would disagree with the verdict of the 19th century traveller and writer George Borrow:

"Perhaps in all the world there is no region more picturesquely beautiful."

ABERDOVEY

Also commonly known by its Welsh name, **Aberdyfi**, this now quiet resort, at the mouth of the River Dovey (or Dyfi), was once one of the most important ports along the Welsh coast. Shipbuilding flourished here alongside the busy port, whose records show on one particular occasion having 180 ships unloading or waiting for a berth. The town has been attracting holiday-makers since Edwardian times, when the railways made such seaside trips possible for many more people. It is a gentle, civilised spot, with all the best attributes of a seaside resort and none of the kiss-me-quick tat of many larger places. Aberdovey has given its name to a Victorian ballad called 'The Bells of Aberdovey', recounting the legend that the sea drowned a great kingdom here and how on quiet summer evenings the bells can be heard ringing out from beneath the waves.

BALA

A pleasant town that's a good stopping off point when exploring Snowdonia National Park. Tourism is certainly an important part of the town's economy but it also remains a market place for the local farming communities. To the southwest of the town, **Llyn Tegid (Bala Lake)** is the largest natural lake in Wales and feeder of the River Dee. Four miles long, nearly three quarters of a mile wide and up to 150 feet deep, the Lake is a popular centre for all manner of watersports; it is also the home of Tegi, the Welsh version of Scotland's Nessie. Along the eastern bank of the lake runs the narrow gauge **Bala Lake Railway**, which provides the perfect opportunity to catch a glimpse of the Tegi.

BANGOR

A cathedral and university city, Bangor incorporates a wide variety of architectural styles that remind the visitor that this is not only an interesting and stimulating place but also one with a long history. The **Bangor Museum and Art Gallery** is the place to discover not only the past 2,000 years of history of this area of Wales but also to see the reconstructions of domestic life in days gone by. The base of the oldest bishopric in Britain, Bangor's **Cathedral** dates from the 13th century and has probably been in continuous use for longer than any other cathedral in Britain. Improvements in the roads and then the coming of the railways to the North Wales coast saw Bangor grow in both stature and impor-

Bala Lake

Menai Straits Bridge

Barmouth was once a small port with an equally small shipbuilding industry. As the fashion for seeking out sea air grew in the 18th century, the character of Barmouth changed to accommodate visitors flocking here for the bracing sea air - those suffering from scurvy were even fed seaweed, which is rich in Vitamin C and grew in abundance in the estuary. However, the Barmouth seen today is, like many other seaside resorts, a product of the railway age and the Victorian architecture is still very much apparent. **Ty Gywn** is one of its older buildings, dating from the 15th century. The house, now the home to a Tudor exhibition, is said to have been built for Henry Tudor, Earl of Richmond, who went on to become Henry VII. It is thought to have been used as the meeting place where the plot to overthrow Richard III was hatched. The town is also home to the **Lifeboat Museum**.

tance. The **Menai Suspension Bridge** was built by Thomas Telford between 1819 and 1826 and was the first permanent crossing of the Menai Strait. The **Britannia Bridge**, a mile further southwest from Telford's bridge, is a combined road and rail crossing built between 1846 and 1850 by Robert Stephenson. Also jutting out into the Menai Strait from the town is the 1,500 foot long **Victoria Pier**, the youngest of the structures, which was built in 1896. To the west of the town and overlooking Beaumaris on the Isle of Anglesey lies **Penrhyn Castle**, a dramatic neo-Norman construction built by Thomas Hopper between 1820 and 1845, and incorporating Doll and Railway Museums.

BARMOUTH

Occupying a picturesque location by the mouth of the River Mawddach,

BEAUMARIS

An attractive and elegant town, Beaumaris was granted a charter by Edward I in 1294 and it adopted the Norman name 'beau marais' which translates as 'beautiful marsh'. The lawned seafront, now with its elegant Georgian and Victorian terraces, was once a marsh that protected the approaches to **Beaumaris Castle**. Often cited as the most technically perfect medieval castle in Britain, Beaumaris Castle was the last of Edward I's Iron Ring of fortresses built to stamp his authority on the Welsh. Now a World Heritage listed site and in the hands of CADW (Welsh Historic Monuments), Beaumaris Castle is still virtually surrounded by its original moat; there was also a tidal dock here for ships coming in through a channel in the marshes - an iron ring where vessels of up to 40 tons once docked still hangs from the wall. Beaumaris was at one time also an administrative and legal centre for the island. The **Courthouse**, dating from 1614, is open to the public during the summer and, although it was renovated in the 19th century, much of its original Jacobean interior remains. Close by is **Beaumaris Gaol**, which was designed as a model prison by Hansom in 1829. An equally interesting place for all the family to visit is the **Museum of Childhood Memories**, a treasure house of nostalgia with a collection of over 2,000 items.

Beaumaris Castle

BETHESDA

This old quarry town takes its name from the Nonconformist chapel that was built here and served many of the 2,300 men (and their families) who worked in the quarry at its peak in 1875. The gouged rock of the **Penrhyn Slate Quarries** forms a huge hillside amphitheatre; it was the largest open cast slate mine in the world and still produces high-quality slate 250 years after it was first worked.

BETWS-Y-COED

A sizeable village at the confluence of four beautiful forested valleys, Betws-y-Coed first came to prominence with the setting up in 1844 of an artists' colony by David Cox and other eminent Victorian countryside painters; their work inspired others, and the coming of the railway in 1868 brought the tourists to what soon became a busy holiday centre. A major attraction is the **Motor Museum**, whose unique collection of vintage and post-vintage cars includes a fabulous Bugatti Type 57. As the village is close to the point where the Conwy, Lledr and Llugwy rivers meet, it seems natural that these waterways should play an important role in the development of Betws-y-Coed. Thomas Telford's **Waterloo Bridge**, a marvellous iron construction, built in 1815, gracefully spans the River

Conwy, while the **Pont-y-Pair**, dating from around 1470, crosses the River Llugwy; further downstream, an iron suspension footbridge spans the river by the church. However, the main attractions that draw people to this area are the waterfalls: the spectacular multi-level **Swallow Falls** on the River Lugwy, **Conwy Falls**, **Machno Falls** and **Fairy Glen Ravine**. Next to the railway station is the **Conwy Valley Railway Museum** and shop, a popular place to visit in the summer. The village's most famous, and certainly most curious, attraction is **Ty Hyll**, the Ugly House, which stands close by the River Llugwy. Apparently this building, which looks like it was literally thrown together, is an example of hurried assembly in order to obtain freehold on common land.

Ffestiniog Railway

BLAENAU FFESTINIOG

This was once the slate capital of the world and the industry still dominates the landscape and economy of this town and the surrounding area. Stretching across from the feet of Manod towards the Moelwyn Mountains, the legacy of the slate industry is visible everywhere - from the orderly piles of quarried slate waste to the buildings in the town.

Today, the industry lives on in two slate mines: **Llechwedd Slate Caverns** and **Gloddfa Ganol Slate Mine** The slate caverns, the winners of many top tourism awards, take visitors underground to explore the world of a Victorian slate miner and the man-made caverns of cathedral proportions, while, on surface, there is a Victorian village to wander through. The Gloddfa Ganol mine, where digging began in 1818, was once the world's largest, and today slate is still being turned into commercial products. At the foot of Manod Bach, beside the waterfall at Bethania, **Pant-yr-ynn Mill** is the earliest surviving slate mill of the Diffwys Casson Quarry. As well as having a mainline train service, Blaenau Ffestiniog is the end, or the starting point, of the narrow gauge **Ffestiniog Railway**, which runs through the vale to Porthmadog. Built to carry slate down to the sea for shipping off around the world, the railway has since been renovated by enthusiasts and volunteers. There are many stopping off points so walkers can take advantage of many beauty spots.

To the northwest of the town, at First Hydro's power station, is the **Ffestiniog Visitor Centre**, the ideal place to discover the wonders of hydro-electricity. Opened in 1963 by Her Majesty the Queen, the station consists of reservoirs and underwater passages constructed inside the mountains and the displays and exhibitions at the centre explain not only how the electrical power is generated but also the development of electricity over the years.

BODNANT

Situated above the River Conwy and covering some 80 acres are the famous Edwardian **Bodnant Gardens**, where the rhododendrons, camellias and magnolias are a magnificent sight in the spring, followed by herbaceous borders, roses and water lilies in summer and glorious colours in the autumn.

CAERNARFON

Situated on the right bank of the River Seiont, Caernarfon is a town steeped in history as well as a bastion of the Welsh language and of national pride. The history of Caernarfon goes back to Roman times and **Segontium Roman Fort**, half a mile from the town centre on the road towards Beddgelert, is the only place in Wales where it is possible to see something of the internal layout of an auxiliary station. However, it is another great construction and symbol of military power - the impressive **Caernarfon Castle** - that still dominates the town today. The most famous of Wales' numerous great fortresses, the Castle was begun in 1283 by Henry de Elreton, who

was also building Beaumaris Castle, under the orders of Edward I; it took some 40 years to complete. It was here in 1284 that Edward I crowned his son the first English Prince of Wales and the castle was once again used for such an investiture when, in 1969, the Queen crowned Prince Charles Prince of Wales. Also at the Castle, and housed in the Queen's Tower, is the **Museum of the Royal Welsh Fusiliers**, the country's oldest regiment.

To the southwest of Caernarfon and overlooking Caernarfon Bay is **Caernarfon Air World**, located on the site of an RAF station that was built in 1940 and which is also the home of the first RAF mountain rescue team. As well as offering pleasure flights to visitors, there is the **Aviation Museum**, housed in one of the great hangars which not only displays over 400 model aircraft but has various planes and helicopters on show and also provides visitors with the opportunity to take the controls in a flight trainer.

COLWYN BAY

A more genteel place than the resorts found to the east, Colwyn Bay was built largely during the 19th century to fill the gap along the coast between Rhos-on-Sea and the village of Old Colwyn. As a result, there are many fine Victorian buildings to be seen, and the beach is served by a promenade along which most of the town's attractions can be found. Colwyn Bay includes among its famous sons ex-Monty Python Terry Jones and a former James Bond, Timothy Dalton. The philosopher Bertrand Russell (1872-1970) was cremated with no ceremony at Colwyn Bay crematorium and his ashes scattered in the sea.

CONWY

Conwy Castle is situated on a rock which overlooks the River Conwy and its estuary, and

Conwy Castle

commands wonderful views of the whole area. Begun in 1283, the castle's construction was largely finished by the autumn of 1287 and, compared with other of Edward's castles, Conwy is of a relatively simple design which relies on its position rather than anything else to provide a defence against attack. Conwy developed within the shadows of its now defunct fortress, and slate and coal extracted from the surrounding area, were shipped up and down the coast from the town. Later, the town fathers approached Thomas Telford, who planned a causeway and bridge, as Conwy's trade and links grew with the outside world. Built in 1826, the elegant **Suspension Bridge** replaced the ferry that previously had been the only means of crossing the river so close to its estuary. The toll house has been restored and furnished as it would have been a century ago. By the side of Telford's bridge stands the Robert Stephenson designed tubular rail bridge of 1846.

Bridges, however, are not the only

architectural gems Conwy has to offer. **Plas Mawr**, an Elizabethan town house on the High Street, is one of the best preserved buildings from that period in Britain. Close by is **Aberconwy House**, a delightful medieval merchant's home that dates from the 14th century. The rooms have been decorated and furnished to reflect various periods in the house's history and the property is now in the hands of the National Trust. Conwy's **Teapot Museum and Shop**, on Castle Street, is an interesting and unusual attraction where visitors can see a unique collection of antique, novelty and humorous teapots that date from the mid-1700s to the present day.

CORRIS

This small village, surrounded by the tree covered slopes of the Cambrian Mountains, was home to the first narrow gauge railway in Wales. Constructed in 1859 as a horse drawn railway, steam locomotives were introduced in 1878 before the passenger service began in 1883. After finally closing in 1948, the

Corris Railway Society opened a **Railway Museum** dedicated to the line in 1970 that explains the railway's history and also the special relationship with the slate quarries through displays, exhibits and photographs. Industry of a different kind can be found at the **Corris Craft Centre**, which is home to a variety of working craftsmen and women. An excellent place to find a unique gift, the craft centre is also home to the fascinating **King Arthur's Labyrinth** - a maze of underground tunnels where visitors are taken by boat to see the spectacular caverns and relive tales of the legendary King Arthur.

CRICCIETH

An attractive Victorian town, Criccieth is dominated by **Criccieth Castle**, which stands on a rocky outcrop with commanding views over the sea. Built in the early 13th century by Llywelyn the Great as a stronghold of the native Welsh princes, it was captured, in 1283, and extended by Edward I but the core of the

Criccieth Castle

structure - the powerful twin towered gatehouse - still exists from the original fortification. One of the best preserved of the 13th century castles that litter the North Wales countryside, the romantic ruins of Criccieth Castle have inspired many artists down the centuries including JMW Turner, who used it as the backdrop for a famous painting of storm wrecked sailors.

DOLGELLAU

Meaning 'meadow of the hazels', Dolgellau is the chief market town for the southern area of Snowdonia. Pleasantly situated beside the River Wnion, with Cadair Idris rising in background, the town is very Welsh in custom, language and location. Owain Glyndwr held a Welsh parliament here in 1404, later signing an alliance with France's Charles VI. Now, the town's narrow streets can barely evoke those distant times and few early buildings remain. However, the seven-arched bridge over the river dates from the early 17th century and, before much of Dolgellau was built in an attempt to lure Victorian holidaymakers to the delights of Cadair Idris, there was a small rural Quaker community here. The **Quaker Heritage Centre** tells the story of this community and also of the persecution that led them to emigrate to Pennsylvania. The local gold mines provided the gold for the wedding rings of both Queen Elizabeth II (then Princess Elizabeth) and Diana, Princess of Wales.

Rising to some 2,927 feet to the southwest of Dolgellau, **Cadair Idris** dominates the local scenery and on a clear day a climb to the summit is rewarded with views that take in the Isle of Man and the Irish coast as well as, closer to home, the Mawddach estuary.

Harlech Castle

FAIRBOURNE

This growing holiday resort lies on the opposite side of the Mawddach estuary from Barmouth and, from the ferry that carries passengers across the river mouth, runs the **Fairbourne Railway**. Originally a horse-drawn tramway, now steam-hauled, this 15″ gauge railway runs from Fairbourne to the mouth of the Mawddach estuary. Its midway halt was given an invented name that outdoes the 59 letters of LlanfairPG by eight. Translated from the Welsh, it means "Mawddach Station with its dragon's teeth on North Penrhyn Drive by the golden sands of Cardigan Bay".

HARLECH

One of Edward I's Iron Ring of fortresses, which was begun in 1283, **Harlech**

Castle is perched on a rocky outcrop close to the sea. If the use of power and strength to impress and intimidate an indigenous population was ever aided by architecture then Harlech is a prime example. Situated 200 feet above sea level, its concentric design, with lower outer walls, by architect James of St George, used the natural defences of its site to emphasise its impregnability. However, in 1404 Owain Glyndwr managed to capture the castle and held it for five years while using the town of Harlech as his capital.

The song, *Men of Harlech*, has immortalised the siege during the War of the Roses when the Castle was held for the Lancastrian side for seven years before it finally became the last stronghold to fall to the Yorkists in 1468. The last time Harlech saw action was 200 years later, during the Civil War, when it again withstood attack and was the last castle in Wales to fall to Cromwell's forces. The panoramic views from the Castle's battlements take in both Tremadog Bay and the mountainous scenery behind the town.

Though not as imposing as the Castle, **The Lasynys Fawr** is another building worth a visit while in Harlech. The home of Ellis Swynne (1671-1734), one of Wales' most famous prose writers, the house is an excellent example of one of its period - it dates from 1600. Some of the scenes in the early James Bond film *From Russia With Love* were shot in Harlech. The famous Royal St David's golf course is just outside the town.

HOLYHEAD

Holyhead Mountain (Mynydd Twr) rises to 720 feet behind this town, which is the largest on Anglesey and is itself on an island - Holy Island. A busy rail and ferry terminal, especially for travellers to and from Ireland, Holyhead has all the facilities for visitors passing through although it is also, despite being something of an industrial and commercial centre, a seaside resort.

While the town itself is not without interest, it is the immediate surrounding area that draws most visitors to Holyhead. **Breakwater Quarry Country Park**, just northwest of the town,

incorporates Britain's largest breakwater and from here there are many walks along the coast, including a route to **South Stack**. This is a reserve of cliffs and heath teeming with birdlife, including puffins, guillemots, razorbills. The RSPB visitor centre is open daily, the café daily in summer, and the lighthouse is open daily in summer for guided tours. Between South Stack and North Stack lies **Gogarth Bay**, where the RSPB sea bird centre includes a cavern, known as Parliament House Cave, which is used by a profusion of sea birds such as puffins, guillemots and even falcons. Aqua diving, windsurfing, water skiing and fishing are some of the many attractions of **Trearddur Bay**, a popular part of Anglesey's extensive coastline that lies just to the southwest of Holyhead.

LLANBERIS

This former slate-producing community

Llanberis

has many attractions to keep the visitor occupied although it is, perhaps, best known as one of the approaches to **Snowdon**. Rising to some 3,560 feet, this is the highest peak in Wales and the most climbed mountain in Britain. On a clear day, the view from the summit is fantastic, with Ireland sometimes visible, but before setting out for the summit it is worth remembering that the weather changes dramatically up here and walkers and climbers should always be prepared. Many reach the summit the easy way, with the help of the **Snowdon Mountain Railway**, a rack and pinion system built in 1896 that has carried millions to the top of the mountain over the years. For those wanting another train ride or are content with a more sedate journey, the **Llanberis Lake Railway** takes a short trip during which there are several different views of the mountain. The railway lies in **Padarn Country Park**, which gives access to 800 acres of Snowdonia's countryside and also includes Llyn (Lake) Padarn. The Kingfisher Trial is designed specifically for wheelchairs. By the side of the lake is Cwm Derwen Woodland and Wildlife Centre, with a woodland discovery trail and

a timewalk exhibition with an audio-visual display. Here, too, is the **Welsh Slate Museum**, which tells the story of the slate industry through a variety of exhibitions, a restored slate-carrying incline, a terrace of quarrymen's cottages, audio-visual shows and demonstrations. The De Winton waterwheel is the second largest in Britain and once provided all the power for **Dinorwig Power Station**, where bus tours take visitors deep into the mountain into the tunnels and the machinery rooms that control the vast quantities of water of this major engineering project.

LLANDUDNO

Originally just a collection of fishermen's cottages, Llandudno - the largest and one of the most popular of the North Wales coast resorts - was developed in the 1850s under the watchful eye of the Liverpool surveyor, Owen Williams. A

Llandudno

delightful place that is a wonderful example of Victorian architecture, Llandudno was planned around a pleasant layout of wide streets and, of course, the Promenade, the essential feature of a resort from that age. A permanent Victorian puppet show can be watched on the promenade close to the **Pier** that, in 1914, the Suffragettes attempted to burn down during their fight for the right of women to vote. Later, Ringo Starr, of Beatles fame, once worked on the pleasure streamers that docked at Llandudno pier, unaware that a few years later his life was to change so radically.

Along the seafront can also be found a statue of the **White Rabbit** from Lewis Carroll's much loved story *Alice In Wonderland*. The tribute is to the real Alice - Alice Liddell - who came here on holiday with her family; it was also at Llandudno that her parents spent their honeymoon. The **Visitor Centre** at **The Rabbit Hole** presents an interesting audio-visual exhibition that is dedicated to Alice and her time in Wonderland.

The massive lime-stone headland of **Great Orme** still dominates the resort today and also separates the town's two beaches. The summit can be reached by the **Great Orme Tramway**, a magnificent monument to

Victorian engineering constructed in 1902 that is Britain's only cable hauled, public road tramway. The **Great Orme Copper Mine** is the only Bronze Age copper mine in the world open to the public.

LLANFAIR PG

Llanfairpwllgwyngyll, often called Llanfair PG, is better known as the village with the world's longest place name. The full, tongue-twisting name is: Llanfairpwllgwyngyllgogerychwyrn-drobwyllllantysiliogogogh and the translation is even longer - St Mary's Church in a hollow of white hazel near to a rapid whirlpool and St Tysilio's Church near the red cave. The name is said to have been invented, in humorous reference to the burgeoning tourist trade, by a local man. The village, overlooking the Menai Strait, is where the Britannia Bridge crosses to the mainland. The **Marquess of Anglesey Column** looks out from here over to Snowdonia and the

Llanfair PG Railway Station

quite splendid views from the top of the column are available to anyone wishing to negotiate the spiral staircase of some 115 steps. The last public toll house, designed by Thomas Telford when he was working on the London-Holyhead road in the 1820s, stands in the village; it still displays the tolls charged in 1895, the year the toll house closed. Next door is the modest building where, in 1915, the Women's Institute was founded.

However, the most famous building in Llanfair PG is undoubtedly its railway station - the often filmed station whose platform has the longest station sign and where the longest platform ticket in Britain was purchased. Today, visitors can see a replica of the Victorian ticket office, examine some rare miniature steam trains and wander around the numerous craft and souvenir shops that can now be found here.

LLANRWST

The market centre for the central Conwy Valley owes both its name and the dedication of its church to St Grwst, a 6th century missionary who was active in this area.

The **Church of St Grwst** dates from 1470, though the tower and north aisle are 19th century. Next to the church lies **Gwydir Chapel**, famous for its richly carved Renaissance interior, and beyond it lies **Gwydir Castle**, a Tudor mansion which has, in its grounds, some fine Cedars of Lebanon planted in 1625 in celebration of the marriage of Charles I to Henrietta Maria of France.

LLANYSTUMDWY

This small coastal village is best known as being the home of David Lloyd George, the Member of Parliament for Caernarfon for 55 years and the Prime Minister who, at the beginning of the 20th century, was responsible for social reform as well as seeing the country through the Armistice at the end of World War I.

Lloyd George's childhood home, **Highgate**, is still just as it would have been when the great statesman lived here, and the **Lloyd George Museum** features a Victorian schoolroom and an exhibition of the life of this reforming Liberal politician.

MENAI BRIDGE

Acting as a gateway to Anglesey, this largely Victorian town grew and developed after the construction of Thomas Telford's **Menai Suspension Bridge**, which connects the island to mainland Wales. The waterfront is a popular place for anglers and for viewing the annual Regatta on the Menai Strait held every August.

NEFYN

Once a fishing village, this resort was granted a charter in 1355, along with Pwllheli, by the Black Prince. It was here in 1284 that Edward I celebrated his conquest over Wales. Housed in St Mary's church, whose tower supports a sailing ship weathervane, is the **Llyn Historical and Maritime Museum**, an excellent place to visit to find out more about an interesting and beautiful part of Wales.

NEWBOROUGH

Founded in 1303 by the former inhabitants of Llanfaes, who had been moved here by Edward I, the village stands on the edge of a National Nature Reserve that covers 1,566 acres of dunes, coast and forest. **Llanddwyn Island** is accessible on foot, but tidal conditions should be carefully studied before setting out. Charles Tunnicliffe, the renowned wildlife artist, had a studio on the island for over 30 years and Anglesey Council has purchased a collection of his marvellous work which can be seen at the Oriel Ynys Môn in Llangefni. Situated between Newborough and Dwyran lies **Anglesey Model Village and Gardens**, a delightful place where visitors can wander through the attractive landscaped gardens and see many of the island's many landmarks - all built to one twelfth scale.

PENMACHNO

This delightful village of picturesque stone cottages, set in a wooded valley, lies on the River Machno, is the site of **Penmachno Woollen Mill**. Visitors to the mill can not only see the working power looms as they

weave the cloth but can also browse through the shop among the finished articles and other Welsh craftwork on display. To the northwest of the village centre and in the secluded Wybrnant valley lies **Ty Mawr Wybrnant**, the birthplace of Bishop William Morgan (1545-1604) who was the first person to translate the Bible into Welsh.

PENMON

On the eastern tip of Anglesey, this is a beauty spot whose lovely views across the Menai Strait go some way to explaining why it was chosen, centuries earlier, as a religious site. **Penmon Priory** was established by St Seiriol in the 6th century and in 1237 Llywelyn the Great gave the monastery and its estates to the prior of Puffin Island. **St Seiriol's Church**, now the parish church, contains wonderful examples of Norman architecture and a carved cross, recently moved to the church from the fields nearby, that shows influences from both Scandinavia

Plas Newydd

and Ireland. A nearby **Dovecote**, built in around 1600 by Sir Richard Bulkeley, contains nearly 1,000 nesting places.

PLAS NEWYDD

The splendid mansion house of **Plas Newydd** is surrounded by gardens and parkland laid out in the 18th century by Humphrey Repton. The house contains an exhibition of the work of Rex Whistler and a military museum with relics of the Battle of Waterloo.

PORTHMADOG

The history of this busy town and its waterfront is described in the **Maritime Museum** where the importance of the trade in slate and Porthmadog's shipbuilding industry is told. Porthmadog is home to both the **Ffestiniog Railway**, the world's oldest narrow track passenger carrying railway, and the **Welsh Highland Railway** which, in 1922, was the longest narrow gauge railway in Wales. Maintaining the theme of transport, the **Madog Car and Motorcycle Museum** displays a gleaming collection of vintage British vehicles.

PORTMEIRION

This very special village, in a wonderful setting on a wooded peninsula overlooking Traeth Bay, was conceived and created by the Welsh architect Sir Clough Williams-Ellis between 1925 and 1972. An inveterate campaigner against the spoiling of Britain's landscape, he set out to illustrate that building in a beautiful location did not mean spoiling the environment. In looks this is the least Welsh place in Wales: the 50 or so buildings, some of which consist only of a façade, were inspired by a visit Williams-Ellis made to Sorrento and Portofino in Italy and they are mainly either part of the hotel or pastel cottages. The village also has shops selling the famous **Portmeirion Pottery**. The cult television series *The Prisoner*

Portmeirion

was made at Portmeirion and wandering around the village, the delightful woodlands and the secluded beaches, those familiar with the programme will recognise the locations.

PRESTATYN

With three miles or so of sandy beaches Prestatyn has proved a popular holiday destination over the years and all types of entertainment are available, making the town an ideal centre for family holidays in the famously healthy air. Prestatyn lies at one end of the massive 8th century earthwork **Offa's Dyke**. It takes its name from King Offa, one of the most powerful of the early Anglo-Saxon kings; from 757 until his death in 796 he ruled Mercia, which covers roughly the area of the West Midlands. He seized power in the period of civil strife that followed the murder of his cousin King Aethelbald and, ruthlessly suppressing many of the smaller kingdoms and princedoms, created a single settled state that covered most of England south of Yorkshire. His lasting memorial is the dyke, which he had built between Mercia and the Welsh lands. With an earthwork bank of anything up to 50 feet in height and a 12ft ditch on the Welsh side, much of this massive feat of engineering is still visible today. The line of the dyke is followed by the **Offa's Dyke Path**, a long distance footpath of some 180 miles that not only crosses the English-Welsh border ten times but also takes in some extraordinarily beautiful countryside.

PWLLHELI

Pwllheli is the chief town of the peninsula and, like Nefyn, was granted a charter in 1355; this was a gift by the Black Prince to Nigel de Loryng, who had helped the Prince win the Battle of Poitiers. A popular holiday resort with all the usual amusements, this is also still a market town, though its once busy port, where wine was imported from the Continent, is now home to pleasure craft, with a 420-berth marina and an annual sailing regatta. As well as being an ancient town, Pwllheli has played its part in the more recent history of Wales. During the National Eisteddfod in 1925, three members of the Army of Welsh Home Rulers met with three members of the Welsh Movement at the town's Temperance Hotel and joined forces to form the political party, Plaid Cymru.

RHIW

This hamlet lies on a miniature pass and overlooks **Porth Neigwl** (Hell's Mouth), a four mile sweep of beach so called because of its reputation for strong currents; it is a favourite spot for surfing. Sheltered from strong gales by Mynydd Rhiw, **Plas yn Rhiw** is a small, part medieval, part Tudor, part Georgian manor house which was given to the National Trust in 1952 by the unconventional Keating sisters from Nottingham. The three spinsters, Eileen, Lorna and Honora, purchased the property in 1938 and lovingly restored it after the house had lain neglected for some 20 years.

RHYL

As well as offering the full range of amusement arcades and seaside attractions, Rhyl is home to two large and exciting complexes: the **Sun Centre**, one of the first all-weather

Rhyl Harbour

leisure attractions in the country, and **Sea Life**, where a thrilling journey of discovery beneath the waves is promised to all. Rhyl's parish church was built by Sir George Gilbert Scott.

SHELL ISLAND

More correctly described as a peninsula that is cut off at high tide, Shell Island is a treasure trove of seashells and wildlife and the shoreline, a mixture of pebble beaches with rock pools and golden sands, is ideal for children to explore. Seals are often seen close by and there is plenty of birdlife; surprising considering the fairly regular aircraft activity from the nearby Llanbedr airfield.

TYWYN

This coastal town and seaside resort on Cardigan Bay has long sandy beaches, dunes and a promenade, as well as being the start (or the end) of the famous

Talyllyn Railway. The area inland from Tywyn is wonderful walking country, and marked walks include the new National Trail that runs between Machynlleth, Welshpool and Knighton. One of the stations on the line is Dolgoch, from which a walk takes in three sets of magnificent waterfalls. Four walks of varying lengths and difficulty start at Nant Gwernol station and provide an opportunity to enjoy the lovely woodlands and to look at the remains of Bryn Eglwys quarry and the tramway that served it.

UWCHMYNYDD

Situated on the wild and beautiful tip of the Llyn Peninsula, it was from here that, in the Middle Ages, the first pilgrims set out to Bardsey Island. The National Trust is responsible for much of the land towards the tip of the Llyn Peninsula, including the ecologically outstanding coastal heath of **Braich-y-Pwll**, where the ruins of St Mary's Church, once used by the pilgrims, can still be seen. This heath is the spring and summer home of a variety of plant life and birds, including fulmars, kittiwakes, cormorants, guillemots and the rare chough. Settlement of Bardsey Island is thought to have begun during the Dark Ages, although it was the death of St Dyfrig, on Bardsey, that saw the beginning of pilgrimages. At one time it was considered that three pilgrimages to this holy island was equivalent to one to Rome. Little remains of the 12th century monastery, and the island is now an important bird and field observatory. Boat trips around the island can be made from Aberdaron.

Valley was thought to have gained its name while Thomas Telford was cutting his road through the small hill here. Centuries earlier this was the home of Iron Age man whose weapons and horse trappings found in the area are now on display in the National Museum of Wales. However, Valley is perhaps better known today for the nearby airfield established here during World War II as a fighter pilot base. In 1943, the American Air Force expanded the base's capability for use as an Atlantic terminal and now the RAF uses it for training flights and for Air/Sea rescue.

AEL-Y-BRYN HOTEL

DYFFRYN ARDUDWY, GWYNEDD LL44 2BE
TEL: 01341 242701 FAX: 01341 242682

Directions: The hotel lies adjacent to the A496 at Dyffryn Ardudwy, midway between Barmouth and Harlech.

Standing in three acres of grounds back from the A496, **Ael-y-Bryn** is a small privately run hotel where proprietors Dolan and Morris have a warm personal welcome for their guests. Each of the eight en suite bedrooms in the mid-Victorian house has its own particular appeal; two rooms are big enough for families, and the four-poster room creates a romantic atmosphere for a honeymoon or a special weekend. Meals are served every lunchtime and evening, with the emphasis on traditional cooking and the use of fresh local produce. The non-smoking restaurant seats 30, and there's room for 30 in the bar and a further 40 in the conservatory. Sizzling steaks from Welsh Black beef are the speciality, and the Sunday roasts always bring in the crowds - booking is essential at the weekend.

The residents' lounge is a perfect spot to relax, and the well-stocked bar, where two or three real ales are always on tap, is a favourite meeting place with both locals and residents. The hotel enjoys magnificent views of Cardigan Bay across to Criccieth, Porthmadog and the Lleyn Peninsula, and the beach is just minutes away. The hotel has its own tennis courts, and there are several golf courses nearby.

The area is rich in history, and Neolithic, Iron Age and Bronze Age remains abound around the village. Also within a short drive of the hotel are the spectacularly sited Harlech Castle, Shell Island, Llanfair Slate Caverns and Snowdonia National Park. Ael-y-Bryn is open throughout the year.

- 🕐 12-11
- 🍴 A la carte
- £ Mastercard, Visa
- 🛏 8 en suite rooms
- 🅿 Off-road parking, tennis courts
- @ www.aelybryn.com
- ❓ Harlech Castle 5 miles, Shell Island 2 miles, Llanfair Slate Caverns 3 miles

ROSE HILL STREET, CONWY LL32 8LD
TEL: 01492 573482

Directions: Conwy lies just off thpressway across the estuary from Llandudno Junction. The inn lies within the town walls opposite the castle.

The Bridge Inn is a handsome black and white building within the town walls and almost opposite historic Conwy Castle. For the past eight years the inn has been in the ownership of Alison and Grant, who offer visitors a warm Welsh welcome, good food and drink and a comfortable bed for the night in well-kept accommodation. The bar and eating area of the Bridge have an inviting, traditional appeal; collections of beer badges and pump clips, framed caricatures of Victorian politicians and memorabilia relating to the town's past are among the interesting items in the bar, where Banks Bitter is among the wide selection of beers, both draught and bottled, that is available. In the non-smoking dining section bar snacks, bar meals and a traditional Sunday lunch are served, with everything freshly prepared

on the premises. Crab cakes, breaded mushrooms or a bowl of soup could get a meal under way, with turkey stroganoff, smoked haddock and spinach bake and peppered pork typifying the tasty, satisfying main courses. A selection of sweets is always available, and wine can be ordered by bottle or glass.

Bedrooms combine practicality with a certain elegance, and they're looking very smart after recent refurbishment. Central heating keeps things cosy, and all the rooms have en suite facilities, tv, hairdryers and beverage trays. So the Bridge is a very pleasant and convenient base for exploring Conwy, which is a delightful place to stroll around at leisure and discover the many places of historic significance. The chief attraction is, of course, the Castle, built as a royal residence, while among others are museums, churches and town houses.

- 🕐 11-11, Sun 12-10.30
- 🍴 Bar snacks and à la carte
- 💷 Mastercard, Visa
- 🛏 6 en suite rooms
- 🅿 Public car park opposite
- @ info@bridge-conwy.co.uk
- ❓ Conwy Castle, Aberconwy House, Plas Mawr (all in town), Colwyn Bay 6 miles, Llandudno 4 miles

THE DOUGLAS INN

TREGELE, CEMAES BAY, ISLE OF ANGLESEY LL67 0DN
TEL: 01407 710724 FAX: 01407 711575

Directions: From Menai Bridge, take the A5025 all the way to the north of the island, through Amlwch to Cemaes. The inn is on the left at Tregele, about half a mile beyond Cemaes.

When David Boardman and Victor Nikitenko took over **The Douglas Inn** early in 2002 they completely revamped it, adding to its appeal as a pub to appeal to all the family. This cheerful 17th century country inn, with views across open countryside from the front, has a very friendly and lively atmosphere and a warm welcome for all ages, families and even dogs in the non-eating areas; children can play in a separate games room. In the large, comfortable bar, where a log fire burns in the cooler months, a good selection of cask ales, beers and lagers is served, and there's an equally good choice of home-cooked food, from light bar snacks to classic pub favourites served in a smart modern restaurant which can be taken over for functions, parties and special occasions.

Food is served from 12 t0 9, with the restaurant menu available from 6 to 10 each evening. There's live entertainment on Friday and Saturday, a quiz on Thursday, and regular theme food evenings. The inn is also a popular place as a base for a holiday, so it's advisable to book well ahead for a room. The inn has four en suite guest bedrooms, all with tv, tea-making facilities and a high standard of decor and furnishings. On a clear day the Isle of Man can be seen, which explains the inn's name.

Nearby Cemaes Bay has two glorious, safe, sandy beaches, while around the headland at the western end of the bay lies Wylfa Nuclear Power Station surrounded by a nature trail. The nature reserve of Cemlyn Bay is home to thousands of terns between April and July.

- 🕐 12-12 (out of season 12-3 & 6-9)
- 🍴 A la carte + bar snacks
- 💷 All the major cards
- 🛏 4 en suite rooms
- 🅿 Car park, disabled facilities
- 🎵 Live entertainment Fri & Sat, quiz nights
- ❓ Cemaes Bay 1 mile, Holyhead 8 miles

GAERWEN ARMS

CHAPEL STREET, GAERWEN, ISLE OF ANGLESEY LL60 6DW
TEL: 01248 421906

North West Wales

Directions: Gaerwen lies just off the A5 about 4 miles west of Menai Bridge.

Chris and Sally Edwards have recently taken over the **Gaerwen Arms**, which has reverted to its original name after a spell as the Tafarn Newborough. Chris had been in charge of the bars and entertainment at the Celtic Royal Hotel in Caernarfon and felt that the time had come to take the plunge by taking over the licence here. The Gaerwen Arms is a traditional inn with lots of character, and the beamed bars feature some splendid period artefacts and memorabilia. John Smith's and Theakston's are the resident cask ales, with additional guest ales appearing in summer, and in the spacious dining room and conservatory a good choice of home-cooked food is served from noon right through to 9 o'clock. Welsh Black Beef curry is one of the favourites dish, and for the really seriously hungry (or two fairly hungry sharers!) the Gaerwen Grill

is a mighty plateful that probably keeps the local butcher in business - gammon, 16 oz steak, lamb and pork, liver and sausage and black pudding, with tomatoes, chips and a salad garnish. The very popular three-course Sunday lunch centres round a choice of three meats for the main course.

The Gaerwen Arms is very much a pub for all ages, and among the facilities for families with children are an outside play park, high chairs and a nappy changing room; children also have their own menu. This is a very sociable and convivial place, with singers performing on Friday and a disco or karaoke on Saturday. The A5, which by-passes this and other villages on its route, offers quick and easy access to Menai Bridge and the mainland to the east, and to Holyhead on the western tip of the island.

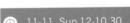

- 🕐 11-11, Sun 12-10.30
- 🍴 A la carte
- 💷 Diners, Mastercard, Visa
- 🅿 Car park, children's play park
- 🎵 Karaoke or disco Saturday, live singers Friday
- ❓ Menai Bridge 4 miles, Llanfair PG 3 miles, Newborough 4 miles

THE GILER ARMS HOTEL

RHYDLYDAN, PENTREFOELAS, NR BETWS-Y-COED,
NORTH WALES LL24 OLL
TEL: 01690 770612

North West Wales

> **Directions:** The inn stands on the A5 1 mile east of Pentrefoelas, 7 miles east of Betws-y-Coed.

Well known to the thousands of Midlanders who have travelled along the A5 to the North Wales coast, **The Giler Arms Hotel** is set in six acres of grounds alongside the River Merddwr. The pub's tenants are John and Sue Cowlishaw, who offer a friendly welcome and Bathams prizewinning ales, as well as an impressive range of whiskies. There is also a slate-floored 'locals' bar with dartboard and tv, and a games room with a pool table. Bar meals are served lunchtime and evening in the comfortable lounge, and in the 60-seat restaurant an extensive menu of excellent home-cooked food is served.

The hospitality and the good food and drink make the Giler Arms a popular place for locals and visitors alike, and it is also an ideal centre from which to tour the region's many attractions, which

range from the working watermill at Pentrefoelas to gardens, castles, slate and copper mines and the scenic glories of Snowdonia. Walking, riding, go karting and white water rafting are among the many outdoor activities available in the vicinity. All the hotel's twin and double rooms have their own shower and toilet, and the doubles enjoy super views across to the Denbigh Moors.

The family room sleeps four in twin and bunk beds, and a travel cot and folding bed can be made available in some rooms. The grounds include pleasant gardens beside the river, a coarse fishing lake stocked with carp and roach (fishing is free to residents) and a small campsite with space for up to five caravans and several tents.

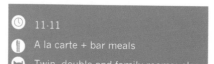

🕐 11-11

🍴 A la carte + bar meals

🛏 Twin, double and family rooms; also caravan and camping site

🅿 Car park, fishing lake

❓ Walking, fishing, Betws-y-Coed 7 miles, Snowdonia National Park 5 miles

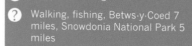

THE GWYDYR HOTEL

BETWS-Y-COED, NORTH WALES LL24 0AB
TEL/FAX: 01690 710777

Directions: The hotel is located in the centre of the town on the main A5.

Built in 1840 as a substantial private residence, **The Gwydyr** has for many years been the choice of discerning visitors to the delightful town of Betws-y-Coed. Since 1984, the handsome greystone hotel has been owned and run by the Wainwright family, who have a warm welcome for all their visitors, whether they have just dropped in to enjoy a drink, to dine in style in the restaurant or to experience the full spread of hospitality by booking in to the comfortable guest accommodation. The hotel's 19 letting bedrooms, all with en suite facilities, television, radio and tea/coffee trays, range from singles to doubles, twins and spacious family rooms.

- 🕐 12-11
- 🍴 A la carte
- 💷 All except Diners
- 🛏 19 en suite rooms
- 🅿 Private parking
- @ e-mail: northwales.gwydyrhotel@tesco.net website: www.betws.org.uk/acc/acc/gwydyr/defaul.htm
- ❓ In Betws-y-Coed: Motor Museum, Railway Museum, Telford's Waterloo Bridge; Swallow Falls 2 miles, Conwy Falls 2 miles, Ty Hill (the Ugly House) 3 miles

The hotel menus offer a wide selection of meals: breakfast is served from 8 o'clock, lunch can be anything from a snack or bar meal to a 3-course luncheon, and evening meals are served in the elegant 40-seat restaurant. The Lounge Bar serves fine wines, beers, spirits and non-alcoholic drinks, while cocktails both classic and unusual are mixed in Banjo's Cocktail Bar. The large Victorian-style drawing room is a perfect place to socialise, to relax after dinner or to indulge in a delicious cream tea (served daily from 2.30 to 5.30). Betws-y-Coed is surrounded by beautiful scenery, and the Gwydyr is a particularly comfortable and civilised base for exploring the wonders of Snowdonia National Park and the Gwydr Forest Park. Miles of rivers provide excellent fishing in the locality, and season tickets can be obtained from the hotel.

KINGS ARMS

HIBERNIA TERRACE, HOLYHEAD, ISLE OF ANGLESEY LL65 1OG
TEL: 01407 762528

> **Directions:** Take the A5 for Menai Bridge to Holyhead on the northwestern tip of the island. The inn is after Newry Beach, on Hibernia Terrace.

The Kings Arms is a traditional old-world hostelry with a black and white frontage, a patio garden and hanging baskets adorning the front in spring and summer. Occupying a prominent site in Holyhead, the inn has been owned and run since 1994 by Tommy Doyle, who is very much at its heart, with a warm greeting for every one of his customers, whether a familiar face or one of the many visitors to the Isle of Anglesey. There's a nautical theme to the spacious panelled bar, which has a non-smoking section and a separate section for watching the major sporting events on a big screen Sky tv. All ages are welcome, and for families with very small children the nappy changing room is a definite bonus.

A good variety of beers and wines is always available, and home-cooked food is served from 12 to 3 and from 5.30 to 9 in the week and all day on Saturday and Sunday. Steaks are a speciality, and the printed menu is supplemented by daily specials; bar snacks cater for smaller appetites or visitors with not much time to spare. But this is really a place to relax and unwind, and for those with business in Holyhead or holidaymakers the Kings Arms makes an excellent base, with neat, practical modern bedrooms, all with en suite facilities, Sky tv and tea/coffee-makers. Entertainment comes in the form of live music on Tuesday and Thursday. Holyhead and the surrounding area have much to offer the visitor, including a maritime museum, clifftop and country walks, safe bathing beaches, South Stack Lighthouse, Holyhead Mountain and the RSPB Centre at Gogarth Bay.

- 🕐 11·11, Sun 12·10.30
- 🍴 A la carte + plus bar snacks
- 💷 All the major cards
- 🛏 All rooms en suite
- 🅿 Car parking
- 🎵 Live music Tuesday & Thursday
- @ 1120efc@aol.com
- ❓ Trearrdur Bay beaches 2 miles, South Stack 2 miles, Gogarth Bay 3 miles

THE KINMEL ARMS

ST GEORGE, NR ABERGELE, NORTH WALES LL22 9BP
TEL: 01745 832207 FAX: 01745 822044

Directions: The village is 1 mile south of the A547 Abergele-Rhuddlan road. Also very close to J24 of the A55.

The Watson family - Lynn and Tim - have in their brief time as owners made **The Kinmel Arms** one of the best and most popular eating places in the whole of North Wales. The 17th century listed buildings oozes style and quality, and in Weston Holmes the Watsons have a chef of great talent. He and his team ensure that all the ingredients are the freshest and the best, and his dishes are prepared with a view to healthier eating, with a reduction in fat, salt and sugar content and an increase in fibre. The lunch and dinner menus change daily, and everything - absolutely everything! - on the lists is worth trying: the fish specials (the choice is greatest on Traditional Friday Fish Night); the famous Weston-style prawn cocktail; the prime Welsh beef steaks; the superb roast Sunday lunches. Sandwiches and lighter meals

are available at lunchtime, along with a small selection from the evening menu. The chefs are experts at catering for groups and parties, organising anything from a finger buffet to a full-scale banquet.

The best food deserves the best drink, and the owners pride themselves on seeking out the best wines, spirits and beers at the best prices. The wine selection includes no fewer than eight house wines, all available by the bottle or two sizes of glass. Three cask ales are always on tap, the resident Tetleys and two fortnightly changing guests. To the west of St George lies Abergele, a quiet holiday resort, while in the other direction is Bodelwyddan with the twin attractions of a Victorian country house that is the Welsh home of the National Portrait Gallery and a village church with a white limestone spire.

- 🕐 12-3 & 7-11, closed Mon except Bank Holidays, also Sunday evenings between Jan & Easter
- 🍴 A la carte
- 💷 Mastercard, Visa
- 🅿 Plenty of adjacent parking
- 🎵 Gourmet evenings
- ❓ Abergele 3 miles, Bodelwyddan 2 miles, Towyn 3 miles

LIVERPOOL ARMS HOTEL

CASTLE STREET, BEAUMARIS, ISLE OF ANGLESEY LL58 8BA
TEL: 01248 810362   FAX: 01248 811135

North West Wales

Directions: A central location in Castle Street, Beaumaris, 4 miles northeast of Menai Bridge on the A545.

Matthew, Sarah and Little Molly Rose are the charming hosts at the **Liverpool Arms Hotel**, a handsome Georgian-fronted building on the main street of Beaumaris. They brought with them many years' experience in the trade when they took over in 2000, and the personal family touch is very evident in the delightfully relaxed atmosphere and the genuine feeling that the customer comes first. The inn's history goes back to 1706, when there was a flourishing trade between Liverpool and Beaumaris; the main feature of the hotel is the splendid and spacious Admiral's Tavern, where traditional real ales and fine malt whiskies are served in a setting of nautical memorabilia and seafaring items, including timbers from Nelson's

flagship HMS Victory and from HMS Conway, which was wrecked in the Menai Strait during a great storm in 1953.

No one goes hungry at the Liverpool Arms, where an appealing and very varied menu changes daily. In summer the well-stocked salad bar is a popular feature, while in winter there are plenty of tasty, warming soups and casseroles. A listed, oak-panelled staircase leads up to the hotel's 10 bedrooms, which include two family rooms and a four-poster suite. All have private bathrooms, tv, telephone, central heating and tea/coffee making facilities. Four more rooms (all doubles) are available in the Lodge, a couple of houses along Castle Street. Beaumaris is a town of wide appeal, with a long and fascinating history, and it is now a popular resort and a yachting centre.

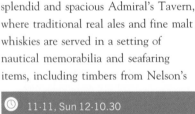

- 🕐 11-11, Sun 12-10.30
- 🍴 A la carte, summer salad bar
- 💷 Diners, Mastercard, Visa
- 🛏 10 bedrooms
- 🅿 Car parking
- @ e-mail: enquiries@liverpoolarms.co.uk web: www.liverpoolarms.co.uk
- ❓ In Beaumaris: Castle, Museum of Childhood Memories, Aquarium; Menai Bridge 4 miles, Puffin Island 4 miles, Red Wharf Bay 5 miles

LLANFAIR ARMS

MILL ROAD, LLANFAIRFECHAN, CONWY LL33 0TT
TEL: 01248 680521

> **Directions:** On the A55 coastal Expressway 6 miles west of Conwy follow the signs for Llanfairfechan; the inn can be found just over the bridge in the centre of the village.

In the heart of a quiet village close to the coast and the coastal Expressway (A55), the **Llanfair Arms** is an attractive stone-built inn that dates back to 1862. The interior is well furnished, comfortable and inviting, and the inn has a splendid suntrap beer garden at the bottom of which flows the Afon Dhu (Black River). Outside or in, visitors can enjoy an excellent selection of drinks from the well-stocked bar, including three real ales on tap (the inn is a member of Cask Marque) and the usual range of beers, lagers and spirits. Solid sustenance is provided by freshly made sandwiches, and tea and coffee are available as an alternative to something stronger - useful for motorists who drop in from the A55 to enjoy a break in their journey.

Very much at the heart of village life, the inn is run by Dafydd and Pebbles Roberts, who were previously in charge of the sailing club in Llanfairfechan, so they know all about hospitality and they know their local clientele. Darts and pool are the favourite pub games, and there are regular quiz nights; football fans can watch premiership action on Saturdays on satellite tv. The inn's location close to the main coastal road means that it is not only popular and easily accessible to the local villages and towns but also a very agreeable stopping off point for motorists and tourists. Llanfairfechan is an excellent base for energetic walks among stunning scenery, and there's a long stretch of sandy beach. Nearby attractions include a nature reserve at Traeth Lafan and a number of prehistoric sites, notably Cefn Coch, one of the best known Bronze Age stone circles in Wales.

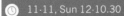

- 11-11, Sun 12-10.30
- Sandwiches
- Street parking
- Quiz nights
- Beach 1 mile, Snowdonia National Park 2 miles, Conwy 6 miles

THE PARCIAU ARMS

MARIAN-GLAS, BENLLECH, ISLE OF ANGLESEY LL73 8NY
TEL: 01248 853766

North West Wales

Directions: From Menai bridge take the A5025 north through Pentraeth to Benllech. The inn is located 2 miles further on towards Amlwch.

Keith and Jan Coulman bought the **Parciau Arms** in the summer of 2001 and have since made steady improvements to the decor and furnishings, making it what it is today - a very pleasant and convivial country pub with a warm welcome for all the family (and the dog, as long as it knows how to behave!). The public areas are cosy and inviting, with an open log fire in the cooler months, and the bar itself is adorned with a fine collection of horse brasses. In the summer, the scene shifts outside to the patio terrace and garden, where there are tables and chairs and play area for children. Tetley's and Abbot real ales head the drinks selection, which also includes the house favourite Anglesey Chardonnay and Shiraz from Australia and a choice of malt whiskies. Food is served from 12 to 2.30 and from 5.30 to 8.30 every day, and the choice

runs from snacks and bar meals to the full menu and daily specials; typifying the bar menu are baguettes, ploughman's lunches, five bean chilli, ham, egg & chips, steak pie, and Welsh Black Beef curry, while the main menu adds the likes of sirloin steak or chicken in white wine sauce, with a roast for Sunday lunch. This is one of the most sociable pubs in the whole region, and more often than not there's something going on, from charity events and a monthly car treasure hunt to regular theme nights, the Sunday evening quiz and live music sessions on Saturday. Pool and darts are played in the bar, and there's also a separate little games room in a corner of the car park. Red Wharf Bay and several lovely secluded beaches are close by, and among other attractions are the substantial remains of a Celtic settlement at Din Lligwy.

- 🕐 12-11, Sun to 10.30
- 🍴 A la carte + bar meals
- 💷 Mastercard, Visa
- 🅿 Car park, children's play area
- 🎵 Live music Saturday, Quiz Sunday, Car treasure hunt 1 Sunday a month
- ❓ Red Wharf Bay 3 miles, Din Lligwy 3 miles, Menai Bridge 10 miles

PENBONT INN

STATION ROAD, LLANRUG, GWYNEDD LL55 4AY
TEL: 01286 674473

> **Directions:** From the A4086 Llanberis-Caernarfon road turn at the Post Office in Llanrug on to Station Road. The inn is on the right, beyond the chapel.

Penbont is an attractive black and white building on a corner site in Llanrug. The tenants are Wendy and Geraint Jones, who took over in the autumn of 2001 and have put a lot of time and effort into redecorating the premises and improving the facilities of this popular spot. Visitors can be sure of a friendly greeting in the bright, roomy bar, where the choice of cask ales includes monthly changing guests and the wines feature well-chosen house selections.

The inn also has a lounge with plenty of room to relax and a games room with a dartboard and pool table. One of the most important enhancements made by Wendy and Geraint is the introduction

of food in the shape of bar meals, basket meals and a children's menu. The public areas are accessible to wheelchairs, and in summer the beer garden is a major attraction. The inn holds live entertainment sessions every Saturday evening. Accommodation in static caravans can be arranged by the tenants, and anyone taking advantage and making a base here has an almost endless list of things to see and do in the locality. Among these are the castle, the museum, the slateworks and the Roman fort in or around Caernarfon; the Greenwood family adventure centre, the little lake railway, the Electric Mountain and Power Station at Llangorse; and the Snowdon Mountain Railway running up the mountain from Llanberis - or there's the walk to the summit.

- 2-11, Fri & Sat 12-11, Sun 12-10.30
- Bar meals
- Static caravan accommodation can be arranged
- Car park; disabled access to bars
- Live music Saturday
- Caernarfon 3 miles, Llanberis 5 miles, Snowdon 4 miles

PENRHYN OLD HALL

PENRHYN BAY, LLANDUDNO, CONWY LL30 3EE

TEL: 01492 549888

Directions: Penrhyn Bay is on the coast road (B5115) between Llandudno and Colwyn Bay. Turn first left off the roundabout to find the hotel.

A medieval manor house is at the heart of **Penrhyn Old Hall**, which enjoys a tranquil, picturesque setting with woods and well-mapped footpaths. At the same time it is virtually a suburb of Llandudno, so the delights of town, country and coast are all close by. Behind its imposing facade, the Hall functions as pub, restaurant and unique venue for parties and special occasions, and the public rooms are warm, inviting and convivial, with bags of historic and old-world appeal. The Tudor Bar and Restaurant, open every day, are atmospheric spots for enjoying a drink or a meal; fresh home-cooked food is served from daily changing menus, including lunches every day, a traditional Sunday lunch and an extensive à la carte choice in the evenings Wednesday to Saturday.

It is said by some that Roderick, grandson of the last King of the Britons, built a palace on this site in the 8th

century. Nothing, of course, of that building survives, but a few parts of the medieval hall are still to be seen, and the whole place is full of architectural and historic interest, including fireplaces, remarkable frescoes, carvings and stained glass. The Marsh family, Ann and George, acquired the property in 1963, and set about major restoration work and the construction of sympathetic extensions. In 1988 they retired, leaving their children Kim and Guy, and Guy's wife Anne, to run the show. One of the extensions houses the nightclub, which can be hired for functions, with room for up to 200 guests. Popular skittles nights are held in the Baronial Hall, which is at other times available for private parties. Places of interest in the vicinity include the resorts of Llandudno and Colwyn Bay and the massive limestone headland of Great Orme.

- 🕐 12-2.30 & 5.30-11.30
- 🍴 A la carte
- 💷 Mastercard, Visa
- 🅿 Car parking
- 🎵 Live music, disco, skittles
- ❓ Conwy Castle 2 miles, Llandudno 3 miles, Colwyn Bay 4 miles

HIGH STREET, BALA, GWYNEDD LL23 7AB
TEL: 01678 520309 FAX: 01678 521135

> **Directions:** The hotel is located on the main street (A494) of Bala, which lies at the northern end of Lake Bala.

On the main street of the popular lakeside town of Bala, **Plas Coch** started life as a coaching inn over 200 years ago. The hotel is owned by the Aykroyd family and run by Edwina Evans, and down the years it has built up a fine reputation for service, comfort and hospitality. Guest accommodation comprises ten bedrooms, all with private bathroom or shower room, tv, tea/coffee making facilities and central heating. Rooms range from singles to family rooms with a double bed, single bed and pull-out bed. The lounge and locals bar are congenial places to meet for a chat or a drink - Worthington Smooth and Carling are the favourites with the regular customers.

The dining area, which is open to residents and non-residents, is open for lunch and dinner and prides itself on traditional cooking and the use of local produce as much as possible, and a good choice of wine to complement the meal. Chef's home-made curry is always a popular choice, and the printed list is supplemented by a daily specials board. Plas Coch is a very agreeable base for touring this lovely part of the world. Bala, 'the Gateway to the Snowdonia National Park', lies on the shores of the largest natural lake in Wales, with sailing, canoeing and windsurfing all available, and the National Whitewater Centre close by. Among the many attractions, apart from the wonderful scenery, is the narrow gauge Bala Lake Railway. This delightful little railway follows the lake for four miles and ends up at Llanuwchllyn.

- 🕐 12-11
- 🍴 A la carte
- £ All except Diners
- 🛏 10 en suite rooms
- @ e-mail: info@plascoch.com
  website: www.plascoch.com
- ❓ Bala Lake Railway, National Whitewater Centre 2 miles, Penllyn Forest 2 miles, sailing, water sports, walking and rambling

THE RED LION HOTEL

LLANSANNAN, NR DENBIGH, CONWY LL16 5HG
TEL: 01745 870256 FAX: 01745 870158

Directions: From the A55 coastal express road turn onto the A548 at Abergele. Follow this road to Llanfair Talhaiarn where it becomes the A544. Llansannan is about 2 miles further on, at the junction with the B5382.

Robert and Alison Jones have a warm Welsh welcome for one and all at the **Red Lion Hotel** on a prominent corner site in the village of Llansannan. It's a lovely old building with its origins in the 13th century, with hanging baskets on its green and cream facade and a beer garden at the rear. Inside, the inn has all the character and atmosphere expected from its great age - and more: open fires, ancient beams, horse brasses and gleaming copper plates, carriage lamps, ornamental shields, mugs, tankards, sporting pictures and prints. there are two open fires with copper hoods, one of them enormous, with rough stone surrounds and ancient implements hanging above.

The bar serving area is, in contrast, quite neat and simple, with black and white decor and comfortably upholstered bar stools. In this most inviting setting regulars and visitors can enjoy the fine range of the J W Lees brewery, including cask ales and original and export beers. In a separate eating area with neatly set little wooden tables home-cooked food is served from a menu and specials board that features plenty of local produce. Major sports events can be viewed on a big-screen Sky tv, and there's live entertainment or karaoke at the weekend. The inn is a good base for a holiday spent walking, climbing and visiting the local places of interest, and it's best to book well in advance for the two comfortable rooms. Denbigh, with its imposing castle ruins, ancient town walls and medieval streets, is a short drive away.

- 11-11, Sun 12-10.30
- Home cooked Pub Grub
- All the major cards
- 2 bedrooms
- Car park
- Live entertainment + karaoke weekends
- jonesa8@aol.com
- Llangernyw 4 miles, Denbigh 7 miles

RHIW GOCH

BRONABER, TRAWSFYNYDD, BLAENAU FFESTINIOG,
GWYNEDD LL41 4UY   TEL: 01766 540374 FAX: 01766 540434

Directions: On the main A470 Dolgellau-Blaenau Ffestiniog road about 9 miles north of Dolgellau. Follow the signs for Trawsfynydd Holiday Village and Ski Slope. The inn is located by the ski slope.

The earliest parts of **Rhiw Goch** date back as far as the 12th century, when it was built as a farmhouse. What is now the locals bar was added in the 13th century, and various later additions include the 1610 wing where the oak-panelled entrance is today. Its history is as interesting as it is long, and the site has at various times also been home of the local MP and the High Sheriff of Merionethshire, a courthouse, the HQ of a Royal Artillery training camp, an officers mess and a hotel. It's now a family friendly inn of great warmth and personality, with the most delightful hosts in Stephen and Sandra Bond, who brought a wealth of experience when they arrived in 1996.

Three bars (wheelchair accessible) provide abundant space and comfort for relaxing with a glass of one of the cask ales and enjoying home-made food prepared to order from an impressively varied menu. Welsh beef and lamb are the basis of many of the dishes, withTex-Mex flavour to some of them; vegetarian options include chilli non carne with 8 kinds of bean, leeks, tomatoes, herbs and spices, topped with cheese and chives. A snack menu, with big baps and a traditional breakfast, is served until 3. The inn has a games room with table football, darts, pool and slot machines, a beer garden and a tennis court. Accommodation is also available in the form of log cabins. The inn stands by the ski slope in the Trawsfynydd Holiday Village; other nearby attractions run the whole gamut from the natural beauty to the local nuclear power station visitor centre.

- 12-11, Sun to 10.30
- A la carte
- All the major cards
- Log cabins on site
- Car park, disabled access, tennis court
- www.rhiwgoch.com
- Adjacent ski slope and holiday village, Nuclear Power Station 2 miles, Snowdonia National Park 2 miles, Blaenau Ffestiniog 6 miles

THE ROYAL OAK HOTEL

HIGH STREET, PENRHYNDEUDRAETH, GWYNEDD LL48 6BL
TEL: 01766 770501

North West Wales

Directions: Penrhyndeudraeth is situated on the A487 4 miles east of Porthmadog. From the A487 turn right into the High Street (Beddgelert Road); the Royal Oak is on the left.

On the High Street in the village of Penrhyndeudraeth, **The Royal Oak** is a bay-windowed end of terrace building in Welsh stone. Once a private residence, it is now a comfortable and convivial hostelry with affable, experienced licensees in Marion and Raymond Jones, at the helm since autumn 2000. In the spacious bar, the Burtonwood range of cask ales and other draught and bottle beers heads the drinks list, while for solid nourishment bar snacks, a full à la carte menu and a children's menu cater for all tastes and appetites. Darts and pool, played in a separate section, are the favourite pub games at the Royal Oak, and other entertainment includes regular quiz nights and live music on Saturdays (sometimes also on Friday and Sunday).

With its two comfortable letting

bedrooms - a double and a twin - the Royal Oak is a very pleasant and convenient base for exploring the numerous attractions of this part of the country. Chief among these are the amazing Italianate village of Portmeirion and the glorious terraced gardens of Plas Tan-y-Bwlch, but this is also an area rich in transport nostalgia. Penrhyndeudraeth is a station on the famous little Blaenau Ffestiniog narrow-gauge railway, which puffs its way along the picturesque Vale of Ffestiniog from Blaenau to Porthmadog. Other attractions to delight transport buffs include the Welsh Highland Railway and the Madog Car & Motorcycle Museum at Porthmadog. To the north, around Beddgelert, the scenery takes on an almost Alpine look, and throughout the region there are reminders of the once-thriving slate industry.

- 🕐 12-11, Sun to 10.30
- 🍴 A la carte + bar snacks
- 🛏 1 double, 1 twin room
- 🎵 Various entertainment at the weekend
- ❓ Portmeirion 2 miles, Blaenau Ffestiniog 3 miles, Porthmadog 4 miles, Beddgelert 5 miles

THE SWAN INN

SWAN SQUARE, LLANFAIR TALHAIARN, CONWY LL22 8RY
TEL: 01745 720233

Directions: From Abergele, take the A548 to Llanfair Talhaiarn (about 4 miles). Over the bridge · The Swan is the second inn on the left.

Annette Tilsley, who has owned the **Swan Inn** since 1999, looks after visitors in the best possible way, combining the role of friendly, welcoming hostess and accomplished cook. At the centre of a quiet, picturesque village just off the A548 Abergele-Llanrwst road, the inn is popular with both locals and tourists, both attracted here by the reputation Annette has established since her arrival. Hanging baskets adorn the 17th century black and white facade in spring and summer, and there's a pleasant beer garden to the rear. Inside, an open fire blazes in the cooler months, and thirsts are quenched by a good selection of traditional beers, including Marsdens Bitter and Banks Mild.

Booking is strongly recommended to be sure of a table in the small non-smoking dining area, where Annette's well-priced bill of fare provides a splendid variety of food catering for all

tastes. To satisfy smaller appetites there are sandwiches and jacket potatoes with a good choice of fillings and 'light-bite' portions of lasagne, broccoli bake, steak pie, burgers, curries and gammon steaks. The wide ranging main menu offers the likes of grilled trout, pan-fried duck breast, lots of steaks and the very popular speciality chicken smokey blue - chicken breast stuffed with stilton, cooked in a smoked bacon and red wine sauce. Sunday lunch, served from 12 till 8, and the Tuesday to Thursday specials list are highlighted by roasts (beef, lamb and alternating pork and chicken): the really ravenous can order a main course of all three meats. This is a particularly peaceful and unspoilt area of North Wales; the inn is surrounded by fine walking country, and fishing is available on the River Elwy. The village itself is the burial place of John Jones, a poet acclaimed as the Welsh Burns.

- 🕐 12-3 & 6-11, Sat 12-11, Sun 12-10.30
- 🍴 A la carte and fixed-price menus
- 🅿 Car parking
- @ e-mail: swaninn@llanfairth.co.uk
  website: www.llanfairth.co.uk
- ❓ Abergele 5 miles, country walks, fishing

THE TOWN HOUSE CAFÉ:BAR

64 MOSTYN STREET, LLANDUDNO, CONWY LL30 2SB
TEL: 01492 862931

North West Wales

Directions: The inn is on the main street in the heart of Llandudno 2 minutes' walk from the beach.

The **Town House** is a popular café and bar on one of the main streets in Llandudno, in the heart of the town and a two-minute walk from the beach. The Davies family have put in a huge amount of time and energy since arriving as leaseholders in June 2002, and the place (previously called Plumes) has quickly become a favourite not only with the local residents but also with the tourists who flock into the area in the summer months. Behind a traditional frontage, the interior is stylishly modern, with effective use of slate and wood. On the ground floor the bar is at the front, the dining area at the back, while upstairs is the restaurant/function room that is available for hire.

The chef Neil Scott keeps a smile on his customers' faces with a good choice

- ⏰ All day, 10.30am-11pm, Sun 12 noon-10.30pm.
- 🍴 A la carte (roasts a speciality)
- Ⓟ Function room (seats up to 60)
- 🎵 Quiz Thursday
- @ e-mail: townhouse@llandudno-wonderland.co.uk
  website: www.townhouse-llandudno.co.uk
- ❓ Great Orme (Copper Mine, Tramway) 1 mile, Colwyn Bay 5 miles, Bodnant Gardens 6 miles

of dishes served from 12 to 3 in the winter and all day until 9 o'clock in the summer. The specialities are the roast meals, well priced and served in generous helpings. On Sundays the Town House stages live entertainment evenings, and Thursday is quiz night, starting at 9 o'clock. This is an excellent spot to relax over a meal, or to pause for a drink while seeing the sights of Llandudno, the largest and most popular of the North Wales coast resorts. Its many attractions include the promenade, the pier, the visitor centre and the museum.

THE WHITE EAGLE

RHOSCOLYN, ISLE OF ANGLESEY LL65 2NJ
TEL: 01407 860267

> **Directions:** leave the A5 at the Valley turn-off. Go to Valley then turn left on to the B4545 signposted Trearddur Bay. About 1 mile along, take the left turn to Rhoscolyn.

The **White Eagle** is a bright, welcoming pub on the west coast of the Isle of Anglesey, an easy drive from the main A5 and not far from Holy Island and Holyhead. The tenants at this splendid inn are Carl and Linsey Owen, who took over in November 2002, but Carl was bar manager for five years before that. Linsey and two other chefs prepare a tempting variety of dishes that cater for all appetites and most tastes, from sandwiches and light snacks to full meals. The home-made pies (steak & kidney, chicken & mushroom) always command a faithful following, and other choices run from meat or vegetable lasagne to gammon and rump steaks, crispy aromatic duck and BBQ ribs served with spicy potato wedges. For many of the regular customers the

Sunday roast special, with roast beef and Yorkshire pudding as the centrepiece, is a treat not to be missed.

On the drinks front, Marston Cask and Bitter are always on tap, along with a rotating guest and other draught beers, lagers and cider. Children are very welcome, and the inn has two non-smoking family rooms. When the weather is kind, the scene shifts to the lawned beer garden, where picnic benches are set out and barbecues are held in the summer. Rhoscolyn has lovely wide, sandy beach that is excellent for swimming and fishing, and the headland is a superb place for cliff walking. From here there are splendid views northwards over Trearddur Bay and southwards over Cymyran Bay. The village holds a charity cricket match every August Bank Holiday.

- 12-3 & 6-11, all day during major holidays
- A la carte and snacks
- Mastercard, Visa
- Off-road parking
- Monthly quiz; themed food nights, charity cricket match August Bank Holiday
- @ www.thewhiteeagle.co.uk
- Beach close by, Holyhead 4 miles

94	The Angel, Llanidloes, Powys		**103**	The New Inn, Llanbadarn Fynydd, Powys
95	The Bull Hotel, Presteigne, Powys		**104**	The Oak, Guilsfield, Welshpool, Powys
96	The Castle Inn, Pengenffordd, Powys		**105**	The Old Ford Inn, Llanhamlach, Powys
97	The Corn Exchange, Crickhowell, Powys		**106**	The Railway Inn, Forden, Powys
98	The Crown Inn, Montgomery, Powys		**107**	The Royal Head, Llandiloes, Powys
99	The George & Dragon, Knighton, Powys		**108**	The Star Inn, Dylife, Powys
100	The Glansevern Arms, Pantmawr, Powys		**109**	Stonecroft Inn, Llanwrtyd Wells, Powys
101	The Green Inn, Llangedwyn, Powys		**110**	Triangle Inn, Cwmdauddwr, Powys
102	Lowfield Inn, Marton, Welshpool, Powys		**111**	The White Swan Inn, Llanfrynach, Powys

Please note all cross references refer to page numbers

POWYS

Once part of the old county of Montgomeryshire, this northern region of Powys is an area of varied landscape and small towns and villages. Situated between the high, rugged landscape of Snowdonia and the farmland of Shropshire, this is a gentle and pleasant region through which many rivers and streams flow. As well as being home to the highest waterfall outside Scotland, Pistyll Rhaeadr, one of the Seven Wonders of Wales, there is Lake Vyrnwy. Built in the 1880s to supply the expanding city of Liverpool with water, this large reservoir is not only famous for its splendid feats of Victorian engineering but also as a location for the film *The Dambusters*.

The major settlement here is Welshpool, a town situated on the banks of the River Severn which is also close to the English border. Originally known as Pool, the prefix was added to ensure that the dispute regarding its nationality was finalised once and for all. From the town leisurely canal boat trips can be taken along the Montgomery Canal but there is also a narrow gauge steam railway running westwards to Llanfair Caereinion. Near the town can be found the splendid Powis Castle, which is famous not only for the many treasures it houses but also for its magnificent gardens.

Montgomery, a tiny anglicised town which gave its name to the county of Montgomeryshire, not only has a splendidly situated ruined borderland castle but it is also close to some of the best preserved sections of Offa's Dyke. Nearby Newtown, which despite its name was founded in the 10th century,

PLACES OF INTEREST

Powys

is another interesting and historic market town that is also the home of the famous High Street newsagents WH Smith. The associated museum tells of the company's growth from its humble beginnings in 1792 and those who are interested

Machynlleth

in history, particularly social history, will find the Robert Owen Memorial Museum well worth a visit.

To the west and beyond the quaint town of Llanidloes lies Machynlleth, the home of Owain Glyndwr's parliament in the 15th century. A visit to the Welsh hero's centre, which is found in the part 15th century parliament house, tells the story of Glyndwr and his struggle against the English.

This is great walking country that takes in some of the finest scenery in Wales. The many marked established trails and walks include a large part of Offa's Dyke Path and Glyndwr's Way, a 123-mile walk that follows a circular route across dramatic landscapes from Welshpool to Knighton by way of Machynlleth.

Llyn Y Fan Fach, Brecon Beacons

This southern region of the large county of Powys is steeped in history and there is evidence aplenty of turbulent times past. From the Celtic standing stones and burial chambers, to the ruined castles at Builth Wells,

Painscastle, Clyro and near Talgarth, the landscape is littered with the buildings and memorials left by many past inhabitants.

Brecon Beacons

In the heart of the county (the northern part of this region) can be found the four spa towns of Llandrindod Wells, Builth Wells, Llangammarch Wells and Llanwrtyd Wells. Still popular tourist centres today, though no longer primarily spas, these places all grew and developed as a result of the arrival of the railways and the Victorians' interest in health. Although the architecture of these towns suggests that they date mainly from the 19th and early 20th centuries, there are the remains of a Roman fort close to Llandrindod Wells, and Builth Wells saw much fighting in medieval times. As well as the spa towns, the region also has the border settlements of Knighton and Presteigne, the second-hand book capital of the world Hay-on-Wye and the ancient cathedral city of Brecon, but it is perhaps for its varied countryside that south Powys is better known. Close to Rhayader, in the Cambrian Mountains, are the spectacular reservoirs and dams that make up the Elan Valley. Built at the end of the 19th century to supply water to the West Midlands, not only are these a great feat of Victorian engineering but the surrounding countryside is home to one of Britain's rarest and most beautiful birds - the Red Kite.

Further south lies the Brecon Beacons National Park, which takes its name from the distinctively shaped sandstone mountains of the Brecon Beacons; but there are two other ranges within the park's 519 square miles. To the east of the Brecon Beacons lie the interlocking peaks of the Black Mountains which stretch to the English border while to the west is Black Mountain, which, though its name is singular, refers to an unpopulated range of barren, smooth humped peaks.

ABERGWESYN

Situated in an isolated spot in the Irfon Valley, Abergwesyn lies on an old drovers' route that twists and climbs through the **Abergwesyn Pass**. Known as the 'roof of Wales', this is a beautiful pathway that centuries ago consisted of nothing more than dirt tracks, along which the drovers would shepherd cattle and other livestock from one market town to the next. There are actually a number of drovers' routes which can be followed - some in part by car. Many of the roads are narrow and in the south one such route begins at Llandovery and travels across the Epynt mountain and crosses the ford at Erwood.

BERRIEW

Berriew's 1870s church contains fine marble effigies of Arthur Price, Sheriff of Montgomeryshire in 1578, and his two wives. The memorial cross of 1933 in the churchyard is by Sir Ninian Comper, whose work can be seen in churches all over Britain. The Gardens at **Glansevern Hall**, entered from the A483 by the bridge over the River Rhiew, were first laid out in 1801 and now cover 18 acres. Noted in particular for the unusual tree species, they also have lovely lawns, herbaceous beds, a walled garden, rose gardens, a lovely water garden and a rock garden

complete with grotto. In the Old Stables are a tea room, a garden shop and a gallery with regular exhibitions of paintings, sculpture and interior design. Surrounding a very handsome Greek Revival house, the gardens are set in parkland on the banks of the Severn.

BRECON

Famous for its ancient cathedral, Georgian architecture and annual Jazz Festival, Brecon lies on the banks of the River Usk, at the confluence of the Rivers Honddu and Tarrell in the heart of the National Park. A walk along the promenade beside the River Usk leads to the remains of medieval **Brecon Castle** which can be found partly in the Bishop's Garden and partly at the Castle Hotel. The town grew up around this castle, which was built in the late 11th century by Bernard of Newmarch. Besieged first by Llywelyn the Last and again during Owain Glyndwr's rebellion in the early 15th century, by the time of the Civil War Brecon considered its growing cloth

Abergavenny Canal, Brecon

trade of paramount importance and remained neutral with the townsfolk going so far as to begin dismantling the castle. **Brecon Cathedral** is a magnificent building that originated from an 11th century cell of the Benedictine monastery at Battle in Sussex. What had been the Church of St John the Evangelist was elevated to cathedral status in 1923 as the Cathedral of the new diocese of Swansea and Brecon. A 16th century tithe barn in the grounds has been restored and now houses the Heritage Centre. In another of the town's old buildings, the elegant former Old Shire Hall, is the **Brecknock Museum** where visitors can see the old assize court and an extensive collection of artefacts and other items from past centuries including a large collection of Welsh love spoons. The town's second museum is equally fascinating and the **South Wales Borderers Museum** features memorabilia of the regiment's famous defence of Rorke's Drift in 1879. Over 300 years of military history are recorded here through various displays that include armoury, uniforms and medals - the regiment has taken part in every major campaign and war and has won 29 Victoria Crosses and over 100 battle honours (nine of the VCs were awarded at Rorke's Drift, where 141 men from the regiment were attacked by 4,000

Zulu warriors). **Monmouthshire and Brecon Canal** is a beautiful waterway that once used to bring coal and limestone into the town. There are attractive walks along the canal towpath along with pleasure cruises on both motorised and horsedrawn barges while the canal basin in the town has been reconstructed and is now proving to be an attraction in its own right. Anyone thirsty from all the sightseeing can either take advantage of the many pubs, inns, restaurant and cafés in the town or pay a visit to the **Welsh Whisky Distillery and Visitor Centre**.

BUILTH WELLS

Builth Wells lies on the River Wye, which is spanned at this point by a six-arched bridge. The discovery of the saline springs in 1830 helped Builth Wells develop from a small market town into a fashionable spa that became more popular with the arrival of the railways towards the end of the 19th century. As

Builth Wells

a result, many of the town's original narrow streets are littered with Victorian and Edwardian buildings.

However, the town's history dates back much further than just a couple of hundred years; it grew up around a Norman castle that changed hands many times during the struggles with the English. At the **Castle Mound** only the earthworks remain of the town's 13th century castle that was built by Edward I on the site of the earlier motte and bailey structure. The earthworks can be reached by a footpath from the town centre.

Since the 1963 opening of the **Royal Welsh Show Ground** at nearby **Llanelwedd**, the annual Royal Welsh Show, held in July, has gained a reputation as being the premier agricultural show in the country.

CARNO

The dress and interior designer Laura Ashley, who was born in Wales, and her husband moved to Machynlleth in 1963 and later settled at **Carno**, which became the site of the headquarters of the Laura Ashley empire. It was in the churchyard of St John the Baptist, close to the factory, that she was buried after her death in 1985. In the hills of Trannon Moor near the village is the National Wind Power's Carno Wind Farm, a site containing dozens of turbines that generate enough electricity to meet the needs of about 25,000 homes. The Carno Wind Farm project was completed in 1996 and comprises 56 wind turbines

each of 600 kilowatts maximum output. The plateau on which the farm is located is visited by over 30 bird species including red kite, hen harrier, buzzard, red grouse, curlew and golden plover.

CRAIG-Y-NOS

The **Dan-yr-Ogof Showcaves**, the largest complex of caverns in northern Europe, lie to the north of this village. Discovered in 1912, the caverns have taken 315 million years to create and they include both the longest and the largest showcaves in Britain. Exploring these underground caverns is only one aspect of this interesting attraction as there is also an award winning **Dinosaur Park**, where life size replicas of the creatures that roamed the earth during Jurassic times can be seen, and the **Morgan Brothers' Shire Horse Centre**, where the massive horses, the wagons they pulled and other farm animals are on show. The replica **Iron Age Farm** gives a realistic idea of how the farmers lived so long ago.

To the east of the village lies **Craig-y-Nos Country Park**, where visitors can enjoy the unspoilt countryside and the landscaped country parkland of the upper Tawe Valley. The mansion in the country park, known as **Craig-y-Nos Castle**, was once the home of the 19th century opera singer Madame Adelina Patti. She bought the estate in 1878 as a home for her and her second husband, the tenor Ernesto Nicolini. She installed an aviary, a little theatre modelled on Drury Lane and a winter garden that was subsequently moved to Swansea's Victoria Park. Patti was born in Madrid in 1843, the daughter of a Sicilian tenor, and achieved fame in New York at an early age. Her first husband was the Marquis de Caux, her second Ernesto Nicolini and her third the Swedish Baron Cedarström, whom she married in the Roman Catholic church at Brecon in 1898.

Crickhowell

CRICKHOWELL

Situated in the beautiful valley of the River Usk and in the shadow of the Black Mountains that lie to the north, Crickhowell is a charming little town with a long history. The town takes its name from the Iron Age fort, **Crug Hywell** (Howell's Fort) that lies on the flat-topped hill above the town that is aptly named Table Mountain. The remains of another stronghold, **Crickhowell Castle** - once one of the most important fortresses in this mountainous region of Wales - can be found in the town's large park. Built in the 11th century, only the motte and two shattered towers remain of the Norman fortress that was stormed by Owain Glyndwr and abandoned in the 15th century.

The picturesque and famous **Crickhowell Bridge**, which dates from the 16th century, spans the River Usk in the heart of the town. Still carrying traffic today, the bridge is unique in that it has 13 arches on one side and only 12 on the other! For the rest, this is a pleasant place, with some fine Georgian architecture which, due to its close proximity to the Black Mountains and the National Park, is popular with those looking for outdoor activities including walking. Close by is **Pwll-y-Wrach Nature Reserve** in a steep-sided valley. Owned by the Brecknock Wildlife Trust, this woodland reserve has a waterfall and also a great variety of flora, for which it has been designated a Site of Special Scientific Interest.

ELAN VILLAGE

The village is close to the beautiful reservoirs of the **Elan Valley** - a string of five dammed lakes that are together around nine miles long and were constructed between 1892 and 1903. Formed to supply millions of gallons of water to Birmingham and the West

Midlands, the first of the dams was opened in 1904 by Edward VII and Queen Alexandra and the final dam, the Claerwen dam, was finished in 1952. Dubbed the 'Lakeland of Wales', the five man-made lakes are surrounded by magnificent scenery and this is a popular area for walkers, cyclists and birdwatchers. The Elan Valley Visitor Centre has an exhibition telling the story of the creation of the reservoirs and lots of information about the red kite, the famous comeback bird. Many houses, including one where the poet Shelley stayed, were submerged by the waters, but traces can be seen when the waters are at a low level.

Hay on Wye

HAY-ON-WYE

This ancient town, tucked between the Black Mountains and the River Wye in the northernmost corner of the Brecon Beacon National Park, grew up around its Norman castle. That was replaced by a stone castle which was all but destroyed by Owain Glyndwr in the early 1400s. A Jacobean manor house was grafted on to part of the surviving walls; close by are traces of a Roman fort. Historic though this town may be, it is as the second hand book capital of the world that Hay-on-Wye is best known. Among the town's many buildings can be found a plethora of book, antique, print and craft shops. The first second-hand bookshop was opened here in 1961 by Richard Booth, owner of Hay Castle, and since then they have sprung up all over the town - the old cinema, many houses, shops and even the old castle are now bookshops, at least 35 in all and with a stock of over a million books. The annual **Festival of Art and Literature**, held every May, draws many to the town, from Germaine Greer and Stephen Fry to Paul McCartney and Bill Clinton. The impressive Hay-on-Wye Craft Centre offers visitors a chance to pit down their books and see craftspeople at work at age-old skills such as glass-blowing, wood-turning and pottery.

KNIGHTON

Situated in the Teme Valley on the border of Powys and Shropshire, Knighton lies on the path of Offa's Dyke. Beginning in Knighton, **Glyndwr's Way** follows the route taken by Owain Glyndwr, one of Wales' favourite sons, as

Knighton Church

Brecon Beacons National Park from displays and presentations; there are also some interesting remains to be seen in the area, including a Bronze Age burial chamber. The Beacons, including the sandstone peaks of **Pen y Fan** and **Corn Du**, were given to the National Trust in 1965 and have become one of the most popular parts of the UK with walkers. The area is also important for sub-alpine plants and is designated a Site of Special Scientific Interest. But the very popularity of the Beacons with walkers has caused great problems, exacerbated by military manoeuvres and the depradations of the sheep that have grazed here since Tudor times. Erosion is the biggest problem, and the National Trust has put in place an ambitious programme of footpath and erosion repair.

he fought the English for Welsh independence in the 1400s. This scenic and important route travels southwest to Abbey-cwm-hir, passing by the ancient abbey ruins, before heading northwards into the old county of Montgomeryshire and the market town of Llanidloes. The 128 miles of the path takes in some of the finest scenery in mid-Wales before reaching Machynlleth, from where it heads southeastwards and finally ends at the border town of Welshpool.

LIBANUS

To the northwest of this attractive hamlet, on Mynydd Illtyd common, lies the **Brecon Beacons Mountain Centre**, where visitors can find out about the

LLANDRINDOD WELLS

The most elegant of the spa towns of mid-Wales, Llandrindod Wells, though not primarily a spa today, is still a popular place that has retained its Victorian and Edwardian character and architecture. It was the Romans who first understood the possible healing powers of Wales' mineral rich waters - saline, sulphur, magnesian, chalybeate - but it was with the coming of the railway in 1867, along with the Victorians' enthusiasm for 'taking the waters', that Llandrindod Wells really developed in to a spa town. People would flock to the town in their thousands (at its peak some 80,000 visitors a year) to take the waters in an attempt to obtain relief from complaints and ailments ranging from gout, rheumatism and anaemia to diabetes, dyspepsia and liver trouble. A complete system of baths and heat and massage treatments were also available. The most famous of the individual spas in Llandrindod during its heyday, **Rock Park** is a typically well laid out Victorian park where visitors coming to the town would take a walk between their treatments.

As well as the evidence of the town's heyday that is all around, visitors can find out more about the spa's history at the **Llandrindod Wells Museum** where not only is there a collection of Victorian artefacts but also relics excavated from Castell Collen. A splendid attraction in the Automobile Palace is the **National Cycle Collection**, an exhibition that covers more than 100 years of cycling history, through an amazing collection of over 200 bicycles and tricycles that date back as far as 1818, spanning every development from the hobby horse and bone-shaker to the high-tech machines of today. Also here are old photographs and posters, historic replicas, the Dunlop tyre story and displays on cycling stars. Each year Llandrindod Wells hosts a Victorian Carnival, which has developed over the years into one of the premier Victorian Festivals in Britain. The aim of the festival is to provide fun for all ages while keeping to a Victorian theme, and the week-long festival ends with a torchlight procession and a fireworks

display over the lake. Wales is famous for its great little railways but it also has some full-size trains. One of the most popular tourist lines is the Heart of Wales line that runs from Shrewsbury to Swansea, billed as 'one line that visits two viaducts, three castles, four spa towns, five counties, six tunnels and seven bridges'.

LLANFAIR CAEREINION

This is one end of the **Welshpool and Llanfair Railway**. Passengers at Llanfair can enjoy reliving the days of steam and then relax in the Edwardian style tea rooms at the station. The narrow-gauge railway was originally opened to carry sheep, cattle and goods as well as passengers. It now travels, without the animals and the goods, along the delightful Banwy Valley, its carriages pulled by scaled-down versions of steam locomotives from Finland, Austria, Sierra Leone, Antigua and Manchester.

LLANGATTOCK

The village church, which was founded sometime during the early 6th century, is dedicated to St Catwg, one of Wales' most honoured saints. Born in around AD 497, by the end of his life, in around 577 Catwg, had become a Bishop and had taken the name Sophias. To the southwest of the village, towards the boundary of the Brecon Beacons National Park lies the **Craig-y-Cilau Nature Reserve**. With over 250 plant species and over 50 kinds of birds

Llangorse Lake

breeding within the reserve, this is one of the richest in the National Park.

LLANGORSE

To the south of the village lies the largest natural lake in South Wales - **Llangorse Lake** (Llyn Syfaddan). Around four miles in circumference and following its way round a low contour in the Brecon Beacons the waters of this lake were, in medieval times, thought to have miraculous properties. Today, the lake attracts numerous visitors looking to enjoy not only the setting but also the wide variety of sporting and leisure activities, such as fishing, horse riding and sailing, that can be found here. There is also a Rope Centre, with climbing, abseiling, potholing, log climbing and a high-level rope course.

Naturally, the lake is associated with a legend and local stories suggest that the land beneath the lake once belonged to a cruel and greedy princess. Though her lover was poor, she agreed to marry him only if he brought her great riches. So the lover set out to complete his task and in so doing robbed and murdered a wealthy merchant, giving the riches to his princess. However, the merchant's ghost returned to warn the happy couple that their crime would be avenged, not on them but on the ninth generation of their family. One night, years later, a great flood burst from the hills, drowning the surrounding land and its inhabitants; it is still said today that a city can been seen under the water.

LLANGYNIDR

Rising to the south of this riverside village on the open moorland of Mynydd Llangynidr, lies the **Chartists' Cave**, where members of the movement stored ammunition during their active years in the mid-19th century.

LLANIDLOES

This peaceful, small market town, which sits at the exact centre of Wales, is certainly one of the area's most attractive, and its adaptability, from a rural village to a weaving town and now to a centre for craftspeople, has ensured that it is likely to remain so for many years to come. John Wesley preached here three times in the mid 1700s and the stone from which he addressed his audience stands outside the town's old **Market Hall**, which dates from 1609 and stands on wooden stilts. It was used by Quakers, Methodists and Baptists before those religious groups had their own premises and has also been a courthouse, a library and a working men's institute. The upper floors of the building now house the **Llanidloes Museum**, where there are displays and information on the textile and mining industries that thrived in the area during the 18th and 19th centuries. In 1839 the town was a focal point of the bitter Chartist Riots after the Reform Bill of 1832 has failed to meet demands that included universal suffrage and social equality. The Chartist Movement had begun in London in 1837 and spread quickly throughout Britain. Marches, riots and petitions followed in the next few years but the movement then went into decline, and the repeal of the Corn Laws in 1846 helped to better the lot of the working classes.

To the northwest of the town lies Llyn Clywedog, a reservoir that was developed in the mid-1960s to regulate the flow of the Rivers Severn and Clywedog. Roads run round both sides of this lake, with the B4518 curving round the slopes of the 1,580ft Fan Hill where the chimneys of the long disused **Van Lead Mine** are still visible. It was once one of the most prosperous mines in this part of Wales, and it is recorded that in 1876 6,850 tons of lead were produced. The deserted houses and chapels of the village that grew up round the mine stand as an evocative reminder of mining days.

LLANRHAEADR-YM-MOCHNANT

Despite its relative isolation this village attracts many visitors who pass through on their way to **Pistyll Rhaeadr**, which lies up a narrow road to the northwest of the village. This is one of the Seven Wonders of Wales and, with a drop of 240 feet, is the highest waterfall in Britain south of the Scottish Highlands. The English translation of the name is Spout Waterfall, an obvious name as the water drops vertically for 100 feet before running into a cauldron, on through a

Pistyll Rhaeadr

Lake Vyrnwy

natural tunnel in the rock and then again reappearing.

LLANWDDYN

The village lies at the southern end of **Lake Vyrnwy** (Llyn Efyrnwy), a four mile stretch of water that was created, in the years following 1881, by the flooding of the entire Vyrnwy Valley, to provide the people of Liverpool with an adequate water supply. Close to the dam, which is 390 yards long, 144 feet high and a splendid testament to Victorian engineering, is a monument that marks the beginning of the **Hirnant Tunnel** - the first stage of a 75 mile aqueduct that carries the water to Liverpool. Another striking building is the Gothic tower designed by George Frederick Deacon, engineer to the Liverpool Water Board. On higher ground is an obelisk that is a monument to the 44 men who died during the construction of the reservoir. To construct this, the first of several massive reservoirs in north and mid-Wales, the original village of Llanwddyn,

home to some 4 souls, was flooded along with the valley. Photographs in the Lake Vyrnwy Hotel show the original village with 37 houses and the church, all now submerged under the Lake's 13,000 million gallons of water. The reservoir's visitor centre not only tells the story of the construction but is also home to an RSPB centre; there are four RSPB hides at various points around the lake and guided tours can be arranged around the estate for schools and groups. With its lovely scenery and coniferous forests, the lake has doubled in films for Switzerland or Transylvania; it was also used for location shots in *The Dambusters*.

LLANWRTYD WELLS

Surrounded by rugged mountains, rolling hills and the remote moorland of **Mynydd Epynt**, it was here, in 1792, that the sulphur and chalybeate spring waters were discovered by a scurvy sufferer. As visitors came here in the 19th century, to take the waters in relief of numerous complaints, the town developed. Llanwrtyd Wells is still a popular holiday centre, particularly with those who enjoy bird watching, fishing and walking. However, anyone visiting Llanwrtyd Wells will be surprised that somewhere so small could have so many events and festivals throughout the year: the 'Man versus Horse' race in May, a

Folk Weekend in spring and a late autumn Beer Festival. However the most unusual of all the events held here is undoubtedly the annual **World Bog Snorkelling Championship** that takes place each August.

On the outskirts of the town lies the **Cambrian Woollen Mill**, which recalls the rich history of Wales' rural past. The first mill was founded in the 1820s, but in its modern form dates from 1918, when it was opened by the Royal British Legion for the benefit of servicemen disabled in the Great War. A tour of the mill allows visitors to see traditional cloths being woven, and in the factory shop a wide choice of beautifully finished items can be bought.

MACHYNLLETH

This small town is a popular but not overcrowded holiday centre in the shadow of the Cambrian Mountains. It was here that Owain Glyndwr held one of his parliaments in around 1404 and, on the site today, stands **Parliament House**, a part 15th century building. Revered as the last native prince of Wales, Parliament House is home to an exhibition of this legendary hero and the **Owain Glyndwr Centre** tells the story of his life, the rebellion he led against the English and details of the parliament from where he controlled most of Wales. Opposite the house is the entrance to **Plas Machynlleth**, an elegant mansion built in 1653 that was given to the town by Lord Londonderry and which is surrounded by attractive gardens open to

the public. This beautifully restored mansion is also home to **Celtica**, a museum and multi-media centre where the history and the legends of the Celts are revealed.

MONTGOMERY

An attractive market town with a pleasant Georgian character, and also some surviving Tudor and Jacobean buildings that are worthy of note. Above the town the ruins of **Montgomery Castle** stand in affirmation of this borderland region's turbulent history. During the Civil War, the castle surrendered to Parliamentary forces but was demolished in 1649 in punishment for the then Lord Herbert's Royalist sympathies. The remains of the Castle are open at all times and entrance is free; access is up steep paths from the town or by a level footpath from the car park, and the visit is worth it for the views alone. Offa's Dyke passes close by and is another reminder of the military significance that this area once held. In Arthur Street, the **Old Bell Museum** has 11 rooms of local history including features on civic and social life, Norman and medieval castles, the workhouse and the Cambrian Railway. Montgomery's 13th century Church of St Nicholas has some interesting features, including wooden carved angels, carved miserere seats and the magnificent canopied tomb of Richard Herbert, Lord of Montgomery Castle. In the churchyard is the famous Robber's Grave: John Davis, hanged in 1821 for murder, proclaimed his innocence and swore that the grass would not grow above his grave for at least 100 years.

NEW RADNOR

Once the county town of Radnorshire, the village is overlooked by the remains of its 11th century motte and bailey **Castle**. Like many other strongholds in this border region, New Radnor Castle suffered at various hands: it was destroyed by King John, rebuilt by Henry III and destroyed again by Owain Glyndwr in 1401. Near neighbour Old Radnor was once home to King Harold. The motte (moat) by the church was the site of his castle, and in the church itself a notable feature is a huge font made from a glacial boulder.

Newtown

NEWTOWN

This was a centre for textiles and weaving and by the 19th century was the home of the Welsh flannel industry that led it to be referred to as the 'Leeds of Wales'. Some of the brick buildings were built with a third or even fourth storey with large windows to let in light for the looms. One such building now houses the town's **Textile Museum**, which tells the story of this once important industry and also gives a very good impression of the working conditions of the people which Newtown's reforming son, Robert Owen, devoted much of his life to changing. His remarkable life is told at the intimate **Robert Owen Memorial Museum** and he was buried by the river in the churchyard of St Mary's. The grave has magnificent Art Nouveau iron railings, and his monument depicts the man with his workers.

Another interesting visit to consider while in Newtown is to the **WH Smith Museum**, where the shop has been restored to its original 1927 layout and devotes much of its space to the history of the booksellers from 1792 onwards. The people of Newtown were clearly an enterprising lot, as it was also here that the first-ever mail order company was begun in 1859 by a man called Pryce-Jones. The business started in a small way with Welsh flannel but expanded rapidly, and Pryce-Jones even obtained the Royal seal of approval by having Queen Victoria on his list. Two miles east of Newtown is Pwll Penarth Nature Reserve, a feeding and nesting site for many species of wildfowl. The reserve has a nature walk and two hides, one of them accessible to visitors in wheelchairs.

PAINSCASTLE

Sometimes known as **Castell Paen**, the early motte built in 1130 by Payn FitzJohn was later rebuilt in stone and, by the late 12th century, was in the hands of the notorious William de Braose. The cruelty of de Braose has earned him a place in Welsh folklore and, while he was given the nickname the Ogre of Abergavenny, his wife Maud is thought to have lived long after his death as a witch.

Close to the castle remains is an altogether more pleasant place to visit, the **Tawny Owl Animal Park and Craft Centre**, which lies in the shelter of beautiful hills. Opened in 1998, the park is named after the wild owls that live in the broad leafed woodlands surrounding the farm and, as well as the owls (which are not caged), visitors can also see a whole range of farm animals at close quarters. On display and for sale are country wares made by traditional methods passed from one generation to the next.

PRESTEIGNE

Once the county town of Radnorshire, Presteigne remains a charming and unspoilt place on the southern bank of the River Lugg. A border town distinguished by its handsome black and white half-timbered buildings, Presteigne grew up around a Norman castle that has long since been destroyed; the site is now occupied by a pleasant park. One of the town's most outstanding buildings is **The Radnorshire Arms**, which dates from 1616. The town also claims the oldest inn in Radnorshire, the **Duke's Arms**, for which records show that an inn on the site was burnt to the ground by Owain Glyndwr in 1401. The rebuilt inn became a local headquarters for the Roundheads during the Civil War and, in later centuries, was an important coaching inn. Although the **Judge's Lodging** only dates from 1829, it is another fascinating attraction in Presteigne. Designed by Edward Haycock and built on the site of the county gaol, this was the judicial centre for Radnorshire and the home of the Radnorshire Constabulary. Today, the house, with its adjoining court, has been furnished as it would have appeared in 1870, and visitors can explore the world of the judges, their servants and the felons.

RHAYADER

Often referred to as the Gateway to the Lakeland of Wales, Rhayader lies at the entrance to the magnificent Elan Valley and the impressive collection of dams and reservoirs it contains. This town, whose name means "Waterfall of the Wye", dates back to the 5th century, though the waterfall all but disappeared with the construction of a bridge over the river in 1780.

Welsh Royal Crystal, a manufacturer of hand-crafted lead crystal tableware and gift items, is located in the town and the factory takes visitors on a guided tour to watch the craftsmen at work. The area around Rhayader is still very rural and on the outskirts of the town lies **Gigrin Farm**, where visitors can see red kites at close quarters as they are feeding.

SENNYBRIDGE

Situated along the southern edge of the Mynydd Epynt and on the northern border of the Brecon Beacons National Park, this village is very much a product of the industrial age as it only began to develop after the railways arrived here in 1872 and Sennybridge became a centre for livestock trading. However, the remains of **Castell Ddu**, just to the west of the village, provides evidence of life here from an earlier age. Dating from the 14th century and believed to stand on the site of an 11th century manor house, this was the home of Sir Reginald Aubrey, a friend of Bernard of Newmarch. Two new waymarked walks have been opened on the Sennybridge army training area, beginning at **Disgwylfa Conservation Centre** on the B4519. The centre has an interactive learning centre and military and conservation displays. One of the walks is accessible for disabled visitors.

ST HARMON

St Harmon is the village where the diarist Francis Kilvert was for a short time the vicar. To the southwest of the village lies **Gilfach**, a lovingly restored traditional Welsh longhouse built of local rubblestone and lying at the centre of an extensive nature reserve. Oak woodland, meadows and moorland

support a rich diversity of wildlife at this important Site of Special Scientific Interest, and at the longhouse there are exhibitions on the building's history and the surrounding wildlife. Opposite the longhouse, across the farmyard, is another fine old building, The Barn, comprising hay barn, byre and stables and built of stone. Parking is available at the farm, and there is wheelchair access to the centre and some of the waymarked trails.

TALGARTH

Lying in the foothills of the Black Mountains, Talgarth is an attractive market town with narrow streets that boasts many historic associations as well as some fine architecture. The 15th century parish **Church of St Gwendoline** has strong links with Hywell Harris (1714-73), an influential figure in the establishment of Welsh Methodism. Harris was also instrumental in establishing a religious community, The Connexion, which was organised on both religious and industrial lines. Although this is now a quiet and charming place, Talgarth once stood against the Norman drive into Wales. Some of the defensive structures can still be seen today - the tower of the church and another tower that is now incorporated into a house - though it has also served time as the jail. On the outskirts of Talgarth lies **Bronllys Castle** a well-preserved centuries old keep built by the Norman baron Bernard of Newmarch. Originally a motte and bailey castle, it was later replaced with a stone edifice and now it is a lone tower standing on a steep mound that is in the hands of CADW - Welsh Historic Monuments.

TALYBONT-ON-USK

Just beyond this attractive village, the Monmouthshire and Brecon Canal passes through the 375 yard long Ashford Tunnel while, further south still, lies the **Talybont Reservoir**. In this narrow wooded valley on the southeastern slopes of the Brecons there are several forest trails starting from the car park at the far end of the reservoir.

TRETOWER

This quiet village in the Usk Valley is the home of two impressive medieval buildings - **Tretower Court and Tretower Castle** (both in the hands of CADW - Welsh Historic Monuments). The elder of these historic sites is the castle where all that remains on the site of the original Norman motte is a stark keep that dates from the 13th century. The castle was built in this valley to discourage Welsh rebellion but, nonetheless, it was besieged by Llywelyn the Last and almost destroyed by Owain Glyndwr in 1403. Adjacent to the bleak castle remains lies the court, a magnificent

15th century fortified manor house that served as a very desirable domestic residence particularly during the less turbulent years following Glyndwr's rebellion. While the 15th century woodwork here and the wall walk, with its 17th century roof and windows, are outstanding, it is the court's **Gardens** that are particularly interesting. The original late 15th century layout of the gardens has been recreated in such a manner that the owner of the time, Sir Roger Vaughan, would have recognised them. Among the many delightful features there is a tunnel arbour planted with white roses - Sir Roger was a Yorkist - and vines, an enclosed arbour and a chequerboard garden. Tretower Court's Gardens are best seen in the early summer.

WELSHPOOL

This bustling market town, which was granted a charter in 1263 by the Prince of Powys, was, for a long time, known as "Pool" - the Welsh prefix was added in

Powis Castle, Welshpool

1835 to settle the long running dispute concerning its nationality as it is so close to the border with England. As is typical with many places in the upper Severn Valley, Welshpool has numerous examples of half-timbered buildings among its other interesting architectural features. Housed in a former warehouse beside the Montgomery Canal is the **Powysland Museum**, which covers various aspects of the region: the development of life in Montgomeryshire from the earliest times to the present. The warehouse is also home to the **Montgomery Canal Centre** where the story of this waterway is told. Another interesting building is the Cockpit, the only one of its kind in Wales to survive on its original site; built in the 18th century, it remained in use until the 'sport' was banned in 1849. Just to the southwest of the town, off the A483, lies one of the best known places in the area - **Powis Castle**. The castle was originally built for the Welsh princes and later became the ancestral home of the Herbert family and then of the Clive family. One of the owners was Edward, son of Clive of India, and the Clive Museum in the castle houses a beautiful collection of treasures from India from the famous man's time there. The castle is perched on a rock above splendid terraces and gardens laid out in 1720 in a style influenced by both French and Italian design.

From the town, the narrow gauge **Welshpool and Llanfair Railway** takes passengers on a steam train journey through the Powis estates and the delightful Banwy valley to Llanfair Caereinion.

YSTRADFELLTE

This small village is a recognised hiking centre in an area of classic limestone countryside that is among the most impressive in the British Isles. To the south of the village is **Porth-yr-Ogof**, a delightful area with a collection of dramatic waterfalls as the River Mellte descends through woodland.

Porth-yr-Ogof

THE ANGEL

3 HIGH STREET, LLANIDLOES, POWYS SY18 6BY
TEL: 01686 412381

Directions: Llanidloes lies on the A470 about 4 miles northeast of Llangurig, and The Angel is on the main street.

Dating from the middle of the 18th century, **The Angel** presents a cheerful face to the world on the main street of a historic town at the very centre of Wales. Behind the black-and-white frontage, the interior is delightfully traditional, and a full range of beers and lagers, including some guest ales, is available in the warm, comfortable lounge bar. Paul and Debbie Lloyd own and run the inn; Debbie is the inspiration in the kitchen, while Paul is mine host at the bar, and between them they assure all their customers of the warmest of welcomes. The bar menu is the popular choice at lunchtime, while in the evening the à la carte menu is served in the restaurant, where neatly laid tables, intimate lighting and well-chosen pictures on attractive floral

wallpaper create a very pleasant, relaxing ambience.

With notice, Paul and Debbie can cater for parties of up to 40, with food and drink and entertainment laid on as required. Visitors to this very appealing part of the world will find it a very simple and pleasant task to work up a thirst and an appetite before dropping in at The Angel. The town of Llanidloes itself has a rich history, and its many places of interest include the museum and the market hall. It lies at the crossing point of two major recreational footpaths, the Severn Way and Glyndwr's Way National Trail, so walkers will be in their element. And, suitably refreshed at the inn, motorists can take a short drive out of town to visit Llyn Clywedog Reservoir and the old workings of Van Lead Mine.

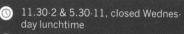

- 🕐 11.30-2 & 5.30-11, closed Wednesday lunchtime
- 🍴 Bar and à la carte menus
- £ All except Amex
- Ⓟ Car park
- ❓ Fan Hill 2 miles, Llan Clywedog 3 miles; walking and cycling on the Severn Way and Glyndwr's National Trail

THE BULL HOTEL

ST DAVIDS STREET, PRESTEIGNE, POWYS LD8 2BP
TEL: 01544 267488

> **Directions:** From the A44 Rhayader-Leominster road, turn on to the B4362 at
> Walton; follow signs to Presteigne (about 5 miles).

Three Grade II listed buildings make up **The Bull Hotel**, the oldest dating back at least to the early 18th century. The name is derived from the bull baiting post which once stood in the market square, where the most recent part of the hotel now stands. The hotel is owned and run by the Jalland family. Tony, who had a long career in education, his wife Jeanette and their daughter Chloë took over in August 2002. They offer their guests excellent hospitality and log-burning fires in the bar lounge help to create a splendidly inviting atmosphere in which to enjoy good conversation and a glass or two of one of the real ales on tap. Evening meals are by arrangement and feature local produce and a menu of

home-cooked dishes.

Guest accommodation comprises six bedrooms - three doubles, one twin, one single and a family room with one double and two single beds. Private fishing on one of the most beautiful stretches of the river Lugg is available to guests (why not take a packed lunch and enjoy the day). The Bull Hotel is a particularly comfortable and civilised base from which to explore the beautiful countryside and surrounding towns and villages steeped in history. Presteigne itself, situated on the River Lugg, which was once the border between England and Wales, was the country's judicial centre and the Judge's Lodging, winner of the 'Interpret Britain' and 'Britain's Local Museum of the Year', is a must for any visitor.

- 🕐 11.30-2.30 & 7-11, Sun 12-2.30 & 7-10.30
- 🍴 A la carte
- 💷 All the major cards
- 🛏 6 bedrooms, including a family room
- 🎵 Folk night every 2nd Wednesday in the month
- ❓ Knighton 5 miles, Old and New Radnor 5 miles, fishing

THE CASTLE INN

PENGENFFORDD, NR TALGARTH, POWYS LD3 0EP

TEL/FAX: 01874 711353

Powys

Directions: From Talgarth, 4 miles south on the A479. From Crickhowell, 8 miles north A40 then A479.

The Castle Inn, which takes its name from the nearby ancient fortress of Castell Dinas, lies on the A479 at the top of a picturesque, unspoilt valley within the Black Mountains, the northern part of Brecon Beacons National Park. A former hill farm, it has its own spring water drinking supply and has been CAMRA recommended since the early 1990s. Paul and Linda Mountjoy are the welcoming hosts, and visitors can relax by an open log fire in the bar and quench their thirsts with one of several traditional ales that are always on tap. Meals are also traditional and mainly home-cooked, and portions are more than sufficient to satisfy appetites generated by days spent in the pure, fresh local air. Typical dishes on the regularly changing evening menu run from home-made soup and garlic mushrooms to

ploughman's salad, curries, pies, baked chicken and pork in cider, with a variety of sweets and children's meals. Packed lunches can be supplied by arrangement.

The area caters well for lovers of the great outdoors, and the inn offers a choice of accommodation. A recent extension houses four en suite Bed & Breakfast rooms decorated in a relaxing pine and white theme, with easy chairs, tv and radio. More basic overnighting is provided in the Trekkers Barn, a 200-year-old stone barn recently converted to provide bunkhouse style accommodation for up to 20 visitors in two rooms. At one end of the barn is a shower block, at the other end male and female toilets and one side opens on to a small field which can be used for camping. Meals are taken at the adjoining inn. There is bike storage and ample safe parking for cars. Local activities are almost endless, from canoeing and sailing to caving, mountain biking to gliding.

- ⊙ 7-11, weekend also 12-3. Longer summer hours.
- ❶ Evening meals, packed lunches
- ⓔ Amex, Mastercard, Visa
- ⊖ 4 en suite rooms + bunkhouse
- Ⓟ Car park, camping site
- @ e-mail: castlepen@aol.com website: www.thecastleinn.co.uk
- ❓ Talgarth 4 miles, Crickhowell 8 miles

THE CORN EXCHANGE

54 HIGH STREET, CRICKHOWELL, POWYS NP8 1BH
TEL: 01873 810699 FAX: 01873 812166

> **Directions:** The inn is located in the heart of Crickhowell, on the A40 a few miles northwest of Abergavenny.

Situated in the shadow of the Black Mountains in the beautiful valley of the River Usk, Crickhowell is a charming place to visit, and the **Corn Exchange** is a perfect spot to pause for refreshment. Easy to find on the High Street, the handsome white-fronted premises date from 1693 and now comprise two adjacent enterprises - the main bar and the café-restaurant. Hancocks HB and a rotating guest head the list of ales, and food is served from Monday to Saturday from opening time right through to 6 o'clock. Leaseholders Fiona and Chris, who have made a this a top-of-the-range establishment since arriving in 1995, share the cooking, and in the 30-cover non-smoking restaurant visitors can make their choice from the printed menu or the specials board. Favourite dishes include the all-day breakfast and Welsh Black Beef steaks. Well-behaved dogs are welcome in the bar area.

The best-known sight in Crickhowell is the picturesque 17th century stone bridge - unique in having 13 arches on one side and only 12 on the other - that spans the Usk below the town. It's a great place to explore on foot, while for more serious walking the Black Mountains beckon. Just outside town is Sugar Loaf Mountain, which reaches up nearly 2,000 feet and affords wonderful views of the valley, the Black Mountains and beyond. Also close by is Pwll-y-Wrach Nature Reserve, a woodland reserve with a waterfall and a great variety of plant life.

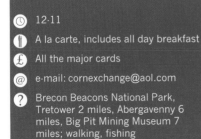

🕐 12-11

🍴 A la carte, includes all day breakfast

£ All the major cards

@ e-mail: cornexchange@aol.com

❓ Brecon Beacons National Park, Tretower 2 miles, Abergavenny 6 miles, Big Pit Mining Museum 7 miles; walking, fishing

THE CROWN INN

CASTLE STREET, MONTGOMERY, POWYS SY15 6PM
TEL/FAX: 01686 668533

Directions: Montgomery stands 7 miles northeast of Newtown at the junction of the B4385 and the B4388. The Crown is on a corner site on the road that runs up to the castle.

Cheerful bright blue signs announce **The Crown**, a 17th century building on a corner site on the road that leads to the castle. Behind the smart cream-painted facade, the public rooms are very traditional in style, with a wealth of exposed beams. The cosy bar has a feature fireplace, and visitors will find an excellent choice of real ales as well as the usual bitters and lagers. Bar snacks are available all day, every day, and on Sunday the lunchtime roasts are a speciality. The cooking is in the safe hands of licensee Pat Lamprell, who also shares duties behind the bar with Trevor.

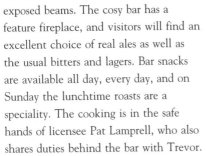

- 11-2 & 7-11, open all day Fri-Sun
- Bar snacks + Sunday lunch
- Mastercard, Visa
- Ample street parking
- Quiz nights, local musicians
- Montgomery Castle 1 mile, Fridd Faldwyn 1 mile, Newtown 7 miles

Pool, darts and dominoes are the favourite games in the bar, and the inn hosts regular music nights and quiz nights. Future plans include bringing on stream some guest bedrooms, which will add considerably to the Crown's scope. The attractive market town of Montgomery is well worth taking time to explore with its handsome Georgian buildings and its fine 13th century Church of St Nicholas. And set on a crag overlooking the town are the ruins of the castle, which was more or less demolished in 1649.

Offa's Dyke passes close by, and to the west of town is the Iron Age fort Fridd Faldwyn; a climb to the top of its 750ft hill is rewarded with splendid views over Cadair Idris and eastwards into England.

THE GEORGE & DRAGON

4 BROAD STREET, KNIGHTON, POWYS LD7 1BL
TEL: 01547 528532

Directions: From the A49 at Ludlow take the A4117 Knighton road. The inn is situated on the left, halfway up the hill towards the clock tower.

On a main street in the centre of Knighton, **The George & Dragon** is a delightful Grade II listed coaching inn and restaurant with a history that goes back as far as the 17th century. The George & Dragon has been owned and personally run since early 1997 by Peter and Angela Vrettos, who have made their pub one of the most popular in the whole region. Flower tubs and hanging baskets adorn the black and white frontage, and the inn's interior is equally appealing. Oak panelling and antique settles provide a lovely traditional ambience in the comfortable little lounge, where visitors will find it no problem at all to relax and unwind. The atmosphere is more lively in the public bar, especially at the weekend, and connoisseurs of real ale will find plenty of choice.

- ⏰ 7-11, Sat & Sun 12-2.30 & 7-11. Longer hours in summer
- 🍴 A la carte
- £ All the major cards
- 🛏 5 en suite rooms
- Ⓟ Street parking
- ❓ In Knighton: Offa's Dyke Centre, Powys Observatory; walking (Offa's Dyke footpath, Glyndwr's Way), fishing, pony trekking, Presteigne 6 miles, Ludlow 12 miles, Rally school 6 miles.

Good wholesome home-cooked meals are served lunchtime and evening, and the regular themed food evenings are always occasions to savour. the non-smoking restaurant is particularly cosy and inviting, with a country cottage atmosphere, a mixture of furnishings and an interesting collection of bric a brac and old tools scattered about the walls and ceiling. The stables at the rear of the pub, once home to up to 20 horses, have been cleverly converted to provide five characterful en suite rooms - three twins and two doubles, all with tv, clock-radio and tea-making facilities. The accommodation - strictly non-smoking - is not suitable for young children or pets. The Welsh border town of Knighton is well worth taking time to explore, and outside town the spectacular scenery of the Teme Valley beckons. The pub will provide guests with packed lunches on request.

THE GLANSEVERN ARMS

PANTMAWR, NR LLANGURIG, POWYS SY18 6SY
TEL: 01686 440240 FAX: 01686 440741

Directions: The hotel is situated on the main A44 four miles west of Llangurig and 19 miles inland from Aberystwyth.

On the A44 west of the village of Llangurig, the **Glansevern Arms Hotel** commands a superb position on the banks of the River Wye, amid the glorious hill scenery of the Plynlimon range. Friendliness and hospitality have long been watchwords at this exceptional old hostelry, a tradition which is being continued in the best possible way by owners Glenys and Alun Davies. Glenys does the cooking and looks after the accommodation, while Alun runs the working farm during the day and is an excellent host at the bar in the evening. As well as the usual range of beers and lagers, the Glansevern Arms keeps real ales and quite a choice of malt whiskies. Log fires burn in the cosy bar and lounge, and the restaurant is a lovely

spot for enjoying a leisurely, relaxing a meal. Glenys sees that nobody ever goes hungry here by offering a menu of bar snacks throughout the day, an evening menu, Welsh teas and roasts for Sunday lunch.

Local produce such as Welsh lamb and Wye salmon features prominently, and the fine food is complemented by some well-chosen wines. The hotel, which has a mile of private fishing on the River Wye, is a peaceful, civilised base for touring an outstandingly beautiful part of the country. The seven bedrooms, all en suite, include a single and four family rooms; children and pets are welcome. The A44 and the nearby A470 put this most agreeable of country inns within easy reach of many local attractions, including the Elan Valley reservoirs, the red kite feeding centre near Rhayader and the coast at Aberystwyth. And the hotel can organise clay pigeon shooting and carriage driving courses.

🕐 11-2 & 6-11 (hotel open from 8am)

🍴 Six course dinner menu at an all inclusive price

£ Mastercard, Visa

🛏 7 en suite rooms

🅿 Car park, fishing

❓ Llangurig 4 miles, Devil's Bridge 7 miles, Llanidloes 7 miles, Aberystwyth 19 miles, Cardigan Bay 19 miles, Red Kite Feeding Centre at Rhayader, Elan Valley, walking, mountain biking, narrow guage railways.

THE GREEN INN

LLANGEDWYN, NR OSWESTRY, POWYS SY10 9JW
TEL: 01691 828234

Directions: Take the A5 south from Llangollen beyond the Oswestry by-pass and on to the A483 to Llynclys (or take the A483 north from Welshpool to Llynclys). At Llynclys take the A495, then on to the B4396 for about 7 miles to Llangedwyn.

The Green Inn is a distinguished 17th century country house in an attractive setting in the valley of the River Tanat. A stream passes through the large garden, while inside, the inn has a wealth of exposed beams and brass, making a comfortable and atmospheric spot in which to enjoy a convivial drink. And the choice is impressive, with five real ales and guests beers as well as the usual range of draught and bottled beers and lagers. Emma and Scott are the joint proprietors, Emma in charge of culinary matters, Scott a friendly presence in the bar. They are great supporters of the local community and have built up a loyal clientele who appreciate what they have to offer. Emma's cooking is

traditional, and the menu of pies, steaks and the like is supplemented by fish specials and seasonal game; a children's menu is also available, making this an excellent choice for a family meal.

The upstairs restaurant has seats for 40 (much more for a special event) but meals can also be taken in the comfortable lounge. Dominoes, darts and card games are played in the bar, and in the summer the Green Inn's large garden is a popular place with families. Other facilities of the inn are a large car park, fishing rights on the River Tanat and mobile phone top-ups. The region around the inn offers a wide range of other outdoor activities as well as some of the loveliest scenery in the whole country. A little way northeast of the village, Sycharth Castle is one of the most nationalistic shrines in Wales, one of Owain Glyndwr's principal houses.

- 🕐 12-3 & 6-11, open all day Sat, Sun & Bank Holidays
- 🍴 Full bar menu, specials board, children's menu
- £ All the major cards
- Ⓟ Large car park, fishing rights on the River Tanat
- @ thegreeninn@btopenworld.com
- ❓ Sycharth Castle 1 mile, Pistyll Rhaeadr Waterfall 6 miles, Oswestry 10 miles, Welshpool 10 miles, Lake Vyrnwy 12 miles; all kinds of outdoor activities

LOWFIELD INN

MARTON, NR WELSHPOOL, POWYS SY21 8JX
TEL: 01743 891313

Directions: From the A458 Welshpool-Shrewsbury road take the B4387 to Westbury then the B4386 to Marton. The inn is half a mile before the village.

The **Lowfield Inn** is a fine old traditional freehouse just outside the village of Marton, on the B4386 that runs down from Shrewsbury to join the A490. Easy to spot with its white frontage and thatched roof, the inn is equally appealing inside, with wall and ceiling beams and horse brasses maintaining the old-world look and a handsome stone fireplace in the main bar. The owners are Martin and Beverley Orson, Martin in charge of the kitchen and Beverley the genial hostess. The inn keeps three cask ales which are changed regularly, as well as a good selection of beers, lagers and wines. Martin keeps his customers happy with his traditional home cooking, and the Sunday roast lunch always brings in a good crowd from the neighbouring towns and villages.

There are seats for 40 in the restaurant, and for special occasions the function room can accommodate up to 180. The Lowfield, which has a large beer garden at the back, is also a popular place to pause for motorists touring this area around the Wales-England border. Those looking for a little light exercise can stride out along the nearby Offa's Dyke, which just east of Welshpool crosses the four-mile Long Mountain. Other outdoor pursuits, including fishing, shooting and mountain biking, are all available nearby, and there's also history aplenty, with Montgomery and Powis Castles within an easy drive. Also at Welshpool is the start of the Welshpool & Llanfair Railway, one of the Great Little Trains of Wales. And when the walking's done and the sights seen, Martin and Beverley are ready to quench thirsts and fill empty stomachs at their delightful old inn.

- 🕐 11-11
- 🍴 A la carte + traditional Sunday lunch
- 💷 Mastercard, Visa
- 🅿 Car park
- 🎵 Occasional live performers
- @ www.lowfieldinn.co.uk
- ❓ Offa's Dyke 2 miles, Montgomery 5 miles, Welshpool 5 miles

LLANBADARN FYNYDD, NR LLANDRINDOD WELLS, POWYS LD1 6YA
TEL: 01597 840378

Directions: From J7 of the M54 take the A5 round Shrewsbury, then the A458 to Welshpool. Turn on to the A483 through Newtown and towards Llandrindod Wells. The inn is situated about 10 miles south of Newtown.

Easily found on the main A483 road south of Newtown, **The New Inn** is a typical old country inn of Welsh stone that has been serving the local community and travellers for many years. A coaching inn in its early days, it offers a great deal more than meets the eye from the road. It occupies a substantial four-acre site which contains attractive gardens and a delightful little waterfall, all the more appealing because they are hidden from the road. Inside, the New Inn is no less inviting, with a number of original features contributing to a winning old world charm. Landlord Stephen Armstrong welcomes one and all into the bar, where real ales are among the drinks on hand to quench thirsts.

Visitors arriving with a hunger are equally well provided for by menus that make excellent use of prime Welsh ingredients in dishes that cater for all tastes and occasions: the bar menu deals in well-filled sandwiches, home-made pies and flavour-packed curries, while the more formal main menu offers an à la carte selection that combines both traditional and contemporary techniques. Sunday lunch is invariably well attended, while visitors with no time to relax over a meal can order a takeaway by phone and roll up to collect it. Favourite pub games are pool, darts and skittles. The New Inn has another string to its bow in providing comfortable overnight accommodation in two letting bedrooms - a double and a twin. This makes it an ideal base for exploring the numerous scenic and historic attractions of the region.

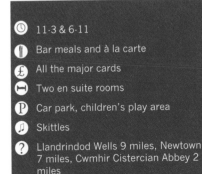

- 🕐 11-3 & 6-11
- 🍴 Bar meals and à la carte
- 💷 All the major cards
- 🛏 Two en suite rooms
- 🅿 Car park, children's play area
- 🎵 Skittles
- ❓ Llandrindod Wells 9 miles, Newtown 7 miles, Cwmhir Cistercian Abbey 2 miles

THE OAK

GUILSFIELD, NR WELSHPOOL, POWYS SY21 9NH
TEL: 01938 553391 FAX: 01938 556724

Directions: From J7 of the M54 take the A5 round Shrewsbury then the A458 to Welshpool. From here take the A290 northwards and after about 2 miles turn right on to the B4392 to Guilsfield. The Oak lies in the centre of the village.

In the centre of the picturesque village of Guilsfield, **The Oak** is a splendid timber-framed building standing back from the road. Built in the 1830s as a farmhouse, the construction is typical of the time, right down to the infill materials of lime, horsehair and cowdung! Records have been traced listing the various licensees over the last few centuries, and in one of the inn's alcoves is a photograph of Mark and Ma Tyler. The Oak is now in the capable hands of Helen and David, who are continuing the tradition of hospitality in fine style. The original interior comprised seven individual little rooms, but during the 1970s these were converted into a single open space, which gives the place a bright, airy spacious feel without

in any way detracting from the building's ancient character and charm - the gnarled beams and the brass ornaments remain eye-catching features.

The bar is well stocked with all the usual drinks, and the inn is also a great place to come for a meal. A splendid selection of home-cooked dishes made from fresh local ingredients is served in the 35-cover restaurant, and the extensive menu is supplemented by a daily specials board. Some of the dishes are pub classics, others more esoteric, so there's something for all tastes. The area in front of the pub, which is now a capacious car park, used to be fields where, among other things, annual sheep dips took place. Other outdoor amenities at this exceptional inn include a patio with plenty of picnic benches, a beer garden and a newly developed children's playground.

🕐 12-11, Sun to 10.30

🍴 A la carte, bar menu and snacks

£ Mastercard, Visa

🅿 Car park, children's play area

@ e-mail: pub@theoakpub.freeserve.co.uk
website: www.welshpool.org

❓ Trelyden Hall 1 mile, Welshpool 2 miles, Powysland Museum 2 miles, Montgomery 9 miles; walking, cycling, riding, fishing, golf, bird watching

THE OLD FORD INN

LLANHAMLACH, NR BRECON, POWYS
TEL: 01874 665391

Directions: From Brecon, take the A40 2 miles in the direction of Abergavenny. From Abergavenny, take the A40 towards Brecon; the Old Ford Inn is located on this road about 10 miles beyond Crickhowell.

Landlord Richard Barnett is maintaining the reputation of the **Old Ford Inn** as place to seek out for relaxation, fine food and drink and comfortable, well-priced overnight accommodation. This ancient coaching inn stands in a dramatic, isolated setting on the main A40, and the views over the surrounding countryside are unsurpassed. The handsome old stone building is fronted by a little grassed area where tables and chairs are set out in summer, and there's plenty of off-road parking. Inside, low beamed ceilings, exposed stone walls and gleaming brassware all add to the atmosphere and old-world charm of the setting, making it a splendid place to pause on a journey or to seek out as a destination. A popular selection of ales, lagers, wines and spirits

is dispensed at the bar, and hungry visitors can look forward to a good choice of food, from light snacks to full three-course meals, all with the true flavour of Wales. Sunday lunches, highlighted by traditional roasts, are particularly popular, drawing devotees from near and far, and booking is essential.

With the Black Mountains and the Brecon Beacons National Park on the doorstep, this is a wonderful area for walking, hiking, climbing or taking in the breathtaking scenery from the comfort of a car, and the Old Ford Inn is an ideal base, with 8 comfortably appointed en suite bedrooms with tv and hospitality tray, let on a Bed & Breakfast basis. The characterful rooms, many sporting old beams, range from singles through doubles and twins to family rooms. One of the main local attractions is Llangorse Lake, the largest natural lake in the region.

- 🕐 12-11
- 🍴 Bar meals and snacks
- £ All the major cards
- 🛏 8 en suite double rooms
- 🅿 Car parking
- @ e-mail: enquiries@theoldfordinn.co.uk
  website: www.theoldfordinn.co.uk
- ❓ Brecon 2 miles, Llangorse Lake 2 miles, Crickhowell 10 miles, walking, fishing, riding

THE RAILWAY INN

FORDEN, NR WELSHPOOL, POWYS SY21 8NN
TEL: 01938 580237 FAX: 01938 580618

> **Directions:** From J7 of the M54 take the A5 round Shrewsbury then the A458 towards Welshpool. At Buttington turn left on to the B4388 and after passing through Kingswood turn right into Forden. The inn is situated ½ mile south of the community centre and village school.

Situated in the pleasant rural village of Forden, **The Railway Inn** is a lively, welcoming place with friendly family owners. Mick and Pam Brewer, daughter Karen and son-in-law Dave take excellent care of their customers, whether regulars from the nearby towns and villages or visitors from all parts of the country and from further afield; Dave and Mick are mine hosts at the bar, while Karen and Pam produce the food. A log fire with a huge copper hood keeps things cosy in the beamed bar lounge, where a full selection of beers, lagers and ciders is available. The extraordinary

collection of jugs went with earlier incumbents, but there's plenty to take the eye, including brass and copper ornaments, pictures and prints. Pool, darts and dominoes are played by the locals, and the inn hosts occasional live music nights.

There's an equally inviting fire in a brick hearth in the restaurant, and the girls keep the customers happy with a wide selection of good home-cooked food. The handsome white-painted building is over 100 years old and took its name from the local railway station. The station closed in the 1960s, but the inn is still clearly very full of life, a state of affairs that should long continue under the Brewer family. The area around the Railway Inn has walking, cycling, riding, fishing or exploring villages such as Berriew.

🕐 12-2 & 7-11 (from 6 Friday), Sat 12-5 & 7-11, Sun 12-3 & 7-10.30. Closed Monday except Bank Holidays

🍴 A la carte

£ All except Amex

🛏 5 rooms, 2 en suite

🅿 Car park

🎵 Occasional live music

@ all@therailwayinn.fslife.co.uk

❓ Montgomery 3 miles, Powis Castle 3 miles, Welshpool 4 miles, Berriew (Glansevern Hall & Gardens) 4 miles; walking, cycling, riding, fishing

SHORTBRIDGE STREET, LLANIDLOES, POWYS SY18 6AD

TEL: 01686 412583

> **Directions:** From the south (Brecon, Builth Wells), take the A470 all the way or leave the A470 at Rhayader and take the B4518 through St Harmon and Tylwch.

The Royal Head is a long black and white half-timbered building that stretches along one of the main streets of a town in the very centre of Wales. The promise of the immaculate exterior is more than fulfilled within, where the lounge bar features a wealth of gnarled black beams. As well as the usual selection of beers and lagers, five traditional ales are among the drinks dispensed at the bar, either by Eileen Hawkins, the licensee, or by members of her family. Eileen also does all the cooking, producing tasty, satisfying bar meals and a Sunday lunch that always brings in the crowds. Darts, dominoes and pool are played in the public bar, where a large screen tv carries the major sporting events.

- 🕐 12-11, Mon from 5
- 🍴 Bar meals + Sunday lunch
- 🛏 5 bedrooms
- Ⓟ Car park
- 🎵 Folk music Wednesday
- @ pubhawk@aol.com
- ❓ Llanidloes Museum, Llyn Clywedog 3 miles, St Harmon (Gilfach longhouse) 6 miles

On Wednesday evenings, these games play second fiddle to the popular folk music sessions. The Royal Head is an excellent place for an overnight (or longer) stay, and the five letting bedrooms range from a single to a family room with four beds. Llanidloes, which developed from a rural village to a weaving town to a craft centre, is an interesting place to explore, and the surrounding area is full of interesting places to see and things to do. To the northwest of town lies the man-made reservoir of Llyn (Lake) Clywedog, close to which can still be seen the chimneys of the now disused Van Lead Mine. And visitors with a sporting inclination will find plenty of activities, including fishing, sailing, golf and clay pigeon shooting.

THE STAR INN

DYLIFE, LLANBRYNMAIR, POWYS SY19 7BW
TEL: 01650 521345

Directions: The inn is located just off the B4518 about 9 miles northwest of Llanidloes. Turn left off the B4518 on a minor road signposted Machynlleth.

Surrounded by some of the most breathtaking countryside in Wales, **The Star Inn** is located just off the B4518. Standing at 1,300 feet above sea level, this is the highest pub in Wales and is an idyllic spot for getting away from it all and revelling in the scenery and the exhilarating fresh air. The charming black-and-white building dates back in part to around 1640, and the atmosphere generated by tenant Sue Ward-Banks is delightfully friendly and relaxed - a major attraction for the regular customers and for the many visitors who come from all parts to this unspoiled part of the country. The inn has two bars, one with an original slate floor and open fire, and a separate dining area. The menu offers a good range of hearty dishes catering to a range of tastes and healthy outdoor appetites, and children have

their own list of dishes.

The Star Inn also offers Bed & Breakfast accommodation in six bedrooms of various sizes, some of them with en suite facilities. Rates are very reasonable and there are discounts for extended stays. Dylife was once a thriving lead mining community, but is now a quiet village surrounded by miles of unspoilt countryside providing spectacular views.

Trout fishing is available on nearby Llyn Clywedog, and the Pennant Valley boasts one of the largest waterfalls in Wales - there is a purpose-made view point at the top of the valley. Pony trekking, golf, sailing, clay pigeon shooting and quad biking can all be arranged locally, but for many visitors the hospitality and good food at the Star are reason enough for a visit.

- 🕐 12.00-14.30, 19.00-23.00 (Phone in Winter time for lunchtime opening)
- 🍴 Lunchtime and evening menus
- £ Visa, Mastercard
- 🛏 2 double en-suite rooms, 1 double, 1 twin, 1 single, 1 family room
- ❓ Llyn (Lake) Clywedog 4 miles, Llanidloes 9 miles

STONECROFT INN

DOLECOED ROAD, LLANWRTYD WELLS, POWYS LD5 4RA
TEL: 01591 610327 FAX: 01591 610304

Directions: The village lies on the A483 about 10 miles northeast of Llandovery.

Peter and Jane Brown and their staff greet visitors to **Stonecroft Inn** and its neighbour **Stonecroft Lodge**. The inn, a traditional country pub, has built up a great reputation for serving excellent meals and bar snacks, and for quenching thirsts with well-kept real ales (a minimum of four) and other draught and bottled beers and ciders. Open fires warm the bar in winter, while for summer sipping the large riverside garden is a great asset. Families are always welcome, and entertainment at the inn includes live music most Saturday evenings. There's a games area with darts and a pool table. Accommodation in the Lodge caters for all a wide range of visitors, from individuals to families and large groups:

bedrooms span all requirements, from two single rooms to family rooms and a first-floor room with six single beds. On the ground floor of the Lodge are a kitchen, lounge/diner, bathroom, cloakroom, washing machine, tv and video, and there's another bathroom and a shower room on the first floor.

The whole house, which has a total bed count of 28 spread over 9 rooms, can also be let on a holiday cottage tariff, making it a perfect spot for a grand get-together, a family party, a reunion or a large group of backpackers, mountain bikers, walkers or bird-watchers. The shops and all the other amenities of the town are just seconds away. Llanwyrtyd Wells, the smallest town in Britain, is also one of the most convivial, with a very full annual calendar of events - beer festivals, folk music gatherings, man v horse marathon, drovers walks and the famous bog snorkelling championships.

- 🕐 5-11, 12-11 Fri-Sun
- 🍴 Bar food and snacks
- 💷 Amex, Mastercard, Visa
- 🛏 Private and shared accommodation in 9 rooms (28 beds)
- Ⓟ Car parking
- 🎵 Live music most Saturdays
- @ e-mail: party@stonecroft.co.uk website: www.stonecroft.co.uk
- ❓ Llanwyrtyd Wells: events and festivals throughout the year, Cambrian Woollen Mill

TRIANGLE INN

CWMDAUDDWR, RHAYADER, POWYS LD6 5AR
TEL/FAX: 01597 810537

> **Directions:** Cwmdauddwr is situated on the B4518 on the Elan Valley road just outside Rhayader. The inn is located on the banks of the River Wye.

Set on the banks of the River Wye, the **Triangle Inn** has a history dating back to the 16th century. Once a halt on the cattle drovers' route from Cardigan to London and a break for monks travelling between Abbeycwmhir and Strata Florida, its fine reputation for hospitality is in the capable and experienced hands of Adrian and Denise Bentley. Along with their dog Chaz, they welcome visitors into the traditional surroundings of the low-beamed bar area, which serves both the blue room, where pretty china takes the eye, and the public bar, where a trap door gives access to a sunken darts pit.

Thirsts are quenched by traditional ales and appetites satisfied by a good selection of home-cooked food; the choice runs from lunchtime sandwiches and jacket potatoes to salads and main courses such as chicken curry, fish dishes, gammon, welsh black steaks, minty lamb pie or roast half duckling with a black cherry and port sauce. Most of the cooking is done by Adrian, but Denise is responsible for the scrumptious desserts, which include vanilla cheesecake topped with seasonal fresh fruit and sticky toffee pudding served with butterscotch sauce. Daily specials supplement the printed menu, Sunday lunch features traditional roasts, and children can choose from their own menu or take small portions from the main menu. The inn has a pleasant terrace for summer drinking, and for visitors wanting to stay overnight a fully furnished self-catering cottage is available opposite the inn. The village of Cwmdauddwr, though small at first sight, is mentioned in the Guinness Book of Records as the largest parish in Great Britain.

- 🕐 12-3 & 6.30-11, Sun 7-10.30
- 🍴 A la carte and bar snacks
- 💷 Diners, Mastercard, Visa
- 🛏 Self-catering cottage opposite the inn
- 🅿 Car park to the side
- ❓ Welsh Crystal factory 1 mile, Gigrin Farm Red Kite centre 2 miles, Elan Valley dams 4 miles, Llandrindod Wells 8 miles

THE WHITE SWAN INN

LLANFRYNACH, BRECON, POWYS LD3 7BZ
TEL: 01874 665276 FAX: 01874 665362

> **Directions:** The Swan Inn is located 3 miles east of Brecon off the A40. Take the B4558 and follow signs to Llanfrynach.

The village of Llanfrynach is tucked away east of Brecon and the short diversion off the A40 is well worth while to find **White Swan Inn**. Easy to spot with its long white-painted stone frontage and sash windows that almost meet the pavement, it is very much a typical Welsh country inn, though on a larger scale than many; the bar area is particularly pleasant and attractive, decorated and furnished to a commendably high standard, and log fires add extra warmth in the cooler months. Visitors can quench their thirsts with an excellent pint of real ale or make their choice from the usual range of draught and bottled beers and a fine wine list.

What makes the White Swan really stand out among its rivals is its first-class food, an asset which has gained it a far-flung reputation and which draws an appreciative crowd of regulars who enjoy their food and know quality when they taste it. That quality is evident in both the selection of ingredients and their preparation, and the frequently changing à la carte menu never fails to excite. A bonus for summer visitors is the secluded beer garden, and for those who would like to stay close by, superb accommodation is available a short distance away at Pencelli Parc. The luxury holiday cottages (Tel: 01874 676470) are set in glorious landscaped surroundings in the heart of the Brecon Beacons National Park and offer top-grade accommodation that has earned 5 Wales Tourist Board dragons. Each is fully equipped for a self-catering holiday, though with the White Swan's cooking in mind, many guests let this admirable inn take the strain at dinner time!

- 🕐 Wed-Sun 11.30-3 & 6.30-11
- 🍽 A la carte
- £ Mastercard, Visa
- 🛏 Self-catering available nearby
- 🅿 Car parking
- 🎵 www.the-white-swan.com
- ❓ Brecon 3 miles, Llangorse Lake 4 miles, Brecon Beacon Mountain centre 6 miles; walking, riding, fishing

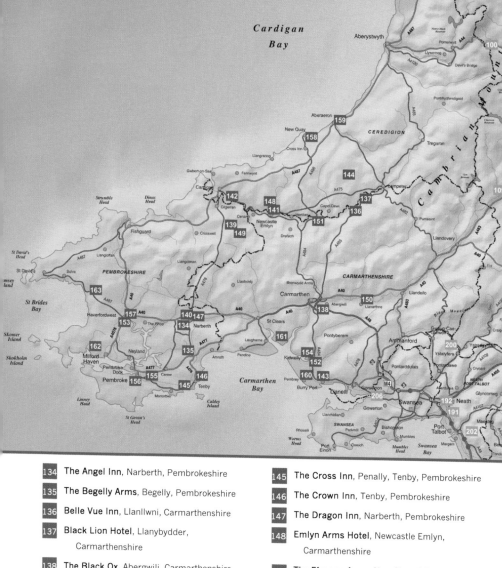

SOUTH WEST WALES

Ceredigion's countryside features some of the most beautiful landscapes in Wales and this county also attracts many rare species of birds, wildlife and plants. In particular, it is home to the graceful red kite and keen birdwatchers are well served by nature reserves around the Teifi and Dyfi estuaries and at Llangranog, New Quay and Cors Caron.

Ceredigion means the land of Ceredig, son of the Celtic chieftain Cunedda. Dating from around AD 415, the region is steeped in history and tradition. It is renowned for its unique brand of Welshness and, within Wales, its inhabitants are affectionately known as "Cardis". The patron saint of Wales, St David, was born in Ceredigion and many famous Welsh princes are buried in the ruins of Strata Florida Abbey. The region is not as well endowed with castles as the counties further north, but Aberystwyth and Cardigan castles both saw fighting before they were left to ruins, and Cardigan is credited with being the venue for the first recorded Eisteddfod in 1176.

Perhaps, though, this county is best known for its coastline on the great sweep of Cardigan Bay. Many of the once fishing villages have now become genteel resorts but few seem to have attained the great degree of brashness that is associated with other seaside holiday destinations. In the north of the county and close to the mouth of the River Dyfi is the great expanse of sand at Borth while, further south, the coastline gives way to cliffs and coves - once the haunt of smugglers.

While much of Ceredigion can be classed as very Welsh and very rural, it is also an important area of learning. St David's College at Lampeter, a world renowned ecclesiastical establishment, is now, as University College, part of the University of Wales, while Aberystwyth is home not only to the first university in Wales but also to the National Library of Wales.

Pembrokeshire, which is known as Sir Benfro in Welsh, is home to Britain's only coastal national park - the Pembrokeshire Coast National Park. Visitors flock to this leading European holiday destination to see the spectacular grandeur and tranquil beauty of the countryside and take in some of the 186 mile coastal clifftop path. The coastal region offers wonderful walking and glorious views and is a paradise for bird-watchers. Incorporating one of the most fantastic stretches of natural beauty in Europe, the Pembrokeshire Coast

Teifi Valley, Cenarth

National Park begins (or ends) on the south facing shoreline near Tenby. Running right around the ruggedly beautiful south western tip of Wales, around St Brides Bay and up along the north facing coast almost to Cardigan, the Park also includes quiet fishing villages, the huge cliffs at

Aberporth

Castlemartin, sweeping golden beaches and small, often busy harbours. Although not strictly on the coast, the labyrinthine Cleddau river system also lies within the Park's boundaries and here there are delightful little villages such as Cresswell and Carew as well as the superb sheltered harbour of Milford Haven.

Offshore there are various islands, including Grassholm, Ramsey, Skokholm and Skomer, which have changed little since they were named by Viking invaders. Many are now bird and wildlife sanctuaries of international importance. Grassholm is home to thousands of gannets, Skokholm has Manx shearwaters, Skomer has shearwaters and puffins. Ramsey harbours such species as choughs and the red-legged crow, and is also the resting place of many Welsh saints. One island, Caldey, has for over 1,500 years been the home of a religious community which continues today to live a quiet and austere life. Between their devotions, the monks of Caldey scrape a living from the land and are famous for their range of perfumes and toiletries inspired by the island's wild flowers. Pembrokeshire is the home of the corgi, which was brought to the notice of the Kennel Club by Captain Jack Howell. He presented Princess Elizabeth with her first corgi, and the rest, as they say, is history.

A county of contrasts, Carmarthenshire has a wealth of interesting places and superb countryside to enchant the visitor. There

Llyn Brianne

are coastal strongholds at Laugharne and Kidwelly, abbey ruins at Talley and Whitland and the famous rugby and industrial centre of Llanelli. Covering some 1,000 square miles, the county also has beautiful clean beaches, seaside towns and villages and rural idylls. A place of myths and

Carreg Sampson, nr Abercastle

legends, Carmarthenshire has remained essentially Welsh in most aspects.

The coastline, which is over 50 miles long, includes the award-winning Pembrey Country Park and beach, once the site of a munitions factory, and Pendine, whose long stretch of sand saw many land speed world records made and broken. Of the seaside villages, Laugharne is certainly the most famous, due mainly to the fact that it is the place where Dylan Thomas lived for the last years of his short life. But the village does not rely solely on its literary links, as it also has one of the country's most handsome castles and offers wonderful views over the estuary of the River Taf.

Inland lies Carmarthen, the county town, whose origins lie back in the time of the Romans. The town is a centre for the agricultural communities of West Wales, and to the east is an area associated with the legends and mysteries of Merlin the magician. Also in this part of Carmarthenshire is one the country's most recent important projects - the National Botanic Garden of Wales. Dedicated to conservation, horticulture, science and education and boasting the largest single-span glasshouse in the world, this is one of the country's newest gardens, while close by lies Aberglasney, one of the oldest, first mentioned in 1477. Evidence of the Roman occupation of Carmarthenshire is most striking at the Dolaucothi Gold Mines, to the northwest of Llandovery. At Cenarth, visitors can see salmon fishermen on the River Teifi still using the coracle, a tiny round boat whose origins are lost in the mists of time. A fascinating museum tells the story of these distinctive little craft.

Situated at the mouth of the River Aeron, this is a delightful small town that was turned by 19th century planning from a small fishing hamlet into a bustling port that also became famous for its shipbuilding. Although the industry here has all but gone, there can

Aberaeron Harbour

be found, on the quay, the **Aberaeron Sea Aquarium** where not only can all manner of sea life be viewed from the shore but the aquarium also offers visitors the chance to discover Cardigan Bay's marine ecology and heritage coast. Just inland from the town lies **Aberaeron Wildlife Park**, the home of llamas, red deer, parrots, owls and Jimmy, who is believed to be the world's only albino crow and who starred in the television series *Gormenghast*.

ABERGWILI

The **Carmarthenshire County Museum** occupies a lovely old house that was previously a palace of the bishop of St David's and visitors to the museum can still see the bishop's peaceful private chapel. Concentrating on Carmarthenshire's past, the museum's displays range from Roman gold through to Welsh furniture and there is also a reconstruction of a school room. The palace's grounds, too, are open to the public, and the delightful parkland is ideal for a stroll and a picnic.

ABERYSTWYTH

The largest town in Cardigan Bay, the seat of local government and the home of the University College of Wales and the National Library of Wales, Aberystwyth is not only the unofficial capital of mid-Wales but also a cosmopolitan coastal resort. Edward I began building **Aberystwyth Castle** and also granted a charter that made the settlement around the new fortification a free borough with a ditch and wall, a guild of merchants, a market and two fairs. Today, the ruins, standing on the rocky headland, remain an impressive sight. Also on Castle Point can be found the town's **War Memorial**, a splendid monument that was commissioned the year after World War I ended. Much of the town's once thriving fishing and boat-building industries have gone, but **Aberystwyth Harbour and Marina** is still a bustling place that can accommodate over 100 vessels, and at the town quay all manner of fish and seafood are landed. The town's 700 foot long **Pier** was constructed in 1864 and the Pavilion at the end was added in 1896 to provide a capacious venue for light entertainment. Just to the north, along the coast from the town centre, lies the Victorian electric **Cliff Railway**, which still carries passengers up the cliff face at a sedate four miles an hour. On the cliff summit is the **Great Aberystwyth Camera Obscura**, a faithful reconstruction of a popular Victorian amusement; the huge 14 inch lens enhances the superb view this excellent vantage point. Aberystwyth is also a seat of learning and is the home of the **National Library of Wales**, one of only six copyright libraries in Great Britain and the keeper of the majority of materials that relate to the Welsh people and their culture. Housed in a beautifully restored Edwardian music hall, right in the centre of the town, is the **Ceredigion Museum**. It tells the history of Cardiganshire through an interesting collection of materials: the history of seafaring, agriculture and silver and lead mining are all well chronicled.

AMROTH

Lying at the south eastern most point of the Pembrokeshire Coast National Park,

this quiet village has a lovely beach overlooking Carmarthen Bay. As well as the delightful surroundings the village is home to the enchanting **Colby Woodland Garden**, an eight acre area of woodland set round a Nash-style house in a secluded valley that is home to one of the finest collections of rhododendrons and azaleas in Wales. The carpets of bluebells follow the displays of daffodils in the spring and there is a mass of colour during the summer when the hydrangeas flower, before the garden is taken over by the rich colours of autumn.

BRONWYDD ARMS

From Bronwydd Arms Station the **Gwili Railway** offers visitors the opportunity to step back in time and take a short steam train journey through the Gwili Valley on part of the old Great Western Railway line. This line originally opened in 1860 and, although it finally closed in 1973, it has, since the late

Gwili Railway

1970s, been run by volunteers. Visitors can enjoy the train journey, and the other end of the line, Llwyfan Cerrig, is the perfect place for a picnic.

CALDEY ISLAND

This peaceful and tranquil island, which along with its sister island of St Margaret's lies just a short distance off the coast from Tenby, has been the home of monks for some 1,500 years. As well as the modern working monastery that is home to a community of 20 monks of the Reformed Cistercian Order, there are the remains of a 13th century monastery which was also founded by the Cistercians. St Illtud's Church, along with the old priory ruins, can be visited, and a small museum on the island tells the history of this beautiful island.

CAPEL DEWI

Close to the village lies **Rock Mills Woollen Mill**, which was established in 1890 by John Morgan and whose descendants still weave here. The machinery is powered by a waterwheel which also drives a small alternator to provide lighting.

CARDIGAN

Once the busiest port in Wales, Cardigan is an ancient borough which received its first charter in 1199 and it was, in the 12th century, a power base of Lord Rhys, one of the last Welsh princes to rule an independent principality. The few remains of **Cardigan Castle**, which stand beside the river, conceal a turbulent history: built in the late 11th or early 12th century by Gryffydd ap Rhys, the fortifications were strengthened around 1170 before it passed into the hands of the Earl of Pembroke in 1240. Thought to be the site of the first Eisteddfod in 1176, the castle fell to Parliament in 1645 during the Civil War.

Housed in an 18th century warehouse on Teifi Wharf, the **Cardigan Heritage Centre** tells the story of this former county town, from prehistoric times through to the present day. Beside the river, just outside the town, lies the **Welsh Wildlife Centre**, a nature reserve that provides a variety of habitats, including reed beds, woodland and meadow.

CAREW

Located on the shores of the tidal mill pond, **Carew Castle** is one of the few such buildings to display the development from Norman fortification (it was built between 1280 and 1310) to Elizabethan manor house. However, this site is much older, as archaeological excavations have found remains which go back some 2,000 years. Various remarkable individuals have connections with the castle, and the Great Tournament held here in 1507 was attended by 600 nobles; but the castle also gives an insight into the lives of servants, craftsmen, priests and common soldiers of the time. During the summer months a wide variety of events is held in the castle grounds, including drama, school projects, holiday activities, battle re-enactments, country fairs and concerts. Here too can be seen one of only three restored tidal mills in Britain. **Carew Tidal Mill** still retains its original machinery, and the story of Milling exhibition traces the history of milling through the ages and the mill's role in the local community. As well as the castle and the mill, the Carew site also incorporates a causeway, a medieval bridge and an 11th century **Celtic Cross** that is one of the best examples of its kind in Wales.

CARMARTHEN

One of the oldest Roman towns in Wales, Carmarthen is the county town of Carmarthenshire and lies at the centre of the West Wales agricultural community. At the site of **Caer Maridunum**, the most westerly Roman fort in Britain, the remains of the amphitheatre can still be seen and the Roman town walls were known to have been visible in the 12th century. However, the historic old part of Carmarthen grew up around **Carmarthen Castle**, which was originally built in around 1109 by Henry I. Overlooking the River Tywi, little remains of the castle today except the early 15th century gatehouse. Among the many attractions in the town are The **Guildhall**, which was built in

1767 to replace the hall of 1583, **Oriel Myrddin**, a contemporary craft gallery and regional art venue, and the **Carmarthen Heritage Centre** which, through displays, multi-media and video presentations, tells the story of the town from the time of the Roman occupation in AD 75 through to the present day.

Carmarthen has a thriving food market, where one of the local specialities on sale is Carmarthen ham, which is air-dried, sliced and eaten raw, like the Spanish Serrano ham.

CENARTH

This ancient village on the banks of the River Teifi - famous for its **Salmon Leap Waterfalls** - has for centuries been associated with fishing and coracles. It is also home to **Cenarth Mill**. Dating from the 18th century, the watermill, which has two pairs of stones (one for barley, the other for oats) is powered by the river close to the salmon leap. Now restored and producing wholemeal flour, the mill complex also houses the

Salmon Leap Waterfalls

National Coracle Centre, where visitors can see a unique collection of these ancient boats from around the world. Dating back to the Ice Age, these little round boats, once covered in skins, are still used for salmon fishing and at the Centre visitors can see demonstrations of coracles at work.

CILGERRAN

The remains of **Cilgerran Castle**, one the most picturesque in Wales, can be seen sitting on a rocky promontory overlooking the River Teifi. A tranquil site today, this land was once hotly disputed territory and the castle's defences reflect this - there are almost sheer drops on two sides of the building, while the 13th century twin round towers and curtain walls protect the flank away from the cliff. One of the first major tourist attractions in Wales - in the 18th and 19th centuries it was fashionable to take a river excursion to the ruins from Cardigan - today, these romantic ruins still provide inspiration to artists, as they have done for centuries.

CROSS INN

To the south of the village lies **New Quay Honey Farm** - the largest honey farm in Wales - which is housed in an old chapel. Visitors here have the chance to see for themselves the amazing life of a honey bee as the top floor of the chapel has been turned into an exhibition illustrating the mysteries of bees and honey. The farm is also home to a colony of leaf-cutting ants.

CROSSWELL

This village, on the northern slopes of the Preseli Hills, is home to **Pentre Ifan Burial Chamber**, one of the grandest megalithic remains in Wales. An ancient chamber with a huge 16-foot capstone, the monument is made of the same Preseli bluestones that somehow found their way to Stonehenge on Salisbury Plain.

DEVIL'S BRIDGE

The terminus of the **Vale of Rheidol Railway**, the narrow gauge railway that runs from Aberystwyth through the Rheidol valley, Devil's Bridge attracts many visitors who come here to see the splendid waterfalls that drop some 300 feet through this breathtaking gorge. While the scenery is marvellous, there are also three interesting bridges here - dating from the 11th, 18th and 20th centuries - which were built one on top of the other.

DREFACH

Drefach is the site of the **Museum of the Welsh Woollen Industry**. One of the most traditional and rural industries, the processes involved in the spinning, weaving and dyeing of wool are explained here, and there are also demonstrations of cloth making and dyeing carried out on 19th century machinery. As well as trying their hand at spinning, visitors can stroll around the sites of the old woollen mills in the village, which still produce flannel cloth and tweeds, and follow the Woollen Mill Trail through the scenic Teifi Valley.

EGLWYS FACH

Found in the sheltered waters of the Dovey estuary, the **Ynyshir RSPB Nature Reserve** is the home of a great many species of birds, in particular waders. It has an extensive network of walks, with bird watching hides, where visitors in winter can observe the reserve's unique flock of Whitefronted Geese from Greenland and also the smaller flock of Barnacle Geese.

FELINWYNT

The village is home to the **Felinwynt Rainforest and Butterfly Centre** where, in a large tropical house, visitors are transported to the jungle to see the beautiful free-flying butterflies that live among the exotic plants.

FISHGUARD

Situated at the mouth of the River Gwaun, from which the town takes its Welsh name Abergwaun, the geography of Fishguard can be somewhat confusing to visitors. The picturesque old harbour, a pretty little quayside lined with fishermen's cottages, is Lower Fishguard, which

was the location for the fictional seaside town of Llareggub used in the filming in the 1970s of Dylan Thomas' play, *Under Milk Wood*, starring Richard Burton. The new harbour, built at the beginning of the 20th century, lies across the bay at Goodwick and it is from here that the ferries depart for Ireland. On the high ground between the two harbours lies the main town of Upper Fishguard, a bustling place packed with shops, restaurants and pubs.

FURNACE

This quaint old village was, in the 18th century, home to a iron ore smelting foundry and, today, **Dyfi Furnace** is an important early industrial site that has one of the country's best preserved charcoal burning blast furnaces.

GWBERT-ON-SEA

This small resort on the eastern banks of the River Teifi estuary is an excellent place for cliff walking and for looking

Fishguard Harbour

out over the estuary and observing its wildlife. To the north of the village, and lying some 200 yards offshore, is **Cardigan Island**, a nature reserve inhabited by wild Soay sheep. Back on the mainland, **Cardigan Island Coastal Farm Park** is an ideal place from which to look out over the island from the headland and also to observe the rare choughs that nest on the cliffs. In the caves below, a colony of seals breed and some lucky visitors may also spot Cardigan Bay's bottle-nosed dolphins.

HAVERFORDWEST

This old county town, with its pleasant rural surrounding, lies on the banks of the labyrinthine Cleddau river system and is more or less in the centre of Pembrokeshire. Lining the steep streets of this hilly town there can be found some fine Georgian buildings that date back to the days when Haverfordwest was a prosperous port trading largely with Bristol and Ireland. Set on a hill overlooking the River Cleddau is the striking landmark of **Haverfordwest Castle**, which was built around 1120 by Gilbert de Clare. The tumbledown remains, whose inner wards were converted into a gaol in 1820, are home to the town's **Museum and Art Gallery**.

HENLLAN

This village is home to the **Teifi Valley Railway**, another of Wales' famous little trains. This narrow gauge railway, which originally served the slate quarries, was created from a section of the Great Western Railway (also known as God's Wonderful Railway) that served the rural areas of West Wales. Today's passengers can enjoy a 40 minute steam train journey through this delightful valley while, at the Henllan terminus, there are plenty of attractions to keep the whole family amused.

KIDWELLY

This historic town, whose charter was granted by Henry I in the 12th century, boasts an ancient church and a 14th century bridge over the River Gwendreath. However, the most interesting and impressive building is undoubtedly the remarkably well preserved Norman **Kidwelly Castle**, which stands on a steep bluff overlooking the river. The castle spans four centuries but most of what remains today is attributed to a Bishop of Salisbury who endeavoured to build a home-from-home from Sherbourne Abbey in Dorset. One of Wales' best kept secrets, Kidwelly Castle gives a fascinating insight into the evolution of a medieval castle into a domestic dwelling of more settled times. On the outskirts of the town, marked by its 164ft redbrick chimney, lies the **Kidwelly Industrial Museum** - housed in an original tinplate works. Here visitors have a unique opportunity to see how the plate was made as well as learning something of the county's industrial past.

LAMPETER

Lampeter has long been the centre for this part of the Teifi Valley and an important meeting place for drovers but today it is best known as being the home of University College. Founded in 1822, **St David's College**, as it was first known, is a world renowned ecclesiastical college that is the oldest institution in Wales. The main university buildings include CB Cockerell's original stuccoed quadrangle of buildings dating from 1827 which were designed to mimic an Oxbridge College; underneath these buildings lies the town's old castle motte. Since 1971, the college has been integrated with the University of Wales - hence its new name **University College** - although the campus still retains its own unique atmosphere.

Dylan Thomas Boathouse

LAUGHARNE

This pretty rural town of Georgian houses on the estuary of the River Taf is home to one of the country's most handsome castles. Originally an earth and timber fortress, **Laugharne Castle** was built in stone around the 13th century and although much of the fortification still remains, it is the transformations undertaken by Sir John Perrot in the 16th century that make this a particularly special site. Granted Laugharne by Queen Elizabeth I, Perrot, an illegitimate son of Henry VIII, turned the castle into a comfortable mansion that after seeing action in the Civil War declined into the ruins seen today. This

coastal town is today a shrine to its most famous resident, Dylan Thomas, who spent the last four years of his life living at **The Boathouse** set in a cliff overlooking the Taf estuary. Discovering this small out-of-the-way place in the 1940s, Thomas famously "got off the bus and forgot to get on again", and it was while in Laugharne that he wrote some of his best works, including *Under Milk Wood*, a day in the life of his imaginary village of Llareggub.

LLANARTHNE

To the southwest of the village lies **Paxton's Tower**, designed by SP Cockerell and built in the early 19th century on the Middleton estate for

National Botanic Garden of Wales

William Paxton; it was dedicated to Lord Nelson. To the south of Llanarthne, and set in the 18th century parkland of Middleton Hall (which no longer exists), is the **National Botanic Garden of Wales** - a Millennium project that covers an amazing 568 acres on the edge of the beautiful Towy Valley. Dedicated to conservation, horticulture, science and education, this national botanic garden, the first to be constructed in Britain for over 200 years, is centred around a great glasshouse that is the largest single span house of its kind in the world. Among the many delights to be found within this old parkland are one of Europe's longest herbaceous borders, a double walled garden, a Japanese garden, lakeside walks and the Physicians of Myddfai, an exhibition that pays tribute to the legendary Welsh healers of the Middle Ages. This is also a garden of the future, and in the Energy Zone there is a biomass furnace using salvaged or coppiced wood for heating the site, and the Living Machine sewage treatment system.

LLANBOIDY

In old stone farm buildings to the north of the village is a chocoholic's dream - the **Welsh Chocolate Farm**, where chocolates of all shapes, sizes and flavours are made. As well as watching chocolate making demonstrations and touring the factory to see just how the chocolate is produced, visitors can buy gifts and treats for family and friends (and selves) at the farm shop, which has the largest selection of chocolates in Wales. And as this is rich dairy country there are also farmhouse cheeses and other dairy delights at the shop (don't even try to resist the homemade fudge!), along with a wide range of hand roasted coffee beans prepared daily.

LLANDEILO

The former ancient capital of West Wales, Llandeilo's hilltop position shows off to best advantage this pretty little market town. Pastel coloured Georgian houses line the main road, which curves elegantly up from the **Tywi Bridge** (its central span is said to be the longest in Wales) to the Church of St Teilo, dedicated to the 6th century saint who gave the town its name. Serving the rich agricultural land which surrounds it, Llandeilo was also one of the original founders of the Welsh Rugby Union, and the so-called Lichfield Gospels, the most perfect Welsh Christian manuscripts, were written here.

To the west of the town lies **Dinefwr Castle**, the ancient seat of the Princes of Deheubarth, one of the three ancient kingdoms of Wales. The castle ruins are surrounded by **Dinefwr Park**. Extensive areas of parkland were landscaped by Capability Brown in 1775 and incorporated the medieval castle, house, gardens and ancient deer park into one breathtaking panorama.

Wildfowl and Wetlands Centre

LLANDOVERY

Llandovery Castle, the remains of which overlook the cattle market, was the most easterly Norman castle within Carmarthenshire, constructed in 1116 by Richard Fitzpons only to be captured and destroyed some 42 years later. Although it was repaired in the late 12th century by Henry II, the castle was left to decay after 1403 and only the tumbledown remains are visible today. Visiting in the 19th century, the author George Borrow called Llandovery "the pleasantest little town in which I have halted". The history of this town, which has pleased many before and since George Borrow, is told at the **Llandovery Heritage Centre** where the legends surrounding the hero Twm Sion Cati - the Welsh Robin Hood are also explored.

LLANELLI

Essentially an industrial town with tinplating, steel, chemical and engineering works, Llanelli is perhaps more famous as the home of the Scarlets, one of the most famous rugby teams in Wales; the saucepan tipped rugby posts at Stradey Park and the Scarlets' anthem, *Sospan Fach*, are both reminders of Llanelli's industrial heritage. Llanelli is not all industry and rugby, as a major new attraction, the **Millennium Coastal Park and Cycleway**, provides all manner of leisure activities and peaceful wildlife havens. To the east of Llanelli lies the **Wildfowl and Wetlands Trust** bird sanctuary, which is one of the eight centres established by the Trust founded by Sir Peter Scott at Slimbridge in 1946.

LLANGLOFFAN

This village is home to the **Cheese Centre** where, in the heart of the Pembrokeshire countryside, traditional Welsh farmhouse cheese is made by the Downey family on their farm. The cheesemaking process - from milk to the finished cheese - begins at 6am and visitors are welcome to view the process from 10am onwards. Llangloffan cheese is sold in specialist shops around the world but visitors to the centre have the chance to sample the cheese at the farm's tea rooms, as well as to look round the museum and meet the friendly farm animals.

LLANGOLMAN

Slate has been quarried in this area for centuries and, housed in a renovated 18th century corn mill, **The Slate Workshop** is a place where the art of handcrafting quality Welsh slate items continues. A wide range of articles is made here, including high quality plaques, sundials, clocks and objets d'art, and many illustrate the great skill required to work and carve the slate.

LLANGRANOG

Lying in a narrow valley and rather reminiscent of a Cornish fishing village, Llangranog is not only one of the most attractive villages along the Ceredigion coast but also one of the most popular resorts in the area. The headland and cliffs to the north of the village (now property of the National Trust) offer

Llywernog Lead and Silver Mine

excellent walks and dramatic scenery. To the east of the village lies the **Walled Garden at Pigeonsford**, a Georgian walled garden which has been replanted with botanical collections of herbaceous plants and shrubs as well as vegetables and fruits.

LLYWERNOG

Just to the north of the village lies the **Llywernog Lead & Silver Mine**, a museum that covers the history of this major rural industry in mid Wales. The mine opened in 1740 and had its most prosperous period between 1850 and 1879. In the slump that followed most of the mines closed for good, but Llywernog refused to die and was briefly reopened in 1903 as a zinc prospect. It was saved in 1973 by the present owners.

South West Wales

MANORBIER

Manorbier is charmingly situated at the head of a valley that reaches down to the shore in a beautiful bay with a safe bathing beach. The village's name is thought to have been derived from Maenor Pyr (Manor of Pyr) and Pyr is believed to have been the first Celtic abbot of Caldey, living in the 5th century. Overlooking the bay of the same name, **Manorbier Castle** was conceived by Odo de Barri in 1095 when he built a wooden hall within a defensive structure but it was his son, William, who began construction of the stone fortification in the early 12th century. Today, life size wax figures placed at various points, including the impressive great hall, the turrets and the chapel, bring the history of this ancient building to life as atmospheric music captures the castle's spirit.

MILFORD HAVEN

Described by Nelson as "the finest port in Christendom", the harbour at Milford Haven offers some of the best shelter in the world to large ships as it is some 10 miles long by up to two miles broad. Norsemen used the harbour as did both Henry II and King John who set sail from here to conquer Ireland, but it was Sir William Hamilton (husband of Lord Nelson's Lady Emma) who, having inherited two nearby manors, saw the potential of the Haven as a major harbour. Although the docks, completed in 1888, failed to attract the hoped for

larger ships, the Neyland trawler fleet moved here and by the beginning of the 20th century, Milford Haven had become one of the country's leading fishing ports. During both World Wars, the Haven was busy with Atlantic convoys but after 1945 there was a decline and trawling also began to disappear. However, since the 1960s Milford Haven has developed as a major oil port and is still used by the leading oil companies.

Aptly housed in a former whale oil warehouse that dates from 1797, the **Milford Haven Museum** has a range of displays that follow the fortunes of the town and dockyard including hands-on exhibits tracing the town's history from a whaling port to a premier oil terminal.

NEWCASTLE EMLYN

In Newcastle Emlyn the first printing press in Wales was set up by Isaac Carter in 1718. The town grew up around **Newcastle Emlyn Castle**, which was built in 1240 beside the River Teifi. On the B4571 a mile north of Newcastle Emlyn lie **Old Cilgwyn Gardens**. This is a 14-acre mixed garden set in 900 acres of parkland that includes a 53-acre Site of Special Scientific Interest. The garden, which was the site of the last duel to be fought in Wales, has ornamental pools and a cast concrete bridge.

PEMBREY

This village lies on the flat lands which border Carmarthen Bay and during World War II a Royal Ordnance Factory produced munitions for the Allied Forces. At the factory's peak, in 1942, it covered some 500 acres and employed 3,000 people; it ceased production in 1965. Since then the land has been landscaped, and as **Pembrey Country Park** it offers visitors an unusual mix of pine forests, sand dunes, beaches and such attractions as a dry ski slope, a toboggan run, a miniature railway and an adventure playground.

PEMBROKE

This historic town, with its long and unbroken line of well-preserved medieval town walls, is dominated by the mighty fortress of **Pembroke Castle**. It was founded in the 11th century by the Montgomerys, who established the first timber castle on a rocky crag above the River Cleddau. Opposite the castle is the charming **Museum of the Home** that houses a unique collection of household utensils and appliances and toys and games that span three centuries.

PEMBROKE DOCK

Once an important naval dockyard, Pembroke Dock stands on the dividing line between the developed and the undeveloped shores of the Milford Haven. Downstream are the large petrochemical plants and oil terminals which take advantage of the Haven's deepwater channels while, upstream, are the much more appealing waters of the Cleddau river system.

PENDINE

The vast expanse of sand which makes Pendine a popular place with families for a day out by the sea was used in the 1920s by Sir Malcolm Campbell and others for attempting land speed records. In 1927, while attempting to break one of Campbell's records, Welshman JG Parry Thomas was decapitated in an accident on the beach and his car, Babs, lay buried in the sand for some 44 years before being unearthed and restored.

Babs can now be seen in all its gleaming glory at the **Museum of Speed**, which explores the history of this stretch of sand where so many records were broken.

Pembroke Castle

PONTERWYD

An inn called the Borrow Arms remembers George Borrow, a noted philologist and linguist who travelled widely overseas, acting for a time as an agent for the British and Foreign Bible Society. Later, he tramped around England and Wales, sometimes with his step-daughter, and in 1862 published his best-known work *Wild Wales*. Close by are a Forest Enterprise centre with forest walks and trails, a mountain bike trail, orienteering course, tea room, local crafts, and picnic and play areas, and the **Kite Country Centre** and feeding station, where at 2 o'clock each afternoon throughout the year the kites swoop down to be fed, joined by other species looking for an easy meal, including crows, buzzards and ravens.

PONTRHYDFENDIGAID

Just a short distance from the village, and close to the ford of the Blessed Virgin, lies **Strata Florida Abbey**, a Cistercian house founded in 1164. This austere order was renowned for seeking out remote and isolated sites for its religious establishments and Strata Florida - the vale of Flowers - is one such site: even though the abbey is in ruins, it is still an evocative place for visitors.

PUMSAINT

Near this hamlet, whose names means Five Saints, is the **Dolaucothi Gold Mines**, which date back some 2,000 years to a time when the open-cast gold workings were secured by the Roman army. Once a likely source of gold bullion for the Imperial mints of Lyons and Rome, the mines are still in a remarkable state of preservation, and visitors to this National Trust site can see both the ancient and modern mine workings, including a number of audits - the horizontal tunnels dug into the hillside for drainage and access. There is also the opportunity to try gold panning, to see an exhibition of vintage mining machinery and to tour the surrounding woodland on a waymarked trail.

SOLVA

Once the departure point for emigrants who sailed to

Strata Florida Abbey

America (price of a one-way ticket: 50p), Solva is a charming old seafaring village that boasts a good range of craft shops. **Solva Woollen Mill**, in the beautiful valley of the River Solfach, has been in continuous production since it opened in 1907; it

Whitesands Bay, St David's

now specialises in carpets and rugs, and visitors can usually see weaving in progress.

ST DAVID'S

Named after Wales' patron saint, St David's is the smallest and the oldest cathedral settlement in Britain. It was here, in the 6th century, that St David founded a religious order and on this site, in 1176, the magnificent **St David's Cathedral** was completed. Situated in a deep hollow below the streets, so that not even its square tower can be seen above the rooftops, the cathedral contains several treasures that include saintly bones which are believed to be those of St Caradog. The undoubted highlight of the cathedral's interior is the oak roof, which displays wonderfully ornate carvings by 15th century crafts-men. Adjacent to the cathedral, in the same grassy hollow, lie the ruins of **St David's Bishop's Palace**, a once impos-

ing building which, even though now in a ruined state, still conveys the wealth and influence of the Church in medieval times.

Quite apart from the religious sites, there are various other attractions at St David's and two, in particular, relate to the sea and the wide variety of creatures found there: the **Marine Life Centre** and the **Oceanarium**, with its sharks and rays.

Just outside the city, in a stunningly beautiful spot overlooking the sea, are **St Non's Well** and the ruins of **St Non's Chapel**. The bay too, is named after St David's mother - St Non - and legend has it that David was born here during a great storm in around AD 520.

Another coastal beauty spot, which is also steeped in legend, is **St Justinian's**, a rock-bound harbour that is home to the St David's Lifeboat Station. Justinian was a 6th century hermit who retreated across to **Ramsey Island**, a short distance offshore, to devote himself to God.

Today, the island is an RSPB reserve that is home to an abundance of wildlife.

ST GOVAN'S HEAD

The cliff scenery is at its most spectacular at St Govan's Head where the tiny religious site of the 13th century **St Govan's Chapel** huddles among the rocks almost at sea level. Accessible by climbing down 52 stone steps, this minute chapel was built on the site of a holy well that once attracted pilgrims who believed the well's waters to have miraculous healing powers.

TENBY

Tenby's Welsh name, Dinbych y Pysgod, means 'Little Fort of the Fishes' and certainly its most photographed scene is the pretty harbour with its pastel coloured Georgian houses. But the whole place is a real delight, prompting many eulogies such as this from the artist Augustus John: "You may travel the world over, but you will find nothing more beautiful: it is so restful, so colourful and so unspoilt." The artist was born in Tenby at Belgrave House, where a collection of his works, and those of his sister Gwen, can be found. The town still retains

its charming medieval character together with the crooked lanes that are enclosed within its surprisingly well-preserved 13th century town walls. On one particular stretch, **South Parade**, the walls are still at their full height and the two tiers of arrow slits are very much visible; the **Five Arches**, a fortified gateway on the walls, is perhaps the most famous feature.

Unfortunately, the same is not true for **Tenby Castle**, the scant remains of which can be found on a small headland. However, the ruins are well worth a visit for the spectacular views out across Carmarthen Bay and along the Pembrokeshire coast. A statue to Prince Albert can also be found on the headland along with **Tenby Museum,** which began life in 1878. As well as having archaeological and historical material relating to the area, the museum has a fascinating maritime section and an impressive art gallery.

Tenby Harbour

Close to the quay lies the **Tudor Merchant's House**, a relic of Tenby's prosperous sea-faring days and a fine example of a comfortable townhouse of the 15th century. Perhaps of more interest to younger visitors to the town is the **Silent World Aquarium and Reptile Collection** housed in an attractive 19th century chapel. In these interesting, if somewhat unusual, surroundings there is a wide range of exotic fish, amphibians and invertebrates on display as well as fish and other creatures that live around the shores of Pembrokeshire.

THE RHOS

The Rhos, the only village in the ancient parish of Slebach, overlooks the Eastern Cleddau and here, close to the river, lies **Picton Castle**, the historic home of the Philipps family which is still lived in by the direct descendants of Sir John Wogan, who had the castle built in the 13th century. Although the principal rooms were remodelled in the mid-18th century, some medieval features remain, and, in the 1790s, the 1st Lord Milford added the wing that now includes the superb dining room and drawing room.

The castle is also home to an **Art Gallery** with a permanent exhibition of paintings by Graham Sutherland. Outside, the gardens are equally impressive and include a walled garden with fish pond, rosebeds, culinary and medicinal herbs and herbaceous borders, and extensive woodland.

THE ANGEL INN

43 HIGH STREET, NARBERTH, PEMBROKESHIRE SA67 7AS
TEL: 01834 860579

Directions: The inn is located on the main street of Narberth, on the A478 about a mile south of the A40 Carmarthen-Haverfordwest road.

David Reynolds brought 30 years' experience in the licensed trade when he took over **The Angel Inn** in October 2001. In a prominent position on the main street of Narberth, the inn serves not only as a popular local with the residents of the town but also as a good base for business or pleasure. Once operating as a jail house where smugglers and other miscreants would be interred, the inn now attracts a more willing clientele with its genuine hospitality, its real ales, its fine food and its comfortable overnight accommodation. There are plenty of seats in the spacious lounge bar, and in summer the beer garden at the back comes into its own; in a separate

games room, pool and darts are played.

David does the cooking, and in his time here he has brought an individual touch to the menus. He always offers his customers a choice that covers most tastes and appetites, but it's the sizzling steaks that his regulars have made a standing dish. The inn's location on the A478, with the A40 close by and easy links in all directions, makes it an ideal choice for an overnight, or longer stay, and the 10 newly refurbished en suite bedrooms provide ample comfort and amenity for guests. Narberth, sited on a steep hill, grew up around its castle, but only a few fragments remain. The little town has in recent years become a flourishing centre of arts and crafts, and within a short walk of The Angel are an acclaimed pottery, a number of antiques centres and a gallery featuring work by local artists and craftspeople.

- 🕐 11-3 & 6.30-11, all day Sat & Sun in summer
- 🍴 A la carte
- 💷 All the major cards
- 🛏 10 en suite bedrooms
- 🅿 Car park
- 🎵 Live music Sat & Sun, also Fri in summer
- ❓ In Narberth: galleries, craft shops and antiques centres; Pembrokeshire Coast National Park 4 miles, Haverfordwest 10 miles, Tenby 10 miles, Carmarthen 14 miles

NEW ROAD, BEGELLY, KILGETTY, PEMBROKESHIRE
TEL: 01834 813285 FAX: 01834 813493

> **Directions:** On the A478 7 miles south of Narberth. From Haverfordwest, take the A40, right on to the B4314 at Robeston Wathen to Narberth, then right on to A478 to Begelly. From Carmarthen, A40, then A478 to Begelly.

Easy to spot on the A478, **The Begelly Arms** is a substantial white-painted building with picnic tables set out on the patio at the front. The inn enjoys plenty of local trade and is also a popular choice with motorists, tourists and holidaymakers, so John and Cheryll Hogan, who has been at the helm since 1999, is busy all year round looking after his customers. An inn since the 1920s, this was previously an undertakers. One of the first landlords after it changed its role did double duty as a dentist - anyone suffering from toothache could pay half a crown (12½p) to have a tooth extracted - presumably after providing plenty of business at the bar! A full range of beers, wines and spirits is served in the bar and lounge, which are warmed by log fires, and in the bright, cheerful, conservatory-style dining area there's ample room to relax and enjoy a meal from the à la carte

menu; the carvery is a popular option.

The Begelly Arms is not only a good spot to break a journey or to make a dining destination, it's also a fine base for both business and leisure visitors staying for one or more nights: of the 24 bedrooms, 8 are of family size and 16 have en suite facilities. Pool and darts are the favourite pub games at the inn, which has a late licence for functions; it's a very popular and well-appointed venue for special occasions, with space for up to 140 sitting or 300+ for a reception. The inn's location on the A478, with easy access to and from the A40, puts it an easy drive away from many of the regions major places of interest, including the historic town of Carmarthen, the old county town of Haverfordwest, the charming seaside town of Tenby and the scenic delights of the Pembrokeshire Coast National Park.

- 🕐 11-11
- 🍴 A la carte
- 💷 Mastercard, Visa
- 🛏 24 rooms (16 en suite)
- 🅿 Car park, late licence for functions
- ❓ Pembrokeshire Coast Path 3 miles, Narberth 7 miles, Tenby 6 miles

BELLE VUE INNE

LLANLLWNI, NR LLANYBYDDER, CARMARTHENSHIRE SA40 9SQ
TEL: 01570 480495

> **Directions:** From J49 on the M4 take the A48 to Carmarthen, then the A485 towards Lampeter. The inn lies about 14 miles along this road, 6 miles before Lampeter.

Located close to the county border with Ceredigion by the main route (A485) between Lampeter and Carmarthen, **The Belle Vue Inne** is very well placed for a large number of the major attractions of the region. Originally built as three cottages, this pleasant Welsh stone inn still has a very homely appearance that is little changed down the years and is helped by the mellow colour of the stones from which it was constructed. Inside, the story is much the same - a warm and inviting place with a friendly, relaxing atmosphere. Very much a favourite with the locals, who gather to catch up on the village news over a pint, the inn is just as welcoming to strangers, who soon become friends of the convivial landlords John George and John Price.

As well as dispensing an excellent selection of beers, ales, lagers and spirits, the two Johns have also built up quite a reputation for the good food they serve. A daily changing specials board supplements the printed menu, on which traditional favourites such as steak & kidney pie share space with more exotic offerings like Madras chicken curry. Everything is prepared on the premises, including some very tempting desserts. The countryside around the inn is largely unspoilt and provides excellent walking. Cycling, fishing and riding are other popular activities, and among the places of interest within easy reach of the inn are Llandysul Woollen Mill, the university town of Lampeter, and the small town of Llanybydder, famous for its weekly sheep and cattle market and even more renowned for its monthly horse sales.

🕐 12-11

🍴 A la carte + snacks

💷 All the major cards

🅿 Car park

❓ Llandysul Woollen Mill 5 miles, Lampeter 7 miles, Welsh Woollen Industry Museum 9 miles; walking, cycling, riding, fishing, birdwatching

BLACK LION HOTEL

MARKET SQUARE, LLANYBYDDER, CARMARTHENSHIRE
TEL/FAX: 01570 480212

South West Wales

Directions: The Black Lion is in the middle of Llanybydder, which is situated on the A485 about 5 miles southwest of Lampeter. From the south (Carmarthen), take the A485 for about 12 miles.

The Black Lion Hotel is a substantial period building with a distinctive whitewashed facade, a capacious beer garden to the side and a large car park. On the market square of a little town famous for its weekly sheep and cattle market and its monthly horse sales, the hotel is owned and run by Joe Turner and his business partner Neil Chidzey, who brought extensive knowledge and experience of the hotel trade when they took over the reins in the summer of 2002. They also brought a generous measure of application and enthusiasm, with personal service the key to the obvious rapport they soon established with their customers. In the cosy bar, made even cosier by a log fire in the cooler months, a fine selection of beers, wines and spirits is dispensed, to enjoy on their own or to accompany something good to eat. That something could be a simple bar snack or a full-scale meal, with anything in between according to

appetite. Among the favourite dishes are hearty warmers such as braised lamb shanks and scrumpy pork hock.

The Black Lion is a popular choice for a special occasion, with room enough (100+ in the function room) and all the facilities on hand. It's also a good base for enjoying the delightful scenery of the surrounding countryside, the invigorating walking and the exceptional salmon and trout fishing that can be arranged nearby. For guests staying overnight the hotel has four well-decorated, spacious bedrooms, and a hearty breakfast sets guests up for a day exploring. Apart from the hills and forests and other natural attractions of the region, there's also plenty of history and culture: the University town of Lampeter is a short drive away, as are several reminders of the woollen industry that was once the mainstay of the local economy.

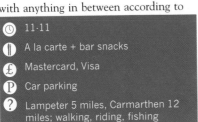

- 🕐 11-11
- 🍴 A la carte + bar snacks
- 💷 Mastercard, Visa
- 🅿 Car parking
- ❓ Lampeter 5 miles, Carmarthen 12 miles; walking, riding, fishing

THE BLACK OX

ABERGWILI, CARMARTHENSHIRE
TEL: 01267 222458

> **Directions:** Abergwili lies 1½ miles east of Carmarthen off the A40.

Carmarthen, the oldest Roman town in Wales, is just along the road, but Abergwili itself is a village of many attractions and the locals rightly put **The Black Ox** among them. Very much at Abergwili's social heart, this attractive white-painted pub with a large car park at the rear has a tradition of hospitality that goes back to the last part of the 18th century, when it served as a resting place for drovers. The old stables are now fulfilling a different role as the inn's restaurant, and sturdy stone walls add to the rustic, old-world feel both here and in the lounge. Mine hostess Catherine Williams takes excellent care of her customers' main requirements, namely food and drink.

The bar is stocked with a good range of real ales and other beers both draught and bottled, and in the restaurant the menu of home-prepared food features some particularly good fish and steak dishes. Carmarthen is rich in history, but visitors to the area would do well to tarry awhile in Abergwili itself, before or after a visit to The Black Ox. The Carmarthenshire County Museum, in a lovely building once occupied by the Bishops of St David's, has many displays concerning the county's history. That's the factual history, while at nearby Merlin's Hill Centre the theme is the legends of the area and the connection with Merlin the Magician. Another popular local attraction is the volunteer-run Gwili Railway, which runs steam-hauled on an old section of GWR track between Bronwydd Arms and Llwyfan Cerrig.

🕐 12-11 Mon-Sat, 12-10.30 Sun
£ All major cards
🍴 A la carte
Ⓟ Car park, patio
❓ Carmarthen 1½ miles, Bronwydd

THE BONCATH INN

BONCATH, PEMBROKESHIRE SA37 0JN
TEL: 01239 841241

> **Directions:** From Newcastle Emlyn take the A484 to Cenarth, then the B4332 for about 5 miles

The Boncath Inn is a grand old slate-roofed stone building fronted by a colourful array of plants and shrubs. The inn and its grounds are floodlit at night, creating an attractive and distinctive landmark that can be seen from miles around. The Boncath Inn is run with great enthusiasm by Philip and Meinir Simpson, who have managed to enhance its appeal and scope without sacrificing any of its period charm and homeliness. The only hostelry in the village, it provides a particularly convivial meeting place for the local communities and is also a popular stopping-off point for motorists in need of a break in their journey. The usual variety of liquid refreshment is available in the bar and the menu of bar meals spans a good range of options to satisfy both light and more serious appetites.

Toasted sandwiches and filled jacket potatoes, both served with a side salad, make tasty quick snacks, while main

dishes run from broccoli and cream cheese bake to cottage pie, lasagne, scampi, salmon in white wine and splendid speciality curries: vegetable, chicken, Welsh lamb & leek, Welsh Black beef – served with rice or chips, or half and half, with a poppadum. All the food is prepared on the premises so freshness is guaranteed, and booking is recommended to be sure of a table on Saturday. The inn has a fascinating secondary role as virtually a museum of local history, with a wealth of old pictures and photographs on the walls and some pieces of old farm machinery standing in the gardens. The area is particularly rich in historic sites, including Newcastle Emlyn Castle, Cilgerran Castle and the Iron Age Fort of Castle Henllys. Other major attractions include the National Coracle Centre and the Salmon Leap waterfalls at Cenarth.

⊙ 5 – 11, Sat & Sun from 12

🍺 Bar menu

🅿 Car park

❓ Bro-Meigan Gardens 2 miles, Newcastle Emlyn 6 miles, Cenarth 5 miles, Pembrokeshire National Park 10 miles

THE BRIDGE INN

COX LAKE, NARBERTH, PEMBROKESHIRE
TEL: 01834 860541,FAX: 01834 869301

Directions: The inn lies on the B4314 road that runs from the A40 at Robeston Wathen to Narberth.

Standing by a stream and the old bridge that gives the pub its name, **The Bridge Inn** is a charming slate-roofed building with planters and hanging baskets adorning its facade. The outside promises plenty of character within, and visitors stepping inside will not be disappointed. The spotlessly kept public areas offer plenty of room and bags of old-world appeal, with stone walls and fireplaces and original beams. The beer garden by the stream is an added delight in the summer. Since arriving with long experience of the licensed trade in 1999, the Evans family have devoted a great deal of time and effort into building an enviable reputation for hospitality and good food and have evolved a menu of wide appeal for their customers to enjoy in the

roomy, comfortable dining area. Fresh fish, including rainbow trout, salmon and plaice, is always guaranteed to have a big following, but there's plenty more besides, including very good chicken and steak dishes and a special menu for children. A full range of drinks is available to accompany the food or to enjoy over a chat in the bar. The Bridge is a short drive from the little town of Narberth, which has in recent years become a thriving centre for arts and crafts and antiques. In the other direction, the A40 is even closer, providing easy access westward to Oakwood and Haverfordwest, with its castle, museum and interesting shops, and eastward to the historic town of Carmarthen.

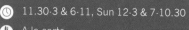

🕐 11.30-3 & 6-11, Sun 12-3 & 7-10.30

🍴 A la carte

£ All the major cards

Ⓟ Car park

❓ Pembrokeshire Coast National Park 4 miles, Haverfordwest 10 miles, Tenby 10 miles, Carmarthen 19 miles

THE BUNCH OF GRAPES

NEWCASTLE EMLYN, CARMARTHENSHIRE SA38 9DU
TEL: 01239 711185

> **Directions:** Newcastle Emlyn is on the A484 about 7 miles southeast of Cardigan, 14 miles northwest of Carmarthen. The inn is right in the centre very close to the castle.

In spring and summer hanging baskets adorn the front of **The Bunch of Grapes**, a 17th coaching inn standing in the centre of town close to the Castle. But the pink and burgundy facade is a cheerful sight at any time of the year, and in the bar Billy Brewer and his staff have a cheerful greeting for all their customers. Home cooking features strongly on an extensive menu that includes daily specials and plenty of choice for vegetarians. Booking is advisable for the traditional Sunday lunch and for the themed food nights that are held regularly throughout the year. The restaurant is non-smoking, but food can also be taken in the bar areas or, in summer, in the garden, where there are occasional barbecues.

A very good wine list complements the food, and real ale fans have a choice of three brews - Courage Directors and two guests. The pub has a separate games room with a pool table, and in the bar there's live music every Thursday. Newcastle Emlyn grew up around its 13th century castle, whose ruins are still a potent attraction. A mile or so north of town are Old Cilgwyn Gardens set in parkland that includes a 53-acre Site of Special Scientific Interest. The garden was the site of the last duel to be fought in Wales. Newcastle Emlyn is located on the A484 Cardigan-Carmarthen road. Attractions close to the inn include The National Coracle Centre at Cenarth Mill, the Salmon Leap Waterfalls on the River Teifi and the Museum of the Welsh Woollen Industry at Drefach.

- 🕐 12-11
- 🍴 A la carte
- 🎵 Live music Thursday
- @ website: www.bunchofgrapes.biz
  e-mail: info@bunchofgrapes.biz
- ❓ Old Cilgwyn Gardens 1 mile, Cenarth 3 miles, Drefach 4 miles, Henllan Steam Railway 2 miles.

THE CARPENTERS ARMS

LLECHRYD, NR CARDIGAN, CEREDIGION SA43 2NT
TEL: 01239 682692

Directions: From Carmarthen take the A484 towards Cardigan. The inn lies along this road about 2 miles before Cardigan.

Situated in the beautiful valley of the River Teifi, **The Carpenters Arms** is a delightful old inn that stands back from the main road through the village. The attractive garden and patio area to the front of the building adds to this pleasant inn's appeal and the whole place is eyecatching and hard to miss while travelling

between Newcastle Emlyn and Cardigan. Although the exterior of this building is traditional – white painted lines and fresh appearance not only create a pleasant drinking area but also a welcoming and inviting atmosphere in which to enjoy the hospitality on offer here courtesy of landlord John Potts and his staff. From the well stocked bar

visitors and locals alike can indulge in their favourite tipple, including real ales, wines, spirits and lagers.

Meanwhile, in the neat, newly appointed restaurant, a traditional menu of delicious pub food is offered throughout the day. Whilst not extensive, this list does contain many favourites including an all day breakfast. However, in the evening the list changes, though all the dishes are still home-cooked, and customers can enjoy a wider variety of tastes including curries, steaks and fish. On Sunday, the carvery takes centre stage. A popular inn, well placed for exploring Cardigan, the coast and Pembrokeshire, The Carpenters Arms can also offer visitors superb accommodation in three en suite double rooms.

🕐 11-11

🍴 Bar meals, snacks, carvery

£ All the major cards

🛏 3 en suite double rooms

🅿 Car park

❓ Pentre Manor Gardens 2 miles, Cardigan 2 miles, beach 6 miles, Teifi Valley Railway 8 miles; walking, cycling, riding, fishing, sailing, bird-watching

CAULFIELD'S HOTEL

11 STATION ROAD, BURRY PORT, CARMARTHENSHIRE SA16 0LR
TEL: 01554 832288 FAX: 01554 830091

Directions: From the M4 (J48) take the A4138 to Llanelli then the A484 to Burry Port (turn off at the garage on the corner). The hotel is ½ a mile on the left.

Caulfield's Hotel is a fine double-fronted end-of-terrace building with a distinctly Irish look - the green paint, the Celtic-style lettering, the map of the Emerald Isle embossed on a window. Richard, formerly a builder, and Caroline, a dental practice manager, spent two years refurbishing the place, and they enter 2003 with a highly attractive finished article. Stained glass windows are a feature in the public and lounge bars, which are served from a central area where the Guinness pumps occupy a place of prominence. To the side is a pool room. The kitchen has been central to the improvement plans, and meals will be available from May

2003 onwards. On the accommodation side are four well-appointed guest bedrooms, two twins and two doubles, all with en suite facilities and modem-adaptable telephones.

A spacious, well-maintained beer garden is closed off from the road by an impressive set of wrought-iron gates. Parking is available for 20 cars at the back of the hotel. The refurbished harbour in Burry Port is well worth a look, and places of interest within easy reach include Pembrey Country Park with attractions for all ages, Kidwelly Castle and Industrial Museum, and the Millennium Coastal Park and Cycleway in Llanelli. With all these amenities within easy reach, and with so many diverse interests catered for, the area is a splendid place to spend a few days, and Caulfield's Hotel is an ideal base to choose.

- 🕐 11-11
- 🍴 Will be available from May onwards
- 🛏 4 en suite bedrooms
- Ⓟ Beer garden with BBQ area
- ♫ Live performers weekly
- ❓ Burry Port harbour, Pembrey Country Park 2 miles, Llanelli 2 miles, Kidwelly 5 miles

CEFN HAFOD

GORSGOCH, LLANYBYDDER, CEREDIGION SA40 9TE
TEL: 01570 434238

Directions: The inn is situated on the B4338 in the village of Gorsgoch. From Lampeter, take the A475 west to Drefach; turn right on to the B4338 and go on to Gorsgoch, about 2 miles.

A private dwelling dating back several centuries has for many years been a cosy, traditional pub at the heart of the small local community of Gorsgoch. **Cefn Hafod** has been owned and run by Geraint and Eiddwen Hatcher since 1991 but has been in their family since 1959. They know all there is to know about the region, so visitors can find out what to see in the neighbourhood while enjoying a drink in the cosy, old-world bar. A full range of beers, wines and spirits is on offer, and Eiddwen keeps the inner man happy with a menu of familiar pub favourites - her chicken curry has plenty of takers whenever it appears on the menu; children have their own list of dishes.

Every Wednesday in the summer the pub hosts one of those old-fashioned games that seem to be played only in British pubs: this one is a form of quoits played with a horseshoe; some of the locals are real experts, and an international match involving England, Scotland and Wales is due to take place at the pub in July 2004. This is very good walking country, and among other activities nearby are fishing and riding; there are also two leisure centres within an easy drive. And the National Six miles south of the pub is the village of Drefach, with Lampeter along the main road (A475), while in the other direction the B4338 leads to Talgarreg and Synod Inn, where it joins the main Cardigan-Aberystwyth road (A487). The bar and toilets at Cefn Hafod are accessible to wheelchair users.

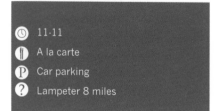

- 🕐 11-11
- 🍴 A la carte
- 🅿 Car parking
- ❓ Lampeter 8 miles

THE CROSS INN

PENALLY, NR TENBY, PEMBROKESHIRE SA70 7PU
TEL: 01834 844665

> **Directions:** From the end of the M4 take the A48 to Carmarthen, A40 to St Clears, A477 then the A478 to Tenby. From Tenby take the A4139; about 1 mile outside Tenby, Penally is signposted opposite a garage. Turn right off this road; the inn is directly behind a phone box.

Christine Feenan spent 12 years in the catering business before taking over her first pub in July 2002. She loves **The Cross Inn** and is rarely away from the premises, and her growing band of regulars also hold the place in high esteem. It's an inviting old-style pub with a cosy bar where the two guest ales change regularly and good conversation is the order of the day. In the separate, spacious restaurant the chef seeks out fresh local produce for a menu that provides plenty of choice for all appetites and tastes. Home-made chicken liver pâté or a pint of prawns could get a meal off to a splendid start, followed perhaps by an omelette, chilli con carne, meat or vegetable lasagne or a full-of-flavour steak pie.

Curries are a particular favourite, and an unusually wide choice includes vegetable tikka masala, chicken korma, lamb balti and even beef Madras, When sea bass is on the menu, fresh landed and simply pan-fried, it should not be missed. Steaks feature top-quality local Welsh Black beef, and the really ravenous customer is sure to be kept happy for some time with the mighty JR Platter consisting of gammon steak, beef steak, sausage, pork chop, mushrooms, onion rings, a fried egg and potatoes. The patio at the front of the pub commands wonderful views over Carmarthen Bay. Penally is very close to the coast, with the many attractions of the delightful town of Tenby just a mile away, and the beautiful and peaceful Caldey Island a short boat trip away.

 12-11

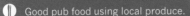 Good pub food using local produce.

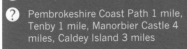 Pembrokeshire Coast Path 1 mile, Tenby 1 mile, Manorbier Castle 4 miles, Caldey Island 3 miles

THE CROWN INN

LOWER FROG STREET, TENBY, PEMBROKESHIRE SA70 7HU
TEL: 01834 842796

Directions: From the end of the M4 take the A48 to Carmarthen, the A40 to St Clears, the A477 then left on to the A478 to Tenby. The inn is in the centre of town.

Good conversation over real ale and good food are the stock in trade of the **Crown Inn**, which has been dispensing hospitality for well over 100 years. The heart and soul of this delightful inn is the friendly, bubbly owner Debbie Donkin, ably assisted by her son Gary and her daughter Suzanne. Debbie has been in the licensed and allied trades since leaving school and has been at the helm since 1999. In the relaxed surroundings of the cosy bar real ale fans are in their element, with a choice of three permanent ales and at least four others that are changed on a regular basis (a framed page from the Tenby Observer dated 1895 shows an advertisement for the Crown selling beer at a penny a pint!).

In the kitchen behind the bar a talented chef prepares a variety of traditional pub dishes; the blackboard specials (chalked up outside the pub as well as in the bar) change daily, and the favourites with the regular customers include his curries and his flavour-packed steak & ale pie. When the sun shines, a small patio at the back of the pub comes into its own. The Crown, which is open all day, every day, is a great place to drop in for a drink and a meal when seeing the sights of this charming old town. These range from the well-preserved 13th century town walls to a 15th century merchant's house and the Silent World Aquarium and Reptile Collection housed in a 19th century chapel.

🕐 11·11, Sun 12·10.30

🍴 Bar menu

🅿 On street parking (public parks close by)

❓ The visitor attractions of Tenby, Caldey Island 3 miles offshore, Manorbier Castle 4 miles

THE DRAGON INN

5 WATER STREET, NARBERTH, PEMBROKESHIRE SA67 7AT
TEL: 01834 861667

Directions: From the end of the M4 take the A48 to Carmarthen, then the A40 for about 15 miles and the A478 to Narberth. The inn is situated on the town square.

The little town of Narberth, situated on a steep hill, is a very pleasant place to explore, and apart from its strong historical and literary associations it has become a thriving centre for antiques shops and arts and crafts galleries. An excellent place to pause while strolling round the town is **The Dragon Inn**,

which enjoys a central location on the market square. Ann Davies has been the tenant since 1990 and she is very much the life and soul of the place: she cooks and she also serves behind the bar, helped by her daughter. Good simple home cooking is the order of the day, with the likes of soup, cottage pie, curries and Sunday roasts satisfying lunchtime appetites. The favourite thirst-quencher among a large selection of beers, lagers and ciders served in the old-fashioned stone-floored bar is Reverend James real ale.

Barbecues are occasionally held in summer in the beer garden, where there are three boules pitches. The Dragon Inn hosts a monthly quiz, and from time to time there are musical evenings. The inn, which dates back about 200 years, once had a half-door from which beer was served to farmers and traders on market day. It also used to serve milk, and the milk licence was relinquished as recently as 2001. Narberth lies only minutes from the main A40, with Haverfordwest to the west and St Clears and Carmarthen to the east. The coast, at Tenby, and the Pembrokeshire Coast National Park are also easily reached.

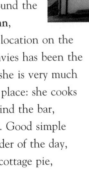

- 🕐 11-11
- 🍴 Lunchtime bar menu + Sunday lunch
- Ⓟ Boules pitches, summer barbecues
- 🎵 Quiz monthly, occasional live music
- ❓ Pembrokeshire Coast National Park 3 miles, Haverfordwest 9 miles, Tenby 10 miles

EMLYN ARMS HOTEL

BRIDGE STREET, NEWCASTLE EMLYN, CARMARTHENSHIRE SA38 9DU
TEL: 01239 710317 FAX: 01239 710792

Directions: Newcastle Emlyn lies on the A484 about 7 miles east of Cardigan. From the south (Carmarthen), take the A484 direct, through Rhos and Henllan, or take the A484 for 5 miles to Cynwyl Elfed, then the B4333.

The Emlyn Arms is a splendid old coaching inn with a whitewashed facade and a history going back more than 300 years. It's now a spacious, comfortable hostelry offering a variety of services - local inn, restaurant and hotel - making it an excellent base for a quick visit, a meal or a base for both business and leisure visits. And it also has a large function room which can host dances, wedding receptions, corporate events and special occasions with up to 200 attendees. Behind every outstanding inn there's likely to be an outstanding landlord, and in the case of the Emlyn Arms it's Barry Byrne, in charge since mid-2001, who is always on hand to add a friendly, personal touch and a warm, genuine greeting.

A full range of drinks is served in the

bars, and in the eating area an à la carte menu and daily specials provide plenty of choice for the hungry visitor. The guest bedrooms are smart, well-decorated and roomy, with en suite facilities. The Castle, which played a part in the Glyndwr rebellion and in the Civil War, is the best known landmark in Newcastle Emlyn, whose other main claim to fame is as the first place in Wales to have a printing press.

There are many other places of interest in the neighbouring towns and countryside. Among the leading attractions are the 18th century watermill, the National Coracle Centre and the famous Salmon Leap Waterfalls on the River Teifi in the ancient conservation village of Cenarth, and the Teifi Valley Railway, one of the Great Little Trains of Wales, in Henllan.

- ○ 11·11
- ◑ A la carte
- £ Mastercard, Visa
- ⊟ En suite bedrooms
- Ⓟ Car park, large function room
- @ www.emlynarmshotel.co.uk
- ? Newcastle Emlyn Castle 1 mile, Cenarth 3 miles, Cardigan 7 miles, Henllan 3 miles

THE FFYNONE ARMS

NEW CHAPEL, BONCATH, PEMBROKESHIRE SA37 0EH
TEL: 01239 841800

> **Directions:** The village of New Chapel is located on the B4332, 3 miles west of Newcastle Emlyn

The Ffynone Arms has been at the heart of village life for almost 300 years, but not always as a hostelry. What is now the lounge for the restaurant was once a court house where farmers paid their dues and the local community came to settle its disputes. There's no dispute nowadays about the convivial, relaxed surroundings of the inn, making it an ideal place for regulars to meet for a chat and for occasional visitors to pause on their journey. The appeal starts with the greystone frontage, with pretty red details for pipes, doors and creeper, and white for window and door surrounds. And the interior does not disappoint, imparting as it does an instant feel of homeliness.

The mood of the pub is definitely set by landlord Billy Scott, an Irishman whose infectious charm makes him

ideally suited for the role, which he shares with his wife Yvonne. A wood fire burns in the slate-floored bar, where a full range of beers and spirits is dispensed, and a varied, frequently changing menu tempts visitors into the cottagey 30-cover restaurant. There's plenty of choice for everyone but in their season salmon and trout specials are never short of takers. The Ffynone Arms is central to many Welsh beauty spots, including the famous Cenarth Falls, and activities in the vicinity include walking, fishing, canoeing and pony trekking. The beaches, bays and coves of the Pembrokeshire coast are also easily reached. With all this in mind, the inn is an excellent place to make a base for a holiday, and a comfortable, economical stay is provided in four letting bedrooms – 2 singles, 1 double and 1 family room. A hearty breakfast starts the day, and packed lunches can be provided.

- 🕐 12·11
- 🍴 Bar menu + à la carte
- 🛏 4 bedrooms
- 🅿 Car park
- @ e·mail:
  ffyone@walestouristonline.co.uk
  web: www.walestouristonline.co.uk
- ❓ Newcastle Emlyn 3 miles, Cenarth Falls 4 miles, Pembrokeshire National Trust Park 12 miles

THE GOLDEN GROVE ARMS

LLANARTHNE, CARMARTHEN, CARMARTHENSHIRE SA32 8JU
TEL: 01558 668551   FAX: 01558 668069

Directions: Llanarthne is on the B4300 about 7 miles east of Carmarthen.

The **Golden Grove Arms** is a well-loved country inn offering friendly service and excellent food and accommodation in the beautiful Tywi Valley. The manager is Keith Brain, who changed course when redundancy forced him out of the local tinplate industry. The move into the licensed trade was one that seems to suit his happy, outgoing personality perfectly, and the growing number of regular customers he has attracted since November 2002 are very pleased that he made the move. Food is a very important part of the business at the Golden Grove Arms, and in the relaxed surroundings of the restaurant the menu includes home-made pies, faggots & peas, Welsh lamb and beef, seasonal game and the superb salmon and sewin from the River Tywi.

In the rustic old-style bars Buckleys Best and Bitter and Brains Mild are on tap, and on one of the open fires Keith can sometimes be seen making traditional Welsh cakes - a sight that amuses regulars and first-timers alike. Once a month in the summer, Keith plans special theme evenings, with Welsh dishes, a harpist and clog dancers. The surrounding area is rich in scenic and historic appeal, and the inn makes a perfect base for a touring holiday. The six well-furnished guest bedrooms, each with its own individual charm, comprise a single, a twin, two doubles and a family room. All have en suite facilities, tv, tea/coffee makers and great views. Golden Grove is the name of a village a short distance east of the inn, on the way to Llandeilo.

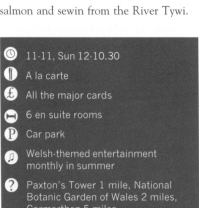

- ⏰ 11-11, Sun 12-10.30
- 🍴 A la carte
- 💷 All the major cards
- 🛏 6 en suite rooms
- 🅿 Car park
- 🎵 Welsh-themed entertainment monthly in summer
- ❓ Paxton's Tower 1 mile, National Botanic Garden of Wales 2 miles, Carmarthen 5 miles

LLWNDAFYDD

SARON, LLANDYSUL, CEREDIGION SA44 5DL
TEL: 01559 371048

> **Directions:** From Carmarthen, take the A484 north for about 12 miles. Stay on this road when it forks with the A486. Saron is about 1½ miles further on.

The **Llwndafydd Inn** is a fine period building with a sympathetic modern extension, standing square on to the A484 north of Carmarthen, between Rhos and Henllan. The owners since early in 2002 have been Tracy and Gethin Williams, a young and enthusiastic couple who provide a warm Welsh welcome and an extensive knowledge of the area which they are happy to impart to their customers. A log fire keeps things warm in the cheerful bar, where among the beers on tap are the Double Dragon range from the local Felinfoel Brewery. The inn has a spacious, comfortable restaurant with seats for up to 100, and a function room that can be used for parties, wedding receptions or other special occasions.

Tracy does the cooking, using local produce as much as possible, and her steaks and home-cooked ham are renowned in the neighbourhood and always in demand; Sunday lunch is usually the most popular time of the week, and it's advisable to book to be sure of a table even in such a roomy restaurant. This is a great place to seek out in its own right for its hospitality and its excellent food, and it also provides a perfect place to pause for refreshment while touring the area. And this is an area full of interesting places to explore: among the nearby attractions are Llandysul with its outstanding scenic views, Victorian town centre, fishing and whitewater canoeing; Henllan, home to the Teifi Valley Railway, one of the Great Little Trains of Wales; Newcastle Emlyn Castle, and Cenarth Falls.

- 🕐 11-11
- 🍴 A la carte
- 💷 Mastercard, Visa
- 🅿 Car park, function room
- @ williss@hotmail.com
- ❓ Llandysul 3 miles, Henllan 3 miles, Newcastle Emlyn 6 miles, Cenarth Falls 10 miles

THE LORD NELSON INN

24 LADY STREET, KIDWELLY, CARMARTHENSHIRE SA17 4UD
TEL: 01554 891532

Directions: From the M4 (J48) take the A4138 to Llanelli, then the A484, by-passing Burry Port, to Kidwelly.

The historic town of Kidwelly is a place of many attractions, and visitors looking for hospitality and refreshment make tracks for the **Lord Nelson Inn**. Opening straight from Lady Street, the mid-terrace pub has an inviting bar in traditional style, with a separate pool room. A small lounge at the front has a log-burning stove set in an imposing stone hearth, while the larger lounge at the back overlooks a spacious patio with a barbecue area, a lawn and a safe children's play area. Brains Brewery provides some of the excellent ales served at the bar, and with the refurbishment of the kitchen bar meals are now available, with steaks, home-made pies and daily specials among the choices.

Endaf Jones was the steward of Kidwelly Bowls Club before taking over the Lord Nelson with his father in 1994; he now runs it with his companion Catrin. The sporting connection remains strong: the pub is the HQ of Kidwelly Town Football Club, who use it for team and committee meetings and for post-match refreshments. The pub also fields a darts team and three pool teams. Other entertainment includes occasional live music evenings. The castle, the church and the Industrial Museum (spot the 164ft redbrick chimney) are the main places of interest in and around Kidwelly, and it's just a short drive to Pembrey Country Park to the south and in the other direction to Tregoning Hill overlooking the estuary created by the Rivers Towy, Taf and Gwendraeth.

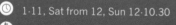

- 🕐 1-11, Sat from 12, Sun 12-10.30
- 🍴 A la carte
- Ⓟ Large patio with children's play area
- 🎵 Occasional live music evenings
- ❓ Kidwelly Castle, Industrial Museum 1 mile, Tregoning Hill 2 miles, Pembrey Country Park 3 miles

THE MASONS ARMS

DALE ROAD, HAVERFORDWEST, PEMBROKESHIRE
TEL: 01437 760815

Directions: The inn is located in the tiny hamlet of Dreen Hill, about a mile southwest of Haverfordwest on the B4327 road to Dale.

The Masons Arms is an irresistibly cheerful sight in summer, with masses of plants in tubs, in hanging baskets and climbing up the trellis on the patio, where picnic tables are set

under parasols. But this is a pub of wide appeal whatever the season, and inside, old Welsh stone walls, a stone fireplace and original beams make for a splendidly traditional ambience. The popularity of the place is due in no small measure to the landlords Lisa and Leighton Davies, who have made it such a favourite with both local residents and visitors from further afield. A full range of drinks is served in the bar and lounge, and non-smokers can enjoy their pint in a smoke-free section of the bar; in a separate games room, pool and darts are played.

The Masons Arms is also a great place for food, and locally sourced produce

features strongly on the printed menu and on the long list of daily specials. Hearty lamb pie and beef casserole, sweet & sour pork and steak & ale pie, all prepared and cooked on the premises, are regular favourites on a menu that is available from 11.30 right through to 9 in the evening (from 12.30 in winter). There's a snack menu for smaller appetites, and children have their own list of dishes, so no matter what time of day no one is in any danger of going hungry at this most welcoming of pubs. The former county town of Haverfordwest is well worth taking time to explore, and it's an easy drive to the villages of Broad Haven and Little Haven, both popular resorts for swimming and boating. The Pembrokeshire Coast Path offers marvellous walks, and inland the scenic attractions of the Pembrokeshire Coast National Park beckon.

- 🕐 11-11
- 🍴 A la carte
- £ Mastercard, Visa
- 🅿 Car park
- ❓ Haverfordwest 1 mile, Broad Haven & Little Haven 4 miles

THE MASONS ARMS

37 WATER STREET, KIDWELLY, CARMARTHENSHIRE SA17 5BX
TEL: 01554 890298

Directions: From J48 of the M4 take the A4138 to Llanelli, then the A484
through Burry Port to Kidwelly. Go through the town centre and over the bridge;
the inn is 600 yards further along this road on the left.

With a history going back
to the 14th century, the
Masons Arms has claims
to being one of the oldest
inns in Wales. It's also
one of the most
distinctive, with a
thatched roof, small-
paned lattice windows
and a big red dragon over
the door. Inside, a mass of

black beams, open fires and copper and
brass ornaments paint a splendidly
traditional picture and create a lovely
atmosphere for enjoying a glass or two
from the fine range of cask ales on tap,
including Felinfoel Mild and Bitter. In
September 2002 28-year-old Mark
Hilbert took over the lease from his
mother and now runs the inn with the
help of his family. Mark does the
cooking, making excellent use of local
produce for dishes chalked up on boards.

Steaks are very popular, so too the
Sunday roasts, and snacks are available
for lighter appetites.

The inn has an ample car park and a
beer garden with a barbecue area. The
historic town of Kidwelly, whose charter
was granted by Henry I in the 12th
century, has much to interest the visitor,
including a 14th century church over the
River Gwendraeth, an ancient church
and the well-preserved Norman castle.
And on the outskirts of town is an
industrial museum with a tall redbrick
chimney. Pembrey Country Park is a short
drive to the south, on the way to Llanelli,
where one of the many attractions is the
Millennium Coastal Park and Cycleway
with a variety of havens for wildlife and
leisure activities for humans.

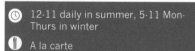

- 🕐 12-11 daily in summer, 5-11 Mon-Thurs in winter
- 🍴 A la carte
- Ⓟ Car park
- ❓ Kidwelly Castle 1 mile, Pembrey Country Park 3 miles, Llanelli 7 miles

THE MILTON BREWERY INN

MILTON, NR TENBY, PEMBROKESHIRE SA70 8PH
TEL: 01646 651202 FAX: 01646 651149

Directions: From the end of the M4 take the A48 to Carmarthen, then the A40 to St Clears; at the roundabout take the A477 Pembroke Dock road. Milton is on this road about 5 miles before Pembroke Dock.

Impossible to miss with its all-over covering of creeper, the **Milton Brewery Inn** is one of the most atmospheric and hospitable inns in the area. The interior has a wonderful old-world look, with beams, low ceilings, exposed stone and all manner of copper and brass ornaments, plates, mugs and glasses. The driving force behind it is the hands-on owner Keith Bailie, who brought with him vast experience in major hotels and restaurants when he took over in December 2002. As a member of the Chefs and Cooks Society and the British Institute of Innkeepers, he takes his job very seriously while at the same time imparting bonhomie in generous measures to his customers. Food is a major part of the business here, and meals are served

throughout from noon to 9 o'clock.

The regularly changing menu runs from snacks to full meals, and Keith's insistence on fresh local produce keeps standards impressively high. The inn is very family friendly, and children have their own menu lunchtime and evening, and a large playground in the attractive garden where they can romp in safety. A separate bistro/wine bar operates in the evenings between 7 and 10. Fine food deserves fine drinks, and the Milton Brewery has a very good selection of beers and wines. Good conversation removes the need for music or other noisy diversions, but sports fans can watch the big events on Sky TV. Milton is located on the A477 about five miles east of Pembroke Dock. There are many places of scenic and historic interest within a short drive, and there's excellent walking in the Pembrokeshire Coast National Park.

- ⏲ 12·11
- 🍴 A la carte + snacks; also evening bistro·wine bar
- £ Mastercard, Visa
- Ⓟ Car park, children's playground
- @ e-mail: goodbeer@themiltonbrewery.co.uk
- ❓ Pembrokeshire Coast National Park 1 mile, Carew Castle 2 miles, Lamphey Palace 3 miles, Tenby 5 miles, Pembroke & Pembroke Dock 5 miles

THE OLD CROSS SAWS INN

109 MAIN STREET, PEMBROKE, PEMBROKESHIRE SA71 4DB
TEL: 01646 682475

South West Wales

Directions: From the end of the M4 take the A48 to Carmarthen, the A40 to St Clears and the A477 to Pembroke Dock. Turn on to the A4075 to the Pembroke one-way system round the town. The inn is on the right just before the road rejoins the A4075.

The cheerful red facade does not deceive, for the **Old Cross Saws Inn** is one of the most social and convivial spots in Pembroke - or indeed in any other town. That is thanks in no small part to the inn's ebullient, hard-working owner Victor Rees, who bought the property at the end of 2001 and runs it with his wife. His presence is guaranteed to bring a warm glow to the single large bar, where the guest ales are changed every two or three days and there's an excellent choice of other draught and bottle beers, lagers and ciders. That takes care of thirsts, and hungers are satisfied by classic pub favourites such as sizzlers and steaks. Vic

may be a one-man entertainment centre, but the Old Cross Saws has much more to offer, with live music on Saturday and a local league quiz on Sunday.

The pub also fields darts and pool teams (both ladies' and gents') in the local leagues, and there's always a full house for the race nights, when there's a lottery every few minutes and the profits go to charity. The historic town of Pembroke, dominated by its impressive Norman castle, demands much more than a passing visit, and here, too, the Old Cross Saws comes into its own. It has five letting bedrooms for B&B, one of them a family room and all with tv, hospitality tray and en suite facilities. The inn has a beer garden, and there's parking for 25 cars across the road.

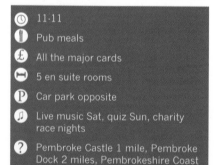

- 🕐 11-11
- 🍴 Pub meals
- 💷 All the major cards
- 🛏 5 en suite rooms
- 🅿 Car park opposite
- 🎵 Live music Sat, quiz Sun, charity race nights
- ❓ Pembroke Castle 1 mile, Pembroke Dock 2 miles, Pembrokeshire Coast Path and National Park 2 miles

THE PEMBROKE YEOMAN

11 HILL STREET, HAVERFORDWEST, PEMBROKESHIRE SA61 1QQ
TEL: 01437 762500

> **Directions:** From the end of the M4 take the A48 to Carmarthen, A40 to
> Haverfordwest. Turn left into the town centre, over the bridge, left into the one-
> way system to the cinema; left again. The inn is on the right.

The old county town of Haverfordwest has plenty to interest the visitor, and one of the best places to pause for a glass of beer and a snack while exploring the place is **The Pembroke Yeoman**. First and foremost a drinking pub, it is a great favourite with the locals, the quiz and dominoes teams enhance the atmosphere. People from all walks of life contribute to a good, lively atmosphere in the bars, where at least four real ales are available at any one time. A varied food menu provides ample nourishment for the healthy appitite. Warming coal fires keep things cosy in the colder months. The Grade II listed building, which started life as a coaching inn, was once called The Three Crowns. It was renamed in 1970 by a

landlord who had been a sergeant in the Pembrokeshire Yeoman Regiment.

The current incumbent, Nigel Brock, has nearly 30 years experience in the business and has been here for 18 years. He has been responsible for restoring many of the inn's original features, including the windows. This is a really splendid place, with bags of atmosphere and a loyal band of customers. It is affectionately known as H.Q. to its regulars. One of the staff, Anne, also deserves a long service medal, being a barmaid for the present owner for nearly 25 years. Haverfordwest grew up around its Norman castle, whose tumbledown ruins now house the town's museum and art gallery. The delights of the countryside are all around, and it's a short drive west on the B4341 to the coast at Broad Haven and Little Haven.

- 🕐 11-11, Sun 12-4 & 7-10.30
- 🍴 Bar meals
- 🅿 Free car park nearby
- 🎵 Dominoes league match Mon, Quiz league Wed
- ❓ Haverfordwest Castle & Museum 1 mile, Little Haven 5 miles, Milford Haven 10 miles

THE PENRHIWLLAN INN

LLANDYSUL ROAD, NEW QUAY, CEREDIGION SA45 9RF
TEL: 01545 560471

> **Directions:** From the A487 Aberystwyth road take the A486 New Quay road. The inn is on the left on the drive into town.

The **Penrhiwllan Inn** is a free house offering genuine hospitality for all the family. Starting life as two cottages around 1750, it has been an inn for at least 150 years. For the last year has been in the very capable hands of David and Angela Russ, a friendly and hard-working couple

who have breathed fresh life into the inn with a top-to-toe refurbishment. Behind the long black-and-white frontage the bar and lounge simply ooze atmosphere, with beams, brasses, exposed stone and open fires - a congenial setting for enjoying a chat and a glass of Felinfoel Double Dragon.

The restaurant is particularly appealing, with an ancient tree trunk supporting the

ceiling and wall lights creating a cosy, intimate ambience. The evening menu, available seven days a week, is prepared by a talented chef who sets great store by local produce, including fish fresh from the harbour. A bar menu, starting with breakfast, is served throughout the day. At the front of the inn picnic benches are set under parasols, while at the back there's plenty more seating in the beer garden. For guests staying overnight there's an en suite double room, or visitors can park their caravans in an adjacent field equipped with all the facilities. The major sporting events are shown at the inn on satellite tv, and live entertainment brings in the crowds at the weekend. There's always plenty to do hereabouts, including boat trips from the harbour for fishing and watching the dolphins.

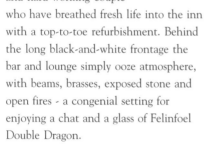

- 🕐 12·11
- 🍴 All day bar menu + evening à la carte
- 🚐 Caravan field
- Ⓟ Full childrens licence
- 🎵 Live entertainment Friday & Saturday
- ❓ Boat trips from the harbour, Aberaeron 5 miles, Llanerchaeron National Trust 7 miles

THE PRINCE OF WALES

1 QUEEN STREET, ABERAERON, CEREDIGION SA46 0BY
TEL: 01545 570366

Directions: Aberaeron lies on the main A487 Aberystwyth-Cardigan road. On reaching the town turn towards the harbour: a large car park is on the left, Queen Street on the right.

Phill and Sonia welcome visitors to **The Prince of Wales**, which stands on a corner site not far from the harbour and the beach. Dating back about 100 years, the building filled various roles before becoming the fine hostelry which today attracts a large clientele of both local residents and tourists. The public bar has a pool table, and there's a small lounge bar with the restaurant attached. The bars are separated by a stone fireplace with a wood-burning stove. Food is an important part of the pub's business, and Phill's main evening offers all-time pub classics such as garlic mushrooms, prawn cocktail, breaded or battered cod, cottage pie, chilli con carne and a splendid steak & ale pie using Welsh beef and Welsh ale. Sirloin and T-Bone steaks can be served plain or with a choice of three sauces - Diane, pepper or creamy Stilton - and for vegetarians spinach and ricotta lasagne and Thai vegetable curry are typical offerings. This menu is also available at lunchtime, when the lighter snack menu is particularly popular with visitors.

To enjoy with the food or on their own are some excellent beverages, including Felinfoel Bitter and Stowford Press strong cider. Aberaeron is a delightful little town with a number of charming Georgian houses. Attractions in the town include the sea aquarium and a craft centre, while just outside is a wildlife park with animals from round the world, nature trails and a miniature railway. The A487 coast road offers easy access north towards Aberystwyth and south towards Cardigan. And the A482 leads inland to the National Trust estate of Llanerchaeron.

- 🕐 11-11, Sun 12-10.30
- 🍽 A la carte + lunchtime snack menu
- 🅿 Free public car park close by
- 🎵 Live band once a month
- ❓ New Quay 5 miles, Llanerchaeron 3 miles

THE RED LION INN

24 RANDELL SQUARE, PEMBREY, CARMARTHENSHIRE SA16 0UB
TEL: 01554 832724

Directions: From J48 of the M4 take the A4138 to Llanelli, then the A484 to Pembrey, by-passing Burry Port. Turn down by the side of the church (one way); the inn is on the right.

The **Red Lion** is a traditional double-fronted inn, looking very smart and attractive after a top-to-toe refurbishment by owners Bob and Diana Spittles. Locals and visitors from further afield can look forward to the warmest of welcomes and an excellent glass of real ale - perhaps the Welsh-brewed Thomas Watkin Dark. In the one main bar, a pool table and dart board provide entertainment, and when there's a big rugby game the locals gather round the big-screen TV and enjoy free cawl (a hearty Welsh broth). Food is an important part of the business at the Red Lion, with home-made pies, steaks, chef's specials, vegetarian meals and a 3-course Sunday lunch among the offerings. And for guests staying overnight in the three letting bedrooms - a double, a twin and a family room - the day starts with an excellent Welsh

breakfast with the Welsh speciality laver bread among the options. Off-road parking is available to residents, otherwise there are parking spaces in the square. The history of the Red Lion goes back 400 years; it was once the local magistrates court, and one of the magistrates' tasks was to collect fines before releasing animals impounded in an enclosure next to the church. A notable attraction almost on the doorstep is Pembrey Country Park, which offers visitors an unusual mix that includes pine forests, sand dunes, beaches, a dry ski slope, a toboggan run, miniature railway and adventure playground. To the east lies Pembrey Saltmarsh, a local nature reserve and a Site of Special Scientific Interest, while a little way north of Pembrey is the historic town of Kidwelly with its castle and its Industrial Museum.

- 🕐 11-3 & 6-11, Sun 12-3 & 7-10.30
- 🍴 A la carte
- 🛏 3 bedrooms
- 🅿 Off-road parking for residents
- ❓ Pembrey Country Park 1 mile, Millennium Walkway, Motor Racing Circuit, Kidwelly Castle 3 miles, Llanelli 4 miles

THE STICKS

LLANSTEFFAN, CARMARTHENSHIRE SA33 5JG
TEL: 01267 241378 FAX: 01267 241398

Directions: Llansteffan is situated 7 miles south of Carmarthen on the B4312 off the A40 between Carmarthen and St Clears.

Mark and Nicole Bowles took over **The Sticks** early in 2001 and have quickly made their mark at this most convivial of spots. The inn acquired its somewhat unusual name in the 1980s after a severe storm which blew all the branches off the nearby pine trees and left them looking like sticks. Behind a long white facade with smart red piping, the bar lounge and separate restaurant attract an excellent cheerful mix of locals and tourists, who come here for the happy, relaxed atmosphere, the fine selection of ales and spirits and the very good food – accorded the Taste of Wales seal of approval. Quick and easy bar snacks provide tasty bites for those short of time or appetite, but its definitely worth taking time to enjoy a leisurely meal from the extensive menu developed by Nicole. Her French background

manifests itself in splendid, satisfying Gallic classics such as lamb provençale or beef bourguignon, with some delectable sweets to round things off.

A leisurely evening can turn into a comfortable night, as the inn has four spacious centrally heated bedrooms – 2 doubles and 2 family rooms – with tv and tea/coffee-making facilities. Some sport original old beams; 2 bathrooms and toilets are adjacent to the bedrooms. The inn provides a fine base for a holiday in the fresh air as Llansteffan lies between the river Towy and the river Taff. The village is guarded by its Norman Castle which offers spectacular views over the estuary. There are walks along the beach and coastal path. Fishing, bird watching, golf, riding and numerous family activities are within easy driving distance.

- 🕐 12 to midnight
- 🍴 A la carte + bar snacks
- 🛏 4 bedrooms
- Ⓟ Car park
- @ www.stickshotel.co.uk
- ❓ Carmarthen 7 miles, St Clears 6 miles, Tenby 17 miles.

THE TABERNA INN

HERBRANDSTON, NR MILFORD HAVEN, PEMBROKESHIRE SA73 3TD
TEL: 01646 693498

Directions: The inn is at Herbrandston, 3 miles west of Milford Haven on the Dale road. Turn left by the school, where the main road takes a 90° right turn; the inn is there on the right.

A warm welcome, good food and drink, peace and quiet and pleasant conversation are watchwords at the **Taberna Inn**, which stands opposite the primary school in the village of Herbrandston. Under previous owners it established a reputation as an excellent Italian restaurant, but when Brenda Absolon and her family took over in 1999 they decided on a change, and they now offer two entirely separate dining choices. Plaice to Meat is a speciality fish restaurant with marine decor and a menu that varies according to the availability of fresh locally landed fish, prepared with skill and imagination by chef James Payne.

Unfishy dishes are also served here, including vegetarian options, while a more traditional menu of pub meals is served daily in the Buffer Stop restaurant, which has a railway theme. Bar snacks and meals are also available in the lounge and bar areas, so this really is a place with something to suit every taste and pocket. Plaice to Meat is open Wednesday to Saturday lunchtimes and Tuesday to Saturday evenings; Buffer Stop every lunchtime and every evening except winter Sundays. The bars stock a wide range of beers, ciders, wines and spirits, with two real ales normally on tap. Pool and darts are played in the public bar, while the lounge bar is the place for quiet conversation. The Taberna also offers three light, airy guest bedrooms - a single, a double and a family room with a sea view, in a self-contained section of the building. The accommodation is available all year round, and the tariff includes a substantial traditional English breakfast.

- 🕐 12-11
- 🍴 A la carte menu, bar meals and snacks
- 💷 All the major cards
- 🛏 3 bedrooms with shared facilities
- 🅿 Car park
- @ e-mail: taberna@inn01.freeserve.co.uk website: www.visitwales.com (search for Taberna Inn)
- ❓ Pembrokeshire Coast Path runs by the Inn, Sandy Haven 1 mile, Broad Haven 3 miles, Milford Haven 3 miles

THE VICTORIA INN

ROCH, HAVERFORDWEST, PEMBROKESHIRE SA62 6AN
TEL: 01437 710426

> **Directions:** From the end of the M4 take the A48 to Carmarthen, the A40 to Haverfordwest and the A487 towards St David's. Roch is 6 miles along this road and the Victoria Inn is in the village on the right.

In the village of Roch, on the main A487 Haverfordwest-St David's road, **The Victoria Inn** presents a very bright and cheerful face to the world. And behind its happy yellow and green frontage the bar is a pleasant spot for a drink, with the bonus of views of St Brides Bay. The beer garden also overlooks the bay, with Ramsay Island in the distance. The inn has a very welcoming and hardworking owner in Julie Roberts, who runs it with the help of family and friends.

Julie's mother and grandmother were both professional cooks, which accounts for Julie's perfectionism and insistence that everything should be just so. That is definitely true of the cooking, and the menu in the 24-cover restaurant features many local specialities, using prime Welsh produce in dishes such as faggots made to a traditional Pembrokeshire recipe, Glamorgan sausages, cawl (a traditional Welsh stew) and a timbale of laver bread, smoked bacon and cockles, topped with Welsh cheddar. Many of the vegetables and salad items are grown on a nearby allotment, so they are as fresh as can be. Sunday lunch brings a choice of roasts and a vegetarian option. Sandwiches, baguettes and jacket potatoes provide lighter or quicker snacks, and children will find plenty of choice on their own menu. There has been a building on the site for more than 200 years, and the original two-room cottage is now the bar. A walk up to the ruins of Roch Castle on a rocky outcrop overlooking the village will build up an appetite that Julie and her helpers are more than ready to satisfy.

- 🕐 12-11
- 🍴 A la carte + snacks
- 💷 Diners, Mastercard, Visa
- 🅿 Car park
- 🎵 Occasional karaoke in winter
- ❓ Roch Castle 1 mile, Pembrokeshire Coast Path 2 miles, Haverfordwest 5 miles, St David's 11 miles

185 **The Angel Inn**, Hendredenny, Caerphilly

186 **The Bear Inn**, Llantrisant, Pontyclun,
   Vale of Glamorgan

187 **The Bridgend Inn**, Brynmawr, Gwent

188 **The Bridgend Inn**, Pontynewynydd,
   Pontypool, Gwent

189 **The Carne Arms**, Llysworney, Cowbridge,
   Vale of Glamorgan

190 **The Cross Keys Inn**, Pontnewydd, Gwent

191 **The Crown Inn & Restaurant**,
   Briton Ferry, Neath, Neath Port Talbot

192 **Glyn Clydach Coach House**,
   Neath Abbey, Neath, Neath Port Talbot

193 **The Goytre Arms**, Penperlleni,
   Monmouthshire

194 **The Monkey Tree**, Blackwood, Gwent

195 **The Mount Pleasant Inn**, Hirwaun,
   Aberdare, Rhondda Cynon Taff

196 **The Mountain Air Inn**, Nantybwch, Gwent

197 **The North Gate Inn**, Caerwent, Monmouthshire

198 **The Old Ferry Inn**, Beachley, Monmouthshire

199 **Rhyd-Y-Blew Inn**, Beaufort, Ebbw Vale, Gwent

200 **The Rose & Daffodil**, Cwmtwrch Isaf, Swansea

201 **The Skirrid Mountain Inn**,
   Llanvihangel Crucorney, Monmouthshire

202 **The Somerset Arms**, Taibach, Neath

203 **The Station Hotel**, Abergavenny, Monmouthshi

204 **The Swan Inn**, Aberkenfig, Bridgend, Bridgend

205 **The Swan Inn**, Nottage, Porthcawl, Bridgend

206 **The West End**, Gorseinon, Swansea, Swansea

207 **The Wingfield**, Llanbradach, Caerphilly

Please note all cross references refer to page numbers

SOUTH WALES

The delightful city of Swansea marks the gateway to the southernmost bulge of Wales, the lovely Gower Peninsula, a region designated an Area of Outstanding Natural Beauty. Much of it is owned by the National Trust. The Gower's southern coastline is made up of a succession of sandy, sheltered bays and along its whole coastline it is dotted with charming and relaxed seaside resorts. The carboniferous limestone coastline is of great importance both for its fossils and for its archaeological remains, and among the many interesting locations are Minchin Hole, a Site of Special Scientific Interest; High Pennard, topped with a prehistoric hill fort; and Three Cliffs Bay with its megalithic burial chamber.

This is also an area rich in natural beauty, with a long history that can be explored not only at the Gower Heritage Centre but also through its various castles, religious sites and ancient monuments. The area has many small family farms that yield some of the finest produce in South Wales; Gower is known in particular for its cockles and its laverbread (edible seaweed). The peninsula was once the haunt of elephants and bears and rhinoceros and other large beasts whose bones have been found in the many caves on the shoreline.

The Vale of Glamorgan is characterised by gentle rolling hills, genteel towns, pretty villages and a splendid natural coastline. An area of rich farmland, the Vale of Glamorgan

Three Cliffs Bay, Parkmill

stands at the foot of the spectacular valleys of south Wales and offers visitors an enticing heritage coastline. This is another area rich in history, where Norman warlords built their castles and where one of the oldest seats of learning was founded at Llantwit Major.

Behind the coastal region lie the valleys of southwest Wales which are known the world over for their coal mining and heavy industry heritage. The best known is the Rhondda Valley, where only one mine survives from the numerous collieries that once powered not just this country but many parts of the world. Though mining has all but gone from the valleys the heritage remains: the towns and villages with their rows of cottages where life revolved around the colliery, the chapel and the music, especially male voice choirs. These famous choirs were formed mainly by communities working in the coalmines and ironworks of the south Wales valleys and in the quarries of north Wales; most of them welcome visitors dropping in on rehearsals as well as attending concerts.

In many cases, nature has reclaimed the hills and vales once scarred by the mining industry and, while the legacy of pride in the industry remains, the various new country parks and nature reserves

Wye Valley

Swansea Marina

developed on the sites of the old mines are giving the area a new appeal.

History, ancient and modern, abounds in the valleys, with the distinguished ruins of Norman fortifications and the remains of the industrial past. An area of contrasts, like much of Wales, it would be easy to pass through this region on a journey to the Gower Peninsula or Pembrokeshire, but that would be to miss out on much of the Welsh heritage.

The valleys of the Wye and Usk offer some truly glorious scenery as well as the equally breathtaking sight of Tintern Abbey. An inspiration for both poets and artists, this abbey was at one time one of the richest in the country and the magnificent ruins beside the River Wye are still a stirring sight. This area, too, is one that saw much contest between the Welsh and the English, so not surprisingly there are numerous fortifications to be seen and explored. The Three Castles - White, Skenfrith and Grosmont - provided a valuable defence from their strong yet isolated positions while most towns of note also had their own fortress.

Along this stretch of coastline lies Cardiff, the capital city of Wales and a place which is successfully blending the ancient

Cardiff Bay

with the modern. The Romans occupied various sites in this area, but it was heavy industry and the influence of the Bute family that made Cardiff such a powerful port. The home of Welsh rugby, the superb Millennium Stadium and a recently rejuvenated waterfront, Cardiff is a city that vibrates with life, energy and enthusiasm. Officially designated the

Ebbw Vale Festival Park

Capital of the Principality by the Queen as recently as 1955, Cardiff has gone from strength to strength as the premier city of Wales, and it is still a busy and important seaport, even though the docks are no longer filled with ships waiting to export their cargoes of coal. The city can boast one of the world's finest civic centres, with buildings of white Portland stone, and the City Hall, the Law Courts, the National Museum of Wales and the Temple of Peace and Health are among many other impressive buildings. But the city's history is still very visible: Cardiff Castle dominates the city centre, and long stretches of the Roman walls are still standing. Close by the edge of the castle park are the headquarters and main ground of Glamorgan Cricket Club, the only first-class cricket club in Wales.

To the north lie the valleys that provided so much wealth until the decline of coal mining and the iron industry. Much of the land that was once an industrial wasteland has been reclaimed by nature, with the help of sensitive human intervention, but there are still some monuments to the great industrial age remaining, chiefly at the Big Pit Mine and Blaenavon Ironworks.

ABERDULAIS

From as early as 1584 the power generated by the magnificent National Trust owned **Aberdulais Falls** has been harnessed for a number of industries, including copper smelting and tin plating. Today, the waterwheel, the largest currently in use for the generation of electricity, makes the Falls self-sufficient in environmentally friendly energy. The Turbine House provides access to a unique fish pass.

ABERGAVENNY

A particularly pleasant and thriving market town, Abergavenny dates back to Roman times when the modest fort of Gobannium was established. Here, too, is the Norman **Abergavenny Castle**, where in 1175 the fearsome Norman lord, William de Braose, invited the Welsh lords to dine and then murdered the lot while they were disarmed at his table. Today, the restored keep and hunting lodge of the castle are home to the **Abergavenny Museum**, where exhibits from prehistoric times to the present day detail the history of the town and surrounding area. Just down the road lies another interesting place to visit - the **Childhood Museum**. Notable treasures in St Mary's Church include medieval choir stalls, fine altar tombs and an imposing wooden figure of Jesse. The church originally belonged to the 11th century Benedictine priory. One of the most accessible gateways to the Brecon Beacons National Park, Abergavenny is a very popular place, particularly in the summer.

BARRY ISLAND

Barry Island is not an island but a peninsula, facing Barry, whose natural, sheltered harbour has been used since Roman times; **Cold Knap Roman Buildings**, to the west of this seaside resort, are all that remains from those days. A popular place for holidaymakers for generations, Barry Island offers its visitors all the traditional seaside resort trappings, from sandy beaches to a funfair, as well as views across the Bristol Channel to the Devon coast. The latest all-weather attraction is the **Barry Island Railway Heritage Centre**, which has opened its extended line from Barry Island into the neighbouring Waterfront Dock Development. To the north of the resort is the **Welsh Hawking Centre**, where 200 birds of prey have their homes and are the stars of regular flying demonstrations.

BLAENAVON

Despite once having been associated with the heavy industries of coal mining and iron working, Blaenavon is set in surprisingly pleasant countryside which can be further explored by taking the **Pontypool and Blaenavon Railway**, the highest standard gauge track to have survived in Wales. Half the site lies within the Brecon Beacons National Park. The oldest colliery in Wales, **Big Pit Mine**, closed in 1980, but has been reopened as a monument to the past, with former miners and engineers from the site giving guided tours accompanied by plenty of anecdotes. The other side of the town's industry, iron working, can be discovered at the **Blaenavon Ironworks,** a marvellous site that not only represents an important aspect of the Industrial Revolution but is also one of Europe's best preserved 18th century ironworks.

BRIDGEND

Known in Welsh as Pen-y-Bont Ar Ogwr (meaning 'the crossing of the River Ogmore'), this bustling market town lies at the confluence of the Rivers Ogmore, Garw and Llynfi and it was once regarded as so vital a route that it had two castles, one on either side of the River Ogmore. The remains of 12th century **Newcastle Castle** lie on the west riverside while the more extensive ruins of 14th century **Coity Castle** stand guard on the other. Bridgend's distinction as a market town dates back as far as the early 16th century and down the ages there have been tanneries, a woollen factory and local potteries in the area.

CAERLEON

Despite its close proximity to Newport, Caerleon has managed to maintain the air of a rural town, but its chief attraction is the remarkable Roman remains. Caerleon is one of the largest and most significant surviving Roman military sites in Europe, set up in AD 75 by the 2nd Augustinian Legion and originally called Isca. A substantial Roman town grew up around the military base and among the remains to be seen at **Caerleon Roman Fortress and Baths** are a large amphitheatre where thousands watched the gladiators, the only surviving barracks to be seen in Europe and a complex system of Roman baths which were the equivalent of today's sports and leisure centres. Finds excavated from the remains are on show at the **Legionary Museum**. Caerleon also has links with King Arthur: one local legend suggests that the Roman amphitheatre was the site of King Arthur's Round Table.

CAERPHILLY

Famous for its distinctive white crumbly cheese which is sadly no longer made

Caerphilly Castle

here, Caerphilly was the birthplace of the much-loved comedian Tommy Cooper. The town's **Visitor Centre**, as well as providing tourist information, has an exhibition on local history and culture, a display of Welsh crafts and a fine Welsh food shop. The town is dominated by the massive **Caerphilly Castle**, which is not only one of Britain's largest castles (only Windsor and Dover are its equal) but is also one of the finest surviving examples of medieval military architecture in Europe. The castle was restored in the 19th century by the Marquess of Bute, but nothing seems to be able to restore the castle's famous leaning tower, which manages to out-lean the leaning tower of Pisa. Today the castle is home to an intriguing display of full size working replica siege engines.

Cardiff Castle

CAERWENT

Close to the Wentwood Forest, this town - which is now more of a village - was the site of **Venta Silurum**, a walled Roman town built by the invaders for the local Celtic Silures tribe. Sections of the Roman defences still remain and are some of the best preserved in Britain, while inside the walls can be seen the remains of the forum basilica and the Romano-Celtic temple. Venta Silurum is thought to have been the largest centre of civilian population in Roman occupied Wales.

CARDIFF

The capital city of Wales is a delightful place with an unexpected beauty, a long history, a sporting tradition and an exciting rejuvenated waterfront that is attracting visitors in their thousands. The Cardiff area was first settled by the Romans in the 1st century, but Cardiff is very much a product of the Industrial Revolution and its story is intertwined with that of the Marquesses of Bute. They controlled the docklands and, as the town began to thrive as a coal exporting port, the family made a vast fortune. Some of this wealth was poured back into the rebuilding, in the 19th century, of **Cardiff Castle** on the site of the previous fortification. Visitors to the castle today also have the opportunity to look around the **Welsh Regiment Museum** and look out over Cardiff from the top of the Norman keep. As might be expected in a capital city, Cardiff is home to many of the national treasures of Wales and at the superb **National Museum and Gallery of Wales** there is a vast collection of archaeology, natural history and ceramics as well as permanent exhibitions on the Evolution of Wales and Man and the Environment. The museum and gallery, along with the City Hall, are located in **Cathays Park**, where there are other civic buildings and also various departments of the University of Wales.

The area once known as Tiger Bay - Cardiff's historic dockland and the birthplace of Shirley Bassey - is one of the country's most exciting and imaginative regeneration developments. Now called **Cardiff Bay**, this revived waterfront is home to the new **National Assembly**, the impressive **Pierhead Building** which was built in 1896 for the Bute Docks Company and the **Cardiff Bay Visitor Centre**. The single most important part in the revival of the Bay is the massive Cardiff Bay Barrage, a barrier that stretches for a kilometre across the mouth of the Bay. Although Cardiff's famous Arms Park, the home of rugby football for so many years, has gone, its replacement, the **Millennium Stadium**, which hosted the last great sporting event of the 20th century, the Rugby World Cup Final in November 1999, is set to become an equally revered shrine to the Welsh national game and is already proving a highly successful replacement for the round-ball events once staged at Wembley. Close to the castle park are the headquarters and main ground of Glamorgan Cricket Club, the only first-class cricket club in Wales.

A mile or so from the city centre stands **Llandaff Cathedral**, a beautiful building set in a grassy hollow beside the River Taff. The cathedral suffered severe bomb damage during World War II and part of its restoration programme included a controversial Epstein sculpture, *Christ in Majesty*, which dominates the interior. Inside, visitors will also find some delightful medieval masonry, a marvellous modern timber roof and some works of art by members of the Pre-Raphaelite movement.

CHEPSTOW

This splendid old market town, which lies on the border with England, occupies a strategic crossing on the River Wye - an important crossing between England and Wales. Situated on a crag overlooking the river are the well-preserved ruins of **Chepstow Castle**, which William Fitzosbern began building in 1067 as a base for the Norman conquest of southeast Wales. Its importance can be judged from the fact that it was built of stone; most Norman fortresses of the time were in motte and bailey form, built of earth and wood. Built at the same time as the castle keep is the Parish and Priory Church of St Mary, which suffered considerable damage after the suppression of the Priory in 1536. The vast three-storey original nave gives some idea of the grand scale on which it was built. The church contains some imposing and interesting monuments. Opposite the castle is **Chepstow Museum**, where the rich and varied history of this border town is revealed. Housed in an elegant 18th century building that once belonged to a wealthy Chepstow merchant family, the museum has displays on the town's many industries, including shipbuilding, fishing and the wine trade.

Chepstow Castle

Throughout the town itself, the medieval street pattern is still much in evidence, along with surviving sections of the town wall, called the Port Wall, and the impressive **Town Gate**. But Chepstow is also a thriving modern town, and its attractions include an excellent racecourse offering both Flat and National Hunt racing; the highlight of the jumping season is the valuable and prestigious Welsh Grand National.

COWBRIDGE

This handsome and prosperous town has been the principal market town of the Vale of Glamorgan since medieval times and today it is noted for its quality shops, crafts and restaurants. The original Norman grid layout of the town is visible to this day, particularly in the mile long main street, and Cowbridge's 14th century town walls and gatehouse still stand.

CRYNANT

In one of the most beautiful and unspoilt valleys of the South Wales coalfield,

Cefn Coed Colliery Museum provides a wonderful opportunity for visitors to discover what life was like for the miners who worked underground in some of the most difficult conditions experienced anywhere in the world.

EBBW VALE

This old steelmaking town, whose member of Parliament was once the formidable orator and social reformer Aneurin Bevan, was transformed by the 1992 Garden Festival. Following the festival, the site was developed into **Festival Park** with houses, shops and a range of leisure activities.

A monument to Aneurin Bevan stands on the outskirts of the town, which still has a number of fine houses which were built by the wealthy steel and coal magnates of the area.

EWENNY

This charming rural village is home to **Ewenny Priory**, which was founded in

1141 by Maurice de Londres, the son of William de Londres of Ogmore Castle. This is one of the finest fortified religious houses in Britain and, while its precinct walls, towers and gateways give the priory a military air, it is believed that they were built for reasons of prestige rather than defence. Close by lies 400-year-old **Ewenny Pottery**, said to be the oldest working pottery in Wales.

KENFIG

This village was originally founded in the 12th century by Robert, Earl of Gloucester, who also built **Kenfig Castle** here. However, just some 300 years later the sands of Kenfig Burrows had swamped the settlement and the medieval town lies buried in the dunes although the remains of the castle keep are still visible. Today, this marvellous area of dunes to the northwest of the present village is the **Kenfig National Nature Reserve**. With over 600 species of flowering plants, including orchids, a freshwater lake and numerous birds, this is a haven for all naturalists as well as ramblers.

LLANRHIDIAN

Near the wild and lonely north coast of the Gower Peninsula, where some of the finest beaches in the country can be found, this village is also close to **Weobley Castle**. Dating from the early 14th century and built by the de Bere family, Weobley is more a fortified manor house than a castle and stands today as one of the few surviving such houses in Wales. On an isolated site overlooking the eerie expanse of Llanrhidian Marsh, this house has been remarkably well preserved and visitors can gain a real insight into the domestic arrangements of those days.

LLANTHONY

In the beautiful Vale of Ewyas, also known as Llanthony Valley, **Llanthony Priory** was built on a spot which has links with the beginnings of Christianity in Wales, and in the 6th century was chosen by St David for a cell. The Priory was founded by the Norman William de Lacy in the 11th century when he established a hermitage that evolved into the priory whose wonderful ruins can be

The Royal Mint

seen today. The beauty and tranquillity of the location have inspired many: Eric Gill and Walter Savage Landor are among those who made their homes here.

LLANTRISANT

Though some of the traditional heavy industry still remains, Llantrisant is best known nowadays for being the home of **The Royal Mint**, which transferred here from Tower Hill, London in 1967. At the **Model Centre**, a craft and design gallery, there is a permanent Royal Mint display along with a shop, café and a programme of events and exhibitions.

LLANTWIT MAJOR

This delightful town is perhaps the Vale of Glamorgan's most historic settlement and it was here, in AD 500, that St Illtud founded a church and school. The only remains of his original church to have survived are the dedication stones, but the imposing **Church of St Illtud** seen today is a combination of two buildings, one an early Norman structure and the other dating from the late 13th century.

LLANVETHERINE

To the south of the village lies one of the famous Three Castles, **White Castle**, which is so called because when it was built the masonry was rendered with gleaming white plaster, patches of which can still be seen. Starting life as a simple earthwork not long after the Norman Conquest, White Castle was rebuilt in

stone during the late 12th and 13th centuries to provide, along with Skenfrith and Grosmont castles, a triangle of fortresses to control this strategic entry point into Wales. Situated in a beautiful and isolated place, the ruins are still able to conjure up the romance of the Middle Ages.

MAESTEG

This ancient market town was the centre of iron making in the 1820s, but the last great furnace was 'blown out' in 1886; one of the ironworks is now a sports centre. Maesteg was once linked to the coast at Porthcawl by a tramway, traces of which can be seen at Porthcawl. The Tabor chapel in Maesteg was where *Land of My Fathers* was first sung in public in 1856. The Welsh words were written by Evan James, the music by his son James James. For 112 years, Talbot Street was the only alcohol-free high street in Britain, so covenanted in the will of the teetotal spinster after whom the street was named. In the summer of 2002, a restaurant owner challenged the covenant, and the magistrates ruled in his favour.

MARGAM

In **Margam Country Park** are several interesting buildings of various ages, including **Margam Abbey Church** (all that remains of an abbey that once stood here), a classical 18th century orangery and a restored Japanese garden from the 1920s. This huge recreational area - the park covers some 800 acres - also includes a visitor centre, waymarked trails, a deer park, bird of prey centre and the **Margam Stones Museum**, where visitors can see a collection of early Christian memorials dating from Roman times through to the 10th and 11th centuries.

MERTHYR TYDFIL

This former iron and steel capital of the world was once the largest town in Wales, and there are many reminders of this heritage. Described as "the most impressive monument of the Industrial Iron Age in Southern Wales", **Cyfarthfa Castle** is a grand mansion situated in beautiful and well laid out parkland. Built in the 1820s, this was the home of the Crawshay family, who constructed their grand house to overlook their ironworks, which at the time were the largest in the world. Today, this mansion is home to a **Museum and Art Gallery** which not only covers the social and industrial history of Merthyr Tydfil and the surrounding area but also has an extensive collection of fine and decorative art. **Joseph Parry's Ironworker's Cottage**, in Chapel Row, provides a contrasting view of life in Merthyr Tydfil during its heyday. A superb example of a skilled ironworker's home, the cottage gives

an interesting insight into the living conditions of those days. It was here that Joseph Parry, the 19th century composer famous for writing the haunting hymn *Myfanwy*, was born and on the first floor is an exhibition of his life and work.

MONMOUTH

This prosperous and charming old market town grew up at the confluence of three rivers - the Wye, Monnow and Trothy - which are all noted for their fishing. The River Wye is crossed by a five arched bridge built in 1617 but the Monnow boasts the most impressive of the town's bridges. **Monnow Bridge** is one of Monmouth's real gems, and its sturdy fortified gatehouse, dating from the 13th century, is the only one of its kind in Britain. Long before the bridge was constructed, the Normans built **Monmouth Castle** here in around 1068. Later rebuilt by John of Gaunt in the late 1300s, the castle was the birthplace of his grandson, later Henry V, in 1387.

Monnow Bridge, Monmouth

Much later, in the 17th century, **Great Castle House** was built by the 3rd Marquess of Worcester from the ruins of the castle and he lived here while his other homes, Badminton and Troy House, were being rebuilt. Today, the castle houses both the **Castle Museum** and the **Regimental Museum** where the histories of the castle and the Royal Monmouthshire Royal Engineers are explored. Another interesting building in the town is the 14th century **St Mary's Church**, whose eight bells are said to have been recast from a peal which Henry V brought back from France after his victory at Agincourt..

The Mumbles

Also in the town is the **Nelson Museum**, where a fascinating collection of material and artefacts about the great Admiral can be seen.

MUMBLES

This charming Victorian resort grew up around the old fishing village of Oystermouth, which has its roots in Roman times and where the Normans built a castle to defend their land. **Oystermouth Castle** is surrounded by small but beautiful grounds overlooking the bay, and the ruins are now the scene of re-enactments which chart the history of the castle and, in particular, the siege of the fortress by Owain Glyndwr. An unusual attraction in Mumbles is the **Lovespoon Gallery**, where visitors will find an amazing variety of these unique love tokens. Lovespoons were traditionally carved from wood by young men and presented to their sweethearts as a token of their devotion. The custom dates back many centuries, but in these less romantic days the spoons are often bought simply as souvenirs of Wales. The **Mumbles Passenger Railway** was the world's first, and from 1807 to its closure in 1960 the five-mile line used horse, sail, steam, battery, petrol, diesel and electricity. On Bank Holidays in the mid-Victorian period it was known to carry up to 40,000 passengers.

Beyond The Mumbles lies the lovely **Gower Peninsula**, designated an Area of Outstanding Natural Beauty. Gower's southern coast is made up of a succession of sandy, sheltered bays and the first of these, **Langland Bay**, is just around the headland from the village.

NEATH

While Neath's industrial history dates back to the late 16th century, when the first copper smelter in South Wales was built here by Cornishmen, the town has its origins in Roman times. Remains of Roman Nidum can still be seen close to the ruins of **Neath Abbey**, which was founded in the 13th century on land seized from the Welsh in around 1130. Housed in the Old Mechanics Institute, the **Neath Museum and Art Gallery** has permanent displays on the history of the town, including finds from the time of the Roman occupation, as well as regularly changing art and photographic exhibitions. The Museum has many hands-on activities, including grinding corn, using a Celtic loom and making a wattle fence.

Held each September, **Neath Fair** is the oldest such event in Wales, founded by Gilbert de Clare in 1280.

NEWPORT

The Romans settled in the area of Newport in the 1st century and the town's **St Woolos Cathedral Church**, splendidly situated on the hilltop, is just the latest building on a site which has been a place of worship since the 6th century.

The history of Newport's docks is explored at the **Pillgwenlly Heritage Community Project**, while at the **Newport Museum and Art Gallery** there is a range of displays on the town's origins, including a Roman mosaic floor which was excavated close by. An impressive reminder of Newport's more recent past is the massive **Transporter Bridge** across the River Usk. Specially designed in 1906 by Ferdinand Arnodin to allow traffic to cross the river without disrupting the movement of shipping, the bridge is one of very few of its kind. To the west of the town lies **Tredegar House and Park**, the home of the influential Morgan family for more than 500 years. The present dignified red brick house dates from the 17th century and is one of Wales' architectural wonders. Visitors can tour the rooms and discover just what life was like here, both above and below stairs, as well as finding out something of this great Welsh family. Its more colourful and famous members include Sir Henry Morgan, the notorious pirate, Godfrey, the 2nd Lord Tredegar, who survived the Charge of the Light Brigade and whose horse is buried in the grounds, and Viscount Evan, whose menagerie included a boxing kangaroo.

OXWICH

One of Gower's prettiest villages, Oxwich lies huddled along a lane at the western end of a superb three mile long beach. The village has some picturesque cottages of the traditional Gower style which include one that was once occupied by John Wesley. To the south of the village lies **Oxwich Castle**, a grand Tudor manor house built around a courtyard. For walkers there are plenty of footpaths to explore and the walk to **Oxwich Point**, in particular, provides some magnificent views of the Gower Peninsula. Close to the beach lies part of the **Oxwich Nature Reserve**, home to many rare species of orchid as well as other plant life and a variety of birds.

Penarth Medieval Village

PARKMILL

This village is home to the **Gower Heritage Centre** which is itself centred around a historic water mill built in the 12th century by the powerful le Breos family, the Norman rulers of Gower. Originally constructed to supply flour for nearby Pennard Castle, this water mill is a rare survivor in Wales of a rural complex that would once have been found in most villages and hamlets. The Heritage Centre has displays on the history of this beautiful region along with a farming museum.

PENARTH

Often described as the 'garden by the sea', Penarth is a popular and unspoilt seaside resort which developed in Victorian and Edwardian times. Built for the wealthy industrialists of Cardiff's shipyards, this once fashionable town has lost none of its late 19th and early 20th century elegance and style typified by the splendidly restored pier, the promenade and the formal seaview gardens. If the town seems to have been lost in a

time warp, a visit to the **Washington Gallery**, housed in an old cinema, will dispel this view through its exciting collection of modern and contemporary art.

To the south of Penarth lies a **Medieval Village** which is slowly being uncovered by archaeologists. This village is located in **Cosmeston Country Park**, an area of lakes, woodlands and meadows created from a disused limestone quarry. A peaceful and tranquil habitat for many birds and animals, with a wide range of plant life, the country park has a visitor centre, picnic areas and a café.

In 1897, **Lavernock Point**, to the southeast of the country park, was the site of Marconi's early experiments in radio transmission and the scene of the historic reception of the words "Are you ready?", which were transmitted to **Flat Holm**, an island some three miles away.

PONTYPOOL

Known to have been in existence before the time of the Normans, Pontypool is credited with being the home of the Welsh iron industry. The first forge here is believed to have been in operation as early as 1425, and the first ironworks opened in 1577. The town's industrial heritage can be explored at the **Pontypool Valley Inheritance Centre** where both the industrial and social history of the town and surrounding Torfaen valley is detailed. The museum is located in the late-Georgian stables of **Pontypool Park**, a 19th century landscaped park whose main attractions include a shell grotto and a unique double-chambered ice house. The formal Italian gardens have recently been restored with the help of Heritage Lottery funding.

PONTYPRIDD

This friendly valley town is justly proud of its past, which is revealed in the **Pontypridd Museum** housed in an old chapel close to Pontypridd's historic stone bridge over the River Taff. As well as its industrial heritage, the town has a long tradition of music and in the main park are two statues commemorating Evan and James James, a father and son songwriting team who were responsible for composing the words and music for the Welsh National Anthem, *Land of my Fathers* (*Hen Wlad fy Nhadau*).

Perhaps better known to today's visitors, however, are the two opera stars Sir Geraint Evans and Stewart Burrows, who were born in the same street in nearby Clifynydd, and the durable singer Tom Jones. Just outside Pontypridd, at

Fforest Uchaf Farm, Penycoedcae, is the **Pit Pony Sanctuary**, where visitors can meet more than 25 horses and ponies, including several retired pit ponies. Also here are pit pony memorabilia and a reconstruction of a typical pony-powered Welsh drift coalmine.

PORT TALBOT

Well known for its steel industry, Port Talbot was named after the Talbot family, who were responsible for the development of the town's docks in the 19th century. Now called the Old Docks, this area saw significant expansion again in the 20th century when a new deep water harbour was opened by the Queen in 1970. Today Port Talbot is home to factories and processing plants, and also to the solar centre of **Baglan Bay Energy Park**, which explains the history of the area and its power generating potential.

PORTHCAWL

One of South Wales' most popular resorts, Porthcawl has much to attract the traditional British seaside holidaymaker. There are award winning clean sandy beaches at Sandy Bay, Trecco Bay and the quieter Rest Bay, along with an amusement park that provides a wide variety of rides, from white knuckle roller coasters to more gentle carousels. This is also a haven for surfers, sailors and fishing enthusiasts, while the headlands above Rest Bay are the site of the famous Royal Porthcawl Golf Club. The history of the town can be discovered at **Porthcawl Museum**, where there is a fascinating collection of artefacts, costumes and memorabilia on display, while at **Porthcawl Harbour** there are still several historic buildings which date from the heyday of this busy port. During the summer, two veteran steamships leave the harbour for trips along the Bristol Channel and across to Lundy Island.

RAGLAN

To the north of this pretty village of shops and inns lies **Raglan Castle**, one of the finest late medieval fortresses in Britain. Built towards the end of the Middle Ages, and thus in relatively peaceful times, the castle was also constructed with comfort in mind and it represents wealth and social aspirations as much as military might.

RHOSSILI

This village, on the westernmost area of the Gower Peninsula, is thought to have been named after St Fili, who is said to have been the son of St Cenydd. Inside the small church is a memorial plaque to a Gower man, Edgar Evans, who is perhaps better known as Petty Officer Evans, who died in the ill-fated expedition to the Antarctic led by Captain Scott in 1912.

To the west of Rhossili lies **Worm's Head**, an island which is a National Nature Reserve. Reached by a causeway at low tide, there is public access to the island, but those making the crossing should take great care not to be cut off by the tide. Worm's Head marks the southern edge of Rhossili Bay, whose beach can be reached by a steep downhill climb. At low tide, the remains of several wrecks can be seen, most notably the *Helvetia*, which was wrecked in 1887. The area is very popular with fishermen, surfers and bathers, and behind **Rhossili Beach** lies **The Warren**, under the sands of which are the remains of old Rhossili village and church.

RISCA

To the south of Risca, at High Cross on the Monmouthshire Canal, is the **Fourteen Locks Canal Centre**, where this complicated systems of locks was constructed to raise and lower barges some 168 feet in just half a mile with only the minimal wastage of water.

Rhossili Beach

There are several walks from the centre, which take in the locks, ponds, channels, tunnels and weirs, as well as the country-side in which the centre is sited.

ST FAGANS

On the outskirts of Cardiff, this pictur-esque village is home to the **Museum of Welsh Life** in the large grounds of St Fagans Castle, a splendid Elizabethan mansion. Founded in 1948, this is a museum unlike most other museums as it contains an assortment of buildings, collected from all over Wales, which have been re-erected in these glorious surroundings.

SWANSEA

Swansea, the second city of Wales, is an attractive and welcoming place with an appealing blend of traditional and modern. It was founded in the late 10th century by Sweyne Forkbeard, King of Denmark. **Swansea Castle**, which gained notoriety in the 18th century when the northern block became a debtors' prison, was first built by the Norman Henry de Newburgh in the late 11th century. However, it was all but destroyed by Owain Glyndwr in the early 1400s when he ransacked the town that had grown up around the fortification.

As early as the 14th century, ship-building and coalmining were important industries in the area and by 1700 Swansea was the largest port in Wales. Smelters from Cornwall arrived here, attracted by the plentiful supply of coal, and copper works also flourished;

Swansea City Centre

Nelson's ships were covered in Swansea copper. At one time 90% of the country's copper was smelted here and, in the heyday of the industry, other metals such as tin, lead, nickel and zinc were imported to the town for smelting and refining. In the 19th century Swansea porcelain was another famous local product. Much of the traditional industry has disappeared and the old dock area has been transformed into a marina surrounded by stylish waterfront buildings. This **Maritime Quarter** is arguably the most impressive part of the town and is alive with cafés, pubs and restaurants. Here, in a former warehouse, is the **Swansea Maritime and Industrial Museum**, where the town's industrial heritage is explored. The town is also home to the oldest museum in Wales, the **Swansea Museum**, which contains a fascinating range of permanent displays ranging from ancient Egyptian Mummies to Swansea and Nantgarw porcelain and pottery. More artefacts from Egypt can be seen at the **Egyptian Centre**, where over 1,000 objects, from impressive painted coffins to everyday household items, can be seen which date back as far as 3500 BC.

However, Swansea does not dwell in the past and at the **Glynn Vivian Art Gallery** a broad spectrum of the visual arts is on display. Swansea has its own Botanical Garden, housed in the walled garden of **Singleton Park**, and at **Plantasia**, visitors can wander around a giant hot house and discover a wide range of colourful exotic plants. The hot house is also home to numerous exotic insects, fish and reptiles, such as leaf cutting ants, and there is a butterfly house where the various colourful species fly freely. **Clyne Gardens**, at Blackpill off the A4067 Mumbles road, are known in particular for their marvellous rhododendrons, including National Collections, their imposing magnolias and an extensive bog garden. No mention of Swansea would be complete without referring to the town's most famous son, Dylan Thomas. In the **Dylan Thomas Centre**, dedicated to the poet's life and works, the exhibitions feature some of his

original manuscripts, letters to friends and family and a moving American documentary about him.

TINTERN PARVA

This riverside village, which nestles among the wooded slopes of the lovely Wye Valley, is a most beautiful place and the whole of the valley, between Monmouth and Chepstow, is designated an Area of Outstanding Natural Beauty. Here are found the enchanting ruins of **Tintern Abbey**, which lie beside the river. The abbey was founded by Cistercian monks in 1131 and largely rebuilt in the 13th century by Roger

Tintern Abbey

Bigod, the Lord of Chepstow Castle. The monks farmed the rich agricultural land as well as remaining dedicated to their rigorous regime of religious devotions right up until the time of the Dissolution. A rich and powerful abbey in its day, Tintern is now a majestic ruin with much delicate tracery and great soaring archways still intact, in a glorious setting that has inspired painters and poets such as Turner and Wordsworth.

TONDU

The nationally important Tondu Ironworks have now been incorporated into the **Tondu Heritage Park**, while the site of an old colliery and open cast coal workings has been developed into the **Parc Slip Nature Reserve**. The reserve's network of paths lead visitors through the various different wildlife habitats, such as grassland, woodland and wetland, where a wide variety of plants, birds and animals have made their homes.

TREHAFOD

When the Lewis Merthyr Colliery closed in 1983, it re-opened as the **Rhondda Heritage Park**, a fascinating place where former miners guide visitors around the restored mining buildings. As well as seeing the conditions in which the miners worked and hearing stories from miners whose families worked in the mines for generations, visitors can also see exhibitions on the role of the women in a mining village, the dramatic history of the 1920s strikes for a minimum wage and the tragedy of mining disasters. Between 1868 and 1919 in Rhondda one miner was killed every six hours and one injured every two minutes. The cultural and social history of a mining community, through brass bands, choirs and the chapel, is explored and visitors also have the opportunity to put on a hard hat and travel down the mine shaft in a cage.

USK

This delightful small town, which takes its name from the river on which it sits, was founded by the Romans in AD 75. Well known for its excellent local fishing - the River Usk is a fine salmon river - the town attracts fishermen from far and wide. Also noted for its floral displays and historic buildings, Usk is home to the **Gwent Rural Life Museum**, housed in several historic buildings, which tells the story of life in this Welsh border region from Victorian times up until the end of World War II.

THE ANGEL INN

WHITE CROSS LANE, HENDREDENNY, CAERPHILLY CF83 2RL
TEL: 02920 882952

Directions: From J32 of the M4 take the A470 Pontypridd road for about 2 miles, then turn on to the A468 Caerphilly road. At the second roundabout turn on to the B4263. White Cross Lane is on the left off this road.

Thelma and Paul brought long experience in the trade when they took over **The Angel Inn** at the end of 2002. Thelma is Caerphilly bred and her interest in the history of the area is evident in the oak-beamed public areas, where the memorabilia include many photographs of Caerphilly and the area in days gone by. And in the beer garden are models depicting local history. Toasties, jacket potatoes and freshly baked pies, pasties and sausage rolls provide tasty hot snacks, while main courses offer all the favourite pub classics, from scampi to lasagne, chilli, curries and steaks. A speciality Welsh menu is available with notice. The restaurant is a non-smoking area, but meals can also be enjoyed in the lounge, where puffing is allowed. To accompany the food, or to enjoy on their

own, are four real ales - resident Flowers IPA and Marstons Pedigree and two weekly changing guests.

Open all day, every day, the Angel is one of the most hospitable and sociable pubs you'll ever find, and there's hardly a day in the week when some entertainment is not laid on! The guitar club meets regularly, and there are pool nights, darts nights, disco nights, karaoke nights and quiz nights; and when the Six Nations rugby internationals are on, the crowd can sometimes enjoy free curry and chips at half time. Caerphilly Castle is one of the leading visitor attractions in this part of the world, and the surrounding countryside provides plenty of opportunities for a little gentle exercise to build up a thirst and an appetite. A mountain walk leads up to the ruins of Castell Morag.

- 🕐 11-11, Sun 12-10.30
- 🍴 A la carte + snacks
- £ All the major cards
- Ⓟ Large car park
- 🎵 Almost every night!
- ❓ Caerphilly 2 miles

HEOL-Y-SARN, LLANTRISANT, PONTYCLUN, SOUTH WALES CF72 8AD
TEL: 01443 222271 FAX: 01443 238695

South Wales

> **Directions:** From J34 of the M4 take the A4119 Talbot Green-Tonyrefail road. Turn right on to the B4595 Llantrisant road. Heol-y-Sarn is the 4th on the left. The pub is on the right, with a prominent statue in front.

The Bear Inn is a well-kept traditional Welsh inn with a very cosy and welcoming feel. Coal fires burn in the bar and lounge, and in winter a glass of mulled wine is guaranteed to bring a warm glow to the coldest customer. The inn is run by Bryden and Margaret Jones, a much travelled couple who decided to settle down here towards the end of 2002. They have a genuine Welsh welcome for everyone, whether a familiar face or a stranger, and real ale enthusiasts have a choice of three brews. No one goes thirsty here, and no one goes hungry, as the inn prides itself on its hearty home-cooked dishes. Sws-y-Ddraig (Kiss of the Dragon) and Tan-y-Ddraig (Fire of the Dragon) are special curries, and the popular mixed grill

comes in three sizes - 24oz Daddy Bear, 18oz Mommy Bear and 12oz Baby Bear. Sunday brings a traditional roast lunch.

The Bear is a family friendly place, with a children's play area at the rear. One of the two guest bedrooms is a family room, the other a double; they share a bathroom. Friday is the night for live entertainment, and on Saturday the locals exercise their vocal chords accompanied by Bryden on the piano. The statue on the roundabout outside the inn is of Dr Price, an eccentric character who was an early protagonist of cremations. The proximity of the M4 puts many of the sights of South Wales in easy reach, and Llantrisant has attractions both ancient and modern, from the scant ruins of the castle to The Royal Mint, which was transferred here from London in 1967.

- 🕐 12-11.30, Sun to 10.30
- 🍴 A la carte
- £ All the major cards
- 🛏 2 rooms sharing a bathroom
- Ⓟ Children's play area
- 🎵 Live entertainment Friday & Saturday
- ❓ The Royal Mint 1 mile, Pontypridd (Museum, Pit Pony Sanctuary) 4 miles, Cardiff 8 miles

THE BRIDGEND INN

8 KING STREET, BRYNMAWR, GWENT NP23 4RE

TEL: 01495 310721

> **Directions:** The inn is located on the edge of Brynmawr, where the A465 meets the A467, about 5 miles west of Abergavenny.

Situated by the roundabout where the A465 and A467 meet, **The Bridgend Inn** is a fine building dating back nearly three centuries. It was originally three cottages and a blacksmith's shop, and later as an ale house it brewed its own beer. When Abilio and Lois Mesquita took over in September 2002 it was their first pub as leaseholders, but Abilio brought many years experience in the catering/licensed trade, and the Bridgend is in very capable and enthusiastic hands. Smartly decorated, with plenty of comfortable seats, the inn serves a good range of ales, including Worthington cask and a rotating guest, two draught lagers and two draught ciders. In the separate non-smoking dining room, with seats for 26, food is served from 11.30 to 3 and from 6 to 10.30.

Abilio is a very talented chef and his dishes are enjoyed by a growing number of happy regular customers, making booking very advisable, and essential at the weekend. Everything chalked up on the blackboard is well worth trying, but the particular favourites are the fresh fish specials and the superb slow-roast Welsh lamb. Abilio and Lois organise occasional themed food evenings and murder/mystery nights. The inn is closed on Mondays. Brynmawr and the surrounding area offer a variety of attractions, with the Brecon Beacons National Park and the Black Mountains to the north and reminders of the industrial past at Tredegar and Blaenavon. And the pleasant old market town of Abergavenny, with its castle and museums, is a short drive west along the A465.

- 🕐 12-3 & 6-11, closed Monday
- 🍴 A la carte
- 💷 Amex, Mastercard, Visa
- 🅿 Car park
- 🎵 Occasional murder/mystery nights
- ❓ Abergavenny 5 miles, Blaenavon 5 miles, Brecon Beacons National Park 1 mile; walking, climbing, fishing

THE BRIDGEND INN

23 HANBURY ROAD, PONTNEWYNYDD, PONTYPOOL, GWENT NP4 6QN
TEL: 01495 757435 FAX: 01495 752938

Directions: The inn is situated in the village of Pontnewynydd, just off the A4043 about 1 mile north of Pontypool in the direction of Blaenavon.

Cottages built in the late 17th century were converted to **The Bridgend Inn** during the following century. Behind the neat white-painted facade the look in the bar is delightfully old-world, with black beams contrasting with white plaster walls. The inn is owned by Rick and Wendy Aldridge. It's their first pub, but they have built up a strong local following since taking over in July 2002. It's open all day, every day, and freshly made sandwiches are available throughout opening hours to accompany the excellent range of drinks; these include Brains SA, Worthington Creamflow, Caffreys and the famous Northumbrian Smooth, until recently only found in the Newcastle area and the House of Commons. The whole place has a very inviting, hospitable feel, and even the two ghosts who have made it

their home are of the friendly variety.

Pool, darts, cribbage, dominoes and shove ha'penny are all played at very sociable inn, and on Friday there's live musical entertainment - and should the mood take anyone at other times, the karaoke machine can be brought out. Sunday night is quiz night, with the proceeds going to charity. The village of Pontnewynydd is situated just off the A4043, a mile or so north of Pontypool on the way to Blaenavon. The tram line that once served Jack Pit and later became a railway line is now the route of a pleasant country walk that goes right up to Blaenavon. Pontypool has plenty to interest the visitor, including a heritage centre where the industrial and social history of the region is presented.

🕐 12-11

🍴 Sandwiches available all day

🅿 Adjacent car park

🎵 Quiz Sunday, live music Friday

@ rickandwendy@thebridgend.fsnet.co.uk

❓ Pontypool 1 mile, Blaenavon 5 miles; walking

THE CARNE ARMS

LLYSWORNEY, COWBRIDGE, VALE OF GLAMORGAN CF71 7NQ
TEL: 01446 773553 FAX: 01446 771573

> **Directions:** From J33 of the M4 take the A4232 to Cardiff then the A48 to Cowbridge. Follow the A48 towards Bridgend and, about 2 miles beyond Cowbridge turn left on to the B4268; the Carne Arms is 1 mile down this road.

Dating back over 400 years, the **Carne Arms** is a delightful old inn with open fires and a friendly, warming, cosy ambience. Thought to have originally been part of the local rectory, its name, too, is ancient and is derived from the Cornish 'carn', which means 'rock'. However, in this instance, the inn probably received its name in memory of a wealthy and influential local family rather than from any feature of the local landscape. Situated beside the main road through the village, this historic inn is easy to spot and well worth taking the trouble to find.

- 🕐 12-11, Sun to 10.30
- 🍴 A la carte & snacks
- 💷 Mastercard, Visa
- 🅿 Car park, children's play area
- 🎵 Themed evenings
- @ e-mail: matthew@thecarnearms.co.uk website: www.thecarnearms.co.uk
- ❓ Bridgend 5 miles, Ogmore Castle and Stepping Stones 5 miles, Nash Point 4 miles, Beach 4 miles, walking, cycling, sailing, fishing

Licensees Stephen and Matthew Foster a father and son team are the welcoming hosts at the Carne Arms; well-known locally, it offers customers an excellent choice of beers and ales in the cosy, characterful bar and restaurant. There is also an appealing home-cooked menu of local and traditional dishes along with bar meals for those who want a lighter bite. Among the seasonal favourites are Dover sole - a fish not often seen on pub menus. The curry nights that are held frequently, offering a choice of up to ten different curry dishes, have proved so popular that they need to be booked well in advance; booking is also advised for Friday and Saturday evenings and Sunday lunch. This is definitely a place for the whole family, with a large beer garden and a safe play area.

THE CROSS KEYS INN

55 FIVE LOCKS ROAD, PONTNEWYDD, CWMBRAN, GWENT HP44 1BT
TEL: 01633 861545

> **Directions:** The inn is located by a canal about 2 miles north of Cwmbran; from Cwmbran take the A4051, following signs for Upper Cwmbran.

A popular place with walkers, cyclists, pleasure boaters and bird watchers, the **Cross Keys** stands by the Monmouthshire & Brecon Canal a short drive north of Cwmbran. Leaseholders Chris and Sian Davies, here since the summer of 2002, have a warm welcome for one and all, and in the bright, inviting bar a good range of

drinks is dispensed, to enjoy either inside or out n the large beer garden by the canal. Food is served every day between 11 in the morning and 9.30 in the evening, and the printed menu and specials board offer a good range of generously served, reasonably priced dishes prepared by Sian and the cook Sue. Booking is advisable for Sunday lunch and for parties of 10 or more.

The area round the Cross Keys offers a wide variety of attractions for the visitor, and the inn's three guest bedrooms - one of them a family room - are available all year round. Among the most interesting places to visit are the Llanyrafon Mill and Farm Museum and the Llamtarnam Grange Arts Centre. And the Greenmeadow Community Farm, set within Cwmbran's green belt, is home to all manner of farm animals and provides a splendid day out for all the family. Nearby Caerleon is the site of one of the largest and most important Roman military sites in Europe, while the region's industrial heritage can be explored in the Pontypool Valley Inheritance Centre.

- 🕐 12·11
- 🍴 A la carte
- 🛏 3 upstairs rooms
- Ⓟ Car park, canalside beer garden
- ❓ Cwmbran 1 mile, Greenmeadow Community Farm 2 miles, Pontypool 3 miles, Caerleon 5 miles

THE CROWN INN & RESTAURANT

244 NEATH ROAD, BRITON FERRY, NEATH SA11 2AX
TEL: 01639 813427

South Wales

> **Directions:** Leave the M4 (westbound) at J41 and take the A48 following signs to Briton Ferry. From J42 (eastbound) follow the signs to Briton Ferry; turn left over the bridge, the inn is on the right about ¾ mile along.

The **Crown Inn** is a white-painted two-storey hostelry easily reached from either Junction 41 or Junction 42 of the M4. With its cheerful ambience and its excellent hospitality, it makes a perfect break on a journey, but is also well worth seeking out as a destination for its top-quality food and drink. Landlord Paul Miles, who has been at the helm since 1999, worked in local industry until deciding on a career change, and the locals are very pleased that he did! He takes great pride in his ales, which include Thomas Watkin Whoosh and a large supporting cast of draught and bottled beers and lagers.

Tudor, who has cooked in various capacities since leaving school, does an equally splendid job on the food side. The main menu, served in the separate 50-cover restaurant, offers pub classics ranging from garlic mushrooms and prawn cocktail to steaks (sirloin, fillet or rump) to minted lamb cutlets, lasagne, breaded scampi, sole or plaice, and several ways with chicken: spicy cajun fillet; in a barbecue sauce; roast; filled with smoked cheese and basil wrapped in bacon; kiev; or spatchcocked, chargrilled and served with fresh herbs and spices. Vegetarians have a choice of main courses, and at lunchtime the bar menu offers lighter alternatives such as Cold ham, BLT baguette or faggots with peas. The public areas are mainly very traditional in style and feel, and the walls are hung with all kinds of objects and memorabilia, from family photographs to framed collections of cigarette cards and old advertisements. The restaurant is particularly appealing with its beams, open hearth and exposed stone walls. A large beer garden overlooking the park makes a very peaceful spot for enjoying a drink when the weather is fine.

- 🕐 11.30-11, Sun 12-10.30
- 🍴 Bar and Restaurant menus
- 💷 All the major cards
- 🅿 Off-road parking
- ❓ Aberavon beach 3 miles, Port Talbot 3 miles, Margam Park 5 miles

GLYN CLYDACH COACH HOUSE

LONGFORD ROAD, NEATH ABBEY, NEATH SA10 7AJ
TEL/FAX: 01792 816307

> **Directions:** From J43 of the M4 take the A465 at he first junction exit. Bear left over a bridge to a roundabout; bear left towards Skewen. At the mini-roundabout turn right into Longford Road; the coach house is 2 miles along this road on the right.

Glyn Clydach Coach House is a handsome and substantial redbrick building set in extensive lawned gardens and grounds, with splendid views over the Clydach and Neath valleys. Andrew and Ian, ably assisted by hardworking, professional staff, have overseen a total refurbishment of the premises in the three years since they became the owners, and in that time they have built up a strong following among the local community. Things tend to be on a grand scale here, starting with the ivy-arched entrance and continuing in the imposing hall, the very comfortable lounge, the Regency-style dining room with seats for 84 and the function room, which can accommodate up to 180 guests in comfort and is an ideal venue

for a variety of celebrations including wedding receptions. In the dining room a popular carvery operates on Saturday and Sunday, and the Saturday session is accompanied by a cabaret (booking essential).

During the week meals are served in the lounge bar, which offers a full range of beers and lagers and a comprehensive choice of wines sold by bottle or glass. The specials board changes daily, and the two for the price of one meal deal is rightly very popular. The accommodation at the coach house is also of very generous proportions, and all the rooms enjoy views over the water garden. They comprise a four-poster suite, a VIP suite, a family suite and a suite with facilities for disabled guests. Attractions close by include the ruins of Neath Abbey and Castle and the National Trust's Aberdulais Falls.

- 🕐 11-11, Sun 12-6
- 🍴 Sat & Sun carvery, bar meals Mon-Fri
- 💷 All the major cards
- 🛏 4 en suite suites
- 🅿 Car park, function room
- 🎵 Saturday carvery & cabaret
- ❓ Neath Abbey, Neath 1 mile, Aberdulais Falls 4 miles, Port Talbot 4 miles

THE GOYTRE ARMS

PENPERLLENI, MONMOUTHSHIRE NP4 0AH

TEL: 01873 880376

Directions: In the village of Penperlleni, adjacent to the A4042 midway between Abergavenny and Pontypool.

The premises now occupied by **The Goytre Arms** were originally three cottages, and later an ale shop, a carpenter's shop and a blacksmith's. They date back to the late 18th century, and the well cared for public rooms have a simple, traditional appeal. Wadsworth 6X, Worthington and a guest are the three real ales served, and there's also a full range of draught and bottle beers and lagers, stout and ciders. David, his sister Norma and his niece Tracey have been here as leaseholders since the end of 2001. Tracey and Norma have raised the status of the inn to one of the best places in the area to seek out for good food. The menu, which is changed to compliment the seasons, is available every lunchtime and evening with the exception of Sunday evening during the winter months.

The restaurant seats 65, and food can also be taken in the lounge and bar areas. Booking is recommended at the weekend to be sure of a table. Some dishes are traditional pub classics, while others have a more contemporary ring, and there's always plenty of choice for everyone, including vegetarian optios and a 'Light Bite' selection. Children are very welcome, and the large rear gardens include a secure play area. The inn has baby changing and disabled facilities, and the bar is accessible to visitors in wheelchairs. Abergavenny is an easy drive north along the A4042, while the same road leads south to Pontypool. Those two towns are well worth taking time to explore, but for lovers of the great outdoors the area round the village is great walking country.

- 🕐 12-3 & 6-11
- 🍴 A la carte
- 💷 Amex, Mastercard, Visa
- 🅿 Car park
- 🎵 Occasional musical evenings
- @ goytrearms@tiscall.co.uk
- ❓ Pontypool 5 miles, Abergavenny 6 miles, Blaenavon 7 miles

THE MONKEY TREE

GORDON ROAD, BLACKWOOD, GWENT NP12 1DS
TEL: 01495 230240 FAX: 01495 223342

South Wales

> **Directions:** Blackwood is on the A4048 about 8 miles south of Tredegar. From the centre of Blackwood follow Gordon Road (no through road) up the hill; the inn is on the right.

Known locally as Plas Newydd, this former farmhouse was once owned by the notorious Captain Henry Morgan. It became **The Monkey Tree** in 1997 and has been run for the past two years by Lynwen and Jeff Lacey and their son Chris (Chris also holds the lease of the Crown Inn on the main street of Merthyr Tydfil). Behind a distinctive grey-washed facade, the Monkey Tree has abundant style and character, with beams, panelling and well-chosen prints and ornaments contributing to the traditional look. This is a very popular place for food, which is served in the spacious restaurant or in the lounge bar every session except Sunday evening. Some of the dishes on the restaurant menu are familiar classics such as garlic mushrooms, grilled steaks and

braised lamb shanks, while others add an imaginative dimension to old favourites: trout with pesto and parmesan crumble, salmon fillet with cheese and chives, oriental pork escalope with rice, broccoli and brie rösti.

Alternatively, the bar menu offers sandwiches, jacket potatoes and hot dishes like liver & onions, cod fillet or Yorkshire pudding with a beef and horseradish filling. Booking are needed for Saturday night and Sunday lunchtime, and also for the monthly dinner dance. The Monkey Tree has 17 comfortable en suite guest bedrooms of various sizes, including one family room. Children are very welcome, and they have a play area in the garden. There's something going on most nights of the week: a quiz on Wednesday, musical entertainment on Friday and Saturday, karaoke/disco on Sunday. The large function room is a popular venue for special occasions.

- 🕐 12-11
- 🍴 Bar and à la carte menus
- 💷 Mastercard, Visa
- 🛏 17 en suite rooms
- 🅿 Car park, children's play area
- 🎵 Quiz Wed, music Fri & Sat, karaoke/disco Sun
- @ claceypubs@aol.com
- ❓ Caerphilly Castle 7 miles, Pontypool 7 miles, Risca (Fourteen Locks Canal Centre) 7 miles

THE MOUNT PLEASANT INN & RESTAURANT

PENDERYN ROAD, HIRWAUN, ABERDARE CF44 9RT
TEL: 01685 811944

Directions: From J43 of the M4 take the A465 to Hirwaun then the A4059 Brecon road. The inn is about 200 yards along this road on the left.

Three cottages dating from 1810 have been converted to form the **Mount Pleasant Inn & Restaurant**, which stands just north of Hirwaun at the gateway to the Brecon Beacons National Park. Behind the long, low, white-painted frontage the bars and restaurants have totally refurbished by licensees Mike Fisher and Leanne Pitt, who both have considerable experience in the licensed trade. In the spacious, comfortable bars and lounges a full range of beers, wines and spirits is served, and in the restaurant award-winning chef Lee Modrate keeps the customers happy with his exceptional cooking. Lee, originally from Penywaun (just along the road), gained experience at top hotels in London and Manchester as well as with the British Culinary Olympics Team

before returning to Wales, and his skill and expertise shine through in every dish.

The choice really is mouthwatering, with dishes ranging from smoked chicken and ham terrine to pan-fried breast of duck with cinnamon and black cherries, fillets of plaice topped with a crab mousse served on a saffron sauce, and pink-roasted rump of lamb served on a celeriac cake with a mint-flavoured sauce. The restaurant is open Wednesday to Saturday evenings and for Sunday lunch, and bar meals (also with a great choice) are served Tuesday to Saturday from midday to 9 o'clock in the evening. Mike and Leanne have big plans for the extensive grounds of the inn, including the landscaping of the lawns and beer garden and the creation of a boating lake. Also in the pipeline are a beer festival and open-air summer concerts.

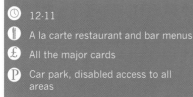

🕐 12-11

🍽 A la carte restaurant and bar menus

£ All the major cards

Ⓟ Car park, disabled access to all areas

♫ Beer festival, open-air concerts

? Brecon Beacons National Park, Garwnant Forest Centre 5 miles

THE MOUNTAIN AIR INN

LLWYN HELYG, NANTYBWCH, TREDEGAR, GWENT NP22 3SD

TEL/FAX: 01495 723116

Directions: From Abergavenny or Merthyr Tydfil take the A465; where this road meets the A4048 on the outskirts of Tredegar take the Trefil turn and find the inn on the right 200 yards along, at the Head of the Valleys.

The **Mountain Air Inn** enjoys a scenic location at the Head of the Valleys a short drive north of Tredegar. Originally a farm and cottages dating back to the mid-17th century, the buildings were converted into an ale house in the following century and became today's inn midway through Queen Victoria's reign. The place has been given a new lease of life by Sian and Joe Elliot, who took over the reins early in 2002. Sian is a local lady, and her father was actually born at the inn. In the delightfully old-world bar and lounge, with a real fire and lots of memorabilia around the walls, Hancocks HB heads the list of drinks, while in the separate non-smoking dining room local produce is prominent in home-cooked dishes chosen from the printed menu or the specials

board. Lasagne, steaks and beef in red wine are among the dishes that have made the inn a very popular place to visit.

Children are welcome if eating, and booking is necessary for Saturday dinner and Sunday lunch. Food is not available on Sunday or Monday evenings. This most convivial of inns is open every lunchtime and evening, and all day when there's a rugby international. On Wednesday evenings the bar resounds with lusty Welsh voices singing along to an accordion, while on Thursday evenings brains are brought into tune for the weekly quiz that starts at 9 o'clock. The Mountain Air Inn is a short distance from Tredegar, famous as the birthplace of Aneurin Bevan. Among the visitor attractions here are a colliery museum and a 600-acre country park with a man-made lake and an abundance of wildlife.

- 🕐 12-3 & 6-11, open all day on Rugby international days
- 🍴 A la carte
- 🅿 Car park
- 🎵 Singalong Wednesday, quiz Thursday
- ❓ Elliot Colliery Winding House 1 mile, Bryn Bach Country Park 1 mile, Ebbw Vale 2 miles

THE NORTH GATE INN

A48 CHEPSTOW ROAD, CAERWENT, MONMOUTHSHIRE NP26 5NZ
TEL: 01291 425292

> **Directions:** The inn is situated on the main A48 at Caerwent, 5 miles west of Chepstow.

Set back from the main A48 between Newport and Chepstow, the **North Gate Inn** is a handsome white-painted building dating back some 60 years. Well furnished and smartly decorated throughout, the inn is in the capable hands of leaseholders Kevin and Lynette Blanks, both of them born and raised in nearby Newport. Both of them cook, and there are separate menus for lunch and dinner, with the daily changing specials board providing additional choice. Everything is good, but the home-made curries are at the top of the popularity stakes, particularly in the cooler months. Two real ales are available - Hancocks HB and a rotating guest - as well as a full range of draught and bottle beers, stouts, lagers and cider. Traditional pub games are played in the bar, and the inn has its own golf team,

The Nags, which always welcomes new members.

The inn is a mere baby compared with some other buildings in Caerwent. Adjacent to it are the ruins of the North Gate (hence the name) that once surrounded the Roman city of Venta Silurum. Sections of the Roman defences still remain and are some of the best preserved in Britain. Among other sites of interest nearby is the Norman Caldicot Castle, and on the way to Chepstow is the renowned St Pierre Golf Club, where many top championship events have been staged over the years, including the Dunlop Masters and Silk Cut Masters, the Epson matchplay and strokeplay tournaments and the Curtis and Solheim Cups. Chepstow itself is best known for its castle, its racecourse and as one end of Offa's Dyke.

- 🕐 12·11
- 🍴 A la carte
- 💷 Mastercard, Visa
- 🅿 Car park
- ❓ Caldicot 2 miles, Chepstow 5 miles, St Pierre Golf Club 3 miles

THE OLD FERRY INN

BEACHLEY, NR CHEPSTOW, MONMOUTHSHIRE NP17 7HH
TEL: 01291 622474 FAX: 01291 628094

Directions: Follow the A48 out of Chepstow until you pass the English border sign. Take the next right turn, signposted Sedbury and Beachley. Follow this road for 2 miles into Beachley; the inn is on the left next to the mouth of the Severn Estuary.

The Old Ferry Inn has a history going back to the early 17th century, and in its time it has been a customs house and a vicarage. It stands by the slipway from which the ferry used to cross the River Severn before the bridge was built in 1962. Owned and run since the summer of 2002 by Linda and Murray, the inn enjoys a magnificent setting in the shadow of the bridge with unbeatable views in all directions. It's open all day for drinks, which include Freeminers cask ale brewed in the Forest of Dean and two draught ciders. And at most times of day there's something good to eat, from morning coffee through lunch to afternoon tea and evening meals (last orders 10pm).

The main menu runs from baguettes with a range of hot and cold fillings to creamy garlic mushrooms, hot smoked mackerel and traditional pub favourites such as sausage 'n' mash, deep-fried haddock, chicken curry and the puff-pastry-topped pie of the day. Other popular choices are the chargrills and the salad bowls, and the home-made cheesecake rounds off a feast in fine style. The restaurant and part of the lounge are non-smoking. With the A48, the M48 and the M4 all within easy reach, the inn is a great base for touring, and its 11 letting bedrooms are available all year round. They range from singles to family rooms, and three have en suite facilities. Children and dogs are welcome.

- 🕐 12-11, closed Monday except Bank Holidays
- 🍴 A la carte and snacks
- £ All the major cards
- 🛏 11 rooms, 3 en suite
- 🅿 Car park
- @ www.theoldferry.co.uk
- ❓ Chepstow 2 miles

RHYD Y BLEW

RASSAU ROAD, BEAUFORT, EBBW VALE, GWENT NP23 5PW
TEL/FAX: 01495 308935

> **Directions:** Beaufort is situated on the A4047 2 miles east of Ebbw Vale, very close to the main A465 Abergavenny-Merthyr Tydfil road.

'A great pub with lots going on.' That's the proud and thoroughly justified boast of the Squire family, who have breathed new life into the **Rhyd y Blew Inn** since acquiring the lease in the autumn of 2000. Three real ales - Wadsworth 6X, a weekly guest ale, Brains 'Skull Attack' SA, with Stella Artois, Castlemaine XXXX and Strongbow the house lagers and cider, head the list of liquid sustenance. Ron and Corrina will see that no one goes hungry with their tasty, well-priced and varied bar menu. Sandwiches, jacket potatoes and prawns (cocktail or mayonnaise) are among the lighter bites, while main dishes run from burgers to the very popular Spicy Cajun Chicken burger, chilli con carne, gammon, breaded scampi and steak & kidney pie served with peas and gravy. Children are welcome in the pub for

meals. Lunch is served 12-2 daily. Speciality evenings are held every month on a Saturday, sampling cuisine the world over, usually 4 courses plus coffee. Numbers for these popular occasions are strictly limited, so advance booking is necessary.

All the major sporting action can be followed on Sky Digital, and regular weekly entertainment includes Quizgo (£50 J pot) and the Millionaire quiz (J pot is produced from ticket sales - the biggest so far was £332). Quizzes start at 8.30pm every Sunday evening. There is a disco on Wednesday and live music on most Fridays and Saturdays. The enterprising and hard-working Squires - Corrina, Ron and their children - have more plans for the inn which include a new restaurant with evening service and a large conservatory/function room for important occassions.

- 🕐 12-3 & 6-11, open all day Sat & Sun
- 🍴 Lunchtime bar meals and snacks
- 💷 All major cards. Cash-back service
- 🅿 Car park
- 🎵 Quiz Sunday, Disco Wednesday
- @ e-mail: cookrjs@easynet.co.uk
  web: squireinns.co.uk
- ❓ Brecon Beacons National Park 2 miles, Ebbw Vale 2 miles, Tredegar 3 miles, Abergavenny 7 miles

THE ROSE & DAFFODIL

43 HEOL TWRCH, CWMTWRCH ISAF, SWANSEA SA9 2TD

TEL: 01639 830067

Directions: From J45 of the M4 take the A4067 to the roundabout at Gurnos, then the A4068 towards Cwmllynfell. The pub is half a mile along this road.

Good hospitality, good conversation and good food are among the chief assets of the **Rose & Daffodil**, a traditional Welsh pub with a welcome for all the family. Owners Paula and Adrian, who took over at the end of 2002, have quickly made this one of the best eating places for miles around, and a very pleasant spot to pause for refreshment. A coal fire blazes merrily in the roomy bar, where a counter in striking modern style dispenses a good range of ales, including a weekly changing guest.

Paula and Adrian (who is an Award winning chef) offer a wide selection of traditional and creative home-cooked dishes using fresh local produce as much as possible. Baguettes with interesting

🕐 12-11, Sun to 10.30; winter 12-3 & 6-11, all day weekend

🍴 A la carte and bar snacks

🅿 Car park at front, children's playground

🎵 Children's drawing competition monthly

❓ Dan-yr-Ogof Showcaves, Dinosaur Park, Shire Horse Centre, Craig-y-Nos Country Park & Castle 4 miles

fillings such as chicken fillet with tomato and garlic pesto make tasty, satisfying snacks, and other dishes - the blackboard selection changes daily - run from duck and pork terrine with a spiced orange compote to roast sea bass with Thai spices, savoury pies, gammon steak with roast sweet figs, and steaks with a choice of sauces - paté and Madeira, black pepper & brandy, Stilton & red wine. Excellent wines complement the fine food. Children have their own menu and an outdoor play area, and each month a children's drawing competition is held and the winning entry framed and displayed on the wall of a long corridor at the back of the pub. The Rose & Daffodil fields pool and darts teams in the local leagues, and all the big sporting events are shown on Sky TV.

THE SKIRRID MOUNTAIN INN

LLANVIHANGEL CRUCORNEY, ABERGAVENNY,
MONMOUTHSHIRE NP7 8DH
TEL/FAX: 01873 890258

> **Directions:** The inn is signposted off the A465 about 5 miles north of Abergavenny.

Easily reached off the A465 north of Abergavenny, the **Skirrid Mountain Inn** has sound claims to being the oldest pub in Wales. It is recorded that a certain John Crowther was tried here for sheep stealing in 1110, and his brother for robbery with violence. John was hanged from a beam at the inn and his brother sent to prison. Owain Glyndwr is also said to have marshalled his troops in the cobbled courtyard before marching on Pontrilas. The mounting stone on to which he climbed, and which is thought to have been used by many royals, can still be seen in the yard. Run since December 2002 by Maria Appleton and her partner, chef Daryl Hardy, the inn is rich not only in history but also in

hospitality and old-world charm. Iin the bar original Welsh slate floors, ancient oak settles and a collection of beaten copper ware add to a lovely setting for enjoying a glass or two of one of the real ales always on tap. The oak beams are made from ships' timbers and the wooden panelling in the non-smoking dining room is said to have come from a British man o' war. Daryl produces top-class dishes for all tastes, including the popular Skirrid Mountain vegetarian loaf, but his real specialities are the dishes based on the excellent local meat and fish - Welsh Mountain lamb and Black Mountain rainbow trout are particular favourites. The inn has three outstanding en suite guest rooms, one a family room, two with four-poster beds. A full Welsh breakfast starts the day. There is a large car park and beer garden.

- ⏱ 12-11
- 🍴 Traditional dishes
- 💷 Mastercard, Visa
- 🛏 3 en suite rooms
- 🅿 Car park
- 🎵 Live music one Saturday a month
- @ e-mail: mistyspooks@aol.com website: www.skirridmountaininn.co.uk
- ❓ Abergavenny (Castle, museums) 5 miles; Offa's Dyke, Brecon Beacons, walking

THE SOMERSET ARMS

COMMERCIAL ROAD, TAIBACH, PORT TALBOT, NEATH SA13 1LP
TEL: 01639 875051   FAX: 01639 898620

Directions: From the M4, J40, take the A4107 Abbey Road and turn left at the traffic lights at the T-junction. The pub is about 800 yards on the left.

A large, comfortable pub with a car park to the side, the **Somerset Arms** enjoys excellent support both from a loyal local clientele and from motorists looking for a break from their journey along the M4. The pub is owned and run by Craig Davies, who started in the trade as a part-time barman while taking a business studies course. He progressed to become a manager with Bass and bought the pub at the beginning of 2001. With the services of two excellent chefs, he has made the Somerset Arms a place to seek out for a really good meal, and in the alcoved eating area customers can take their pick from a wide-ranging menu that includes lasagne, home-made pies, fresh fish specials and a roast of the day.

Among the drinks dispensed at the long bar counter are two guest ales which are changed weekly. The pub has a large function room that's a popular choice for wedding receptions and other special occasions. All the major sports events are shown on a big-screen TV, and the pub has a pool table for 'in-house' entertainment. Thursday night is quiz night. Among the nearby places of interest are Margam Country Park, including the ruins of 13th century Margam Abbey; and the harbour and docks at Port Talbot. Originally called the Somersetshire House Inn, the pub dates back to 1774, when copper was first smelted in the local works and the first terraced houses were built in the village. The pub is also close to several beaches, and the M4 provides quick and easy access east and west.

- 🕐 12-11, Sun to 10.30
- 🍴 A la carte
- £ All except Amex
- Ⓟ Car park, including slots for disabled drivers
- 🎵 Quiz Thursday
- ❓ Margam Country Park and Abbey 2 miles, Port Talbot 2 miles.

THE STATION HOTEL

37 BRECON ROAD, ABERGAVENNY, MONMOUTHSHIRE NP7 5UH
TEL: 01873 854759

South Wales

Directions: The Station Hotel is located on the western outskirts of Abergavenny, a short walk from the centre.

Built around 1850, the **Station Hotel** stood alongside the railway that used to run between Abergavenny and Merthyr Tydfil. That branch line no longer exists - a victim of Dr Beeching's axe in the 1960s and the Station Hotel is no longer a hotel. It's a cheerful local pub that's been run since November 2002 by Malcolm and Elizabeth Woods and their son Matthew; Malcolm was born just a stone's

throw from the premises and used it as his local from 1989 until moving from one side of the bar to the other. Bass, Tetleys, London Pride and Hancocks HB provide plenty of choice for real ale fans, and there's a good choice of other beers both draught and bottled. Those in need of something solid to accompany their drinks can order freshly made sandwiches

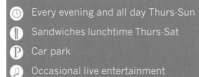

- 🕐 Every evening and all day Thurs-Sun
- 🍴 Sandwiches lunchtime Thurs-Sat
- 🅿 Car park
- 🎵 Occasional live entertainment
- ❓ Abergavenny Castle and Museums, Blaenavon (Big Pit Mine, Ironworks, Pontypool & Blaenavon Railway) 6 miles, Monmouth 12 miles

at lunchtime on Thursday, Friday and Saturday. Darts and cribbage are among the games played in the bar, and the pub hosts occasional nights of live entertainment.

There's a car park at the back of the premises. The thriving market town of Abergavenny is a pleasant place for a stroll and has two interesting museums; one, in the grounds of the Castle, deals with local history, the other, just down the road, is a museum of childhood. The town is also an excellent base for touring the Brecon Beacons National Park. Walking, pony trekking and canal cruising can all be enjoyed nearby, and a little way south of town the 1,840ft Blorenge is a popular tourist spot.

THE SWAN INN

128 BRIDGEND ROAD, ABERKENFIG, BRIDGEND CF32 9AE
TEL: 01656 725612

Directions: From J36 of the M4 take the A4063. Go through the traffic lights and straight over thr roundabout on to the B4281. Turn left after 200 yards into Aberkenfig South. The pub is on the right hand side.

A bright blue and orange frontage proclaims a warm Valleys welcome at **The Swan Inn**, which was built as a pub in 1906. Inside, the look is traditional, with beams, a brick-fronted bar counter and plenty of chairs, banquettes and neatly arranged tables. Above the stone hearth is a framed photograph of the inn. Real ales are among the wide range of drinks dispensed at the bar, where the day's food specials are also listed. The pub's owners are Gareth and Emma Edwards, who have the services of an excellent chef who has helped to make The Swan a popular local choice for anyone looking for a tasty, satisfying home-cooked meal.

Topping the popularity stakes are his savoury pies and curries, lasagne and a mighty 20oz mixed grill that will cope with even the largest appetite. The fish specials are always a good bet, too, and vegetarians usually have a choice of four main courses. Children can choose from their own menu, and visitors with less time or smaller appetites can snack on a filled roll or a burger. Major sports events are shown on a large-screen tv, and regular entertainment at this very sociable place include a quiz on Monday, karaoke on Wednesday and live music on Thursday. The Swan is an ideal place to take a break on a motorway journey, and in the vicinity are plenty of attractions; among those very close by are the Tondu Heritage Centre and Bryngarw Country Park, a secluded park with meadows, lake, woodland and a delightful Japanese garden.

- 🕐 11-11
- 🍴 A la carte + snacks
- £ All the major cards
- 🅿 Car park
- 🎵 Quiz Monday, Karaoke Wednesday, Live music Thursday
- ❓ Tondu Heritage Park and Parc Slip Nature Reserve 1 mile, Bryngarw Country Park 2 miles, Bridgend 3 miles

THE SWAN INN

WEST ROAD, NOTTAGE, PORTHCAWL, BRIDGEND CF36 3SS
TEL: 01656 782568

Directions: From J37 of the M4 take the A4229 towards Porthcawl. Turn right at the third island. 100 yards on, turn right again into the village of Nottage. The Swan is on the left.

The cheerful red and white exterior of **The Swan** promises abundant hospitality within, and owners Julie and Jeff Jenkins provide the warmest of Welsh welcomes for all their customers, whether they are regulars or new faces. Jeff played rugby for Bridgend and Aberavon for 18 seasons, and one corner of the bar is filled with rugby photographs and memorabilia. The other end is richly traditional, with bare stone walls covered with an impressive, gleaming collection of brass plates and ornaments. In between, the long bar counter, topped with shelves of Toby jugs and china plates, dispenses a fine selection of real ales in addition to the usual beers and lagers, wines and spirits.

Food is an important part of the business at The Swan, and the owners are rightly proud of the generous portions and excellent value for money; among the favourites are the home-made pies and curries and a mixed grill that really fills the plate; there are always main courses for vegetarians, and children can be served half-portions. Food for thought is provided by the popular Sunday quiz, and visitors to The Swan can always be sure of some good conversation - and not just about rugby! Just minutes from the motorway, The Swan is a perfect place to take a break on a journey, and for those with more time the area has plenty to offer. Porthcawl has broad, sandy beaches and opportunities for sailing, surfing, fishing and golf, as well as an amusement park and a historic harbour.

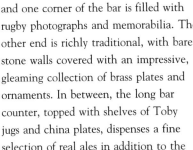

🕐 11.30-11, Sun 12-10.30

🍴 A la carte

🅿 Off-road parking

🎵 Quiz Sunday

❓ Porthcawl 1 mile, Kenfig National Nature Reserve 2 miles, Margam Country Park, Abbey Church and Museum 6 miles,

THE WEST END

1 WEST STREET, GORSEINON, SWANSEA SA4 4AA
TEL: 01792 894217

Directions: From J47 of the M4 take the A4240 to Gorseinon. The West End is located on the left in the centre of the town.

Dating from 1875, **The West End** is a substantial brick building that curves round a corner site in the middle of Gorseinon. Behind the rendered frontage the spacious interior combines original and modern features to pleasing effect, with high Victorian ceilings, some slatted oak floorboards and a smart brick-faced bar counter. In his eight years as proprietor of the pub, Alun Gwenter has made many improvements to the look of the place, and is always seeking ways to improve the facilities. The bar is well stocked with draught and bottle beers, and a good selection of wines is available by glass or bottle.

Alun is fortunate to have the services of an excellent chef who insists on the best local produce for his dishes. Breaded garlic mushrooms, steaks, roast chicken, cod in batter, and salmon with lemon butter are among the classics on the printed menu, along with lasagne in meat or vegetarian form, and the choice is extended by the daily changing specials board: favourites with the regular customers include liver & bacon, corned beef pie and steak & ale pie, and the traditional Sunday lunch is always popular. For those in a hurry or with a smaller appetite, freshly made rolls, toasted sandwiches, filled jacket potatoes and omelettes fit the bill admirably. There's a pool table in the bar, and a DJ spins his selections every Friday and Saturday. For private parties, receptions and other special occasions, the pub has a capacious upstairs function room with space for up to 150. The West End is a very pleasant and convenient place to pause on a journey along the M4 or before embarking on a tour of the lovely Gower Peninsula.

🕐 11-11, Sun 12-10.30

🍴 A la carte

🅿 Car park at side, Function Room

🎵 DJ Friday & Saturday

❓ Swansea 4 miles, Llanelli 4 miles, Gower Peninsula 3 miles

THE WINGFIELD

WINGFIELD TERRACE, LLANBRADACH, NR CAERPHILLY CF83 3NT
TEL: 02920 884165 FAX: 02920 883305

> **Directions:** From J32 of the M4 take the A470 Pontypridd road. Turn right on to the A468 Caerphilly road then left on to the A469. Turn left at the second roundabout; the inn is about 200 yards along on the left.

Standing on its own and backed by the open countryside of the Rhymney Valley, **The Wingfield** is a very distinctive late-Victorian building of close-set stone. In the large, comfortable lounge, the wood-panelled bar is well stocked with drinks, including Thomas Watkins Whoosh and Welsh Bitter. To the side of the lounge is a smartly appointed restaurant where diners can enjoy the excellent cooking of Neil Wright, who owns the inn with his wife Sue. Neil and his enthusiastic team of kitchen staff prepare and cook everything on the premises, with nothing bought in and no short cuts, with the result that the inn has built up a strong following as one of the best eating places in the region. Charcoal grilled steaks and the Sunday roasts are always very popular, along with the bargain two-meal menu that is offered at lunchtime Monday to Friday.

The specials board changes daily, offering such dishes as tempura prawns with a sweet and sour sauce, breaded plaice or chicken Kiev. There's always a good choice of vegetarian dishes, as well as a children's menu and a snack menu. Food is served every lunchtime and evening and all day on Sunday. The inn has plenty of off-road parking, a beer garden with seats for 60 and a function room that can hold up to a 100 for a party or other special occasion. Theme nights are held from time to time, and every month, on a Friday, there's a karaoke session. The inn is located just a few miles north of Caerphilly, a town dominated by the magnificent castle, one of the finest surviving examples of medieval military architecture in Europe.

- 11-11, Sun 12-10.30
- A la carte + snacks
- All the major cards
- Car park
- Monthly karaoke
- Caerphilly Castle 3 miles

ALPHABETICAL LIST
OF PUBS AND INNS

E

F

G

K

L

M

N

O

P

R

S

T

V

W

Accommodation

Accommodation

All Day Opening

NORTH WALES BORDERLANDS

NORTH WEST WALES

POWYS

SOUTH WEST WALES

SOUTH WEST WALES (Cont.)

SOUTH WALES

Childrens Facilities

NORTH WEST WALES

The Douglas Inn	Tregele, Caemes Bay, Isle of Anglesey	56
Gaerwen Arms	Gaerwen, Isle of Anglesey	57
The Parciau Arms	Marian-Glas, Benllech, Isle of Anglesey	64

POWYS

The New Inn	Llanbadarn Fynydd,Powys	103
The Oak	Guilsfield, Welshpool, Powys	104
The Lord Nelson Inn	Kidwelly, Carmarthenshire	152
The Milton Brewery Inn	Milton, Tenby, Pembrokeshire	155

SOUTH WALES

The Bear Inn	Llantrisant, Pontyclun, Vale of Glamorgan	186
The Carne Arms	Llysworney, Cowbridge, Vale of Glamorgan	189
The Goytre Arms	Penperlleni, Monmouthshire	193
The Monkey Tree	Blackwood, Gwent	194
The Rose & Daffodil	Cwmtwrch Isaf, Swansea, Swansea	200

SPECIAL INTEREST LISTS

Credit Cards Accepted

NORTH WALES BORDERLANDS

The Crown Inn	Pant-y-Mwyn, Mold, Flintshire	24
The Drovers Arms	Rhewl, Ruthin, Denbighshire	25
The Eagle & Child Inn	Gwaenysgor, Rhyl, Flintshire	26
The Red Lion Country Inn	Llanasa, Holywell, Flintshire	28
Tyn-Y-Capel Inn	Minera, Wrexham, Denbighshire	29
Wynnstay Arms Hotel	Ruthin, Denbighshire	31

NORTH WEST WALES

Ael-Y-Bryn Hotel	Dyffryn Ardudwy, Gwynedd	54
The Bridge Inn Conwy	Conwy, Conwy	55
The Douglas Inn	Tregele, Caemes Bay, Isle of Anglesey	56
Gaerwen Arms	Gaerwen, Isle of Anglesey	57
The Gwydyr Hotel	Betws -y-Coed, Conwy	59
Kings Arms	Holyhead, Isle of Anglesey	60
The Kinmel Arms	St George, Abergele, Conwy	61
Liverpool Arms Hotel	Beaumaris, Isle of Anglesey	62
The Parciau Arms	Marian-Glas, Benllech, Isle of Anglesey	64
Penrhyn Old Hall	Penrhyn Bay, Llandudno, Conwy	66
Plas Coch Hotel & Restaurant	Bala, Gwynedd	67
The Red Lion Hotel	Llansannan, Denbigh, Conwy	68
Rhiw Goch Gwynedd	Bronaber, Trawsfynydd, Blaenau Ffestiniog, 69	
The White Eagle	Rhoscolyn, Isle of Anglesey	73

POWYS

The Angel	Llanidloes, Powys	94
The Bull Hotel	Presteigne, Powys	95
The Castle Inn	Pengenffordd, Talgarth, Powys	96
The Corn Exchange	Crickhowell, Powys	97
The Crown Inn	Montgomery, Powys	98
The George & Dragon	Knighton, Powys	99
The Glansevern Arms	Pantmawr, Llangurig, Powys	100
The Green Inn	Llangedwyn, Oswestry, Powys	101
Lowfield Inn	Marton, Welshpool, Powys	102
The New Inn	Llanbadarn Fynydd, Llandrindod Wells, Powys	103
The Oak	Guilsfield, Welshpool, Powys	104
The Old Ford Inn	Llanhamlach, Brecon, Powys	105
The Railway Inn	Forden, Welshpool, Powys	106

POWYS (Cont.)

The Star Inn	Dylife, Llanbrynmair, Powys	108
Stonecroft Inn	Llanwrtyd Wells, Powys	109
Triangle Inn	Cwmdauddwr, Rhayader, Powys	110
The White Swan Inn	Llanfrynach, Brecon, Powys	111

SOUTH WEST WALES

The Angel Inn	Narberth, Pembrokeshire	134
The Begelly Arms	Begelly, Kilgetty, Pembrokeshire	135
Belle Vue Inn	Llanllwni, Llanybydder, Carmarthenshire	136
Black Lion Hotel	Llanybydder, Carmarthenshire	137
The Black Ox	Abergwili, Carmarthenshire	138
The Bridge Inn	Narberth, Pembrokeshire	140
The Carpenters Arms	Llechryd, Cardigan, Ceredigion	142
Emlyn Arms Hotel	Newcastle Emlyn, Carmarthenshire	148
The Golden Grove Arms	Llanarthne, Carmarthen, Carmarthenshire	150
Llwndafydd	Saron, Llandysul, Ceredigion	151
The Masons Arms	Haverfordwest, Pembrokeshire	153
The Milton Brewery Inn	Milton, Tenby, Pembrokeshire	155
The Old Cross Saws Inn	Pembroke, Pembrokeshire	156
The Taberna Inn	Herbrandston, Pembrokeshire	162
The Victoria Inn	Roch, Haverfordwest, Pembrokeshire	163

SOUTH WALES

The Angel Inn	Hendredenny, Caerphilly, Caerphilly	185
The Bear Inn	Llantrisant, Pontyclun, Vale of Glamorgan	186
The Bridgend Inn	Brynmawr, Gwent	187
The Carne Arms	Llysworney, Cowbridge, Vale of Glamorgan	189
The Crown Inn & Restaurant	Briton Ferry, Neath, Neath Port Talbot	191
Glyn Clydach Coach House	Neath Abbey, Neath, Neath Port Talbot	192
The Goytre Arms	Penperlleni, Monmouthshire	193
The Monkey Tree	Blackwood, Gwent	194
The Mount Pleasant Inn	Hirwaun, Aberdare, Rhondda Cynon Taff	195
The North Gate Inn	Caerwent, Monmouthshire	197
The Old Ferry Inn	Beachley, Chepstow, Monmouthshire	198
Rhyd-Y-Blew Inn	Beaufort, Ebbw Vale, Gwent	199
The Skirrid Mountain Inn	Llanvihangel Crucorney, Monmouthshire	201
The Somerset Arms	Taibach, Port Talbot, Neath Port Talbot	202
The Swan Inn	Aberkenfig, Bridgend, Bridgend	204
The Wingfield	Llanbradach, Caerphilly, Caerphilly	207

SPECIAL INTEREST LISTS

Garden, Patio or Terrace

NORTH WALES BORDERLANDS

The Butchers Arms	Rossett, Clwyd	23
The Drovers Arms	Rhewl, Ruthin, Denbighshire	25
The Eagle & Child Inn	Gwaenysgor, Rhyl, Flintshire	26

NORTH WEST WALES

The Giler Arms Hotel	Rhydlydan, Pentrefoelas, Betws-y-Coed, Conwy	58
Llanfair Arms	Llanfairfechan, Conwy	63
The Parciau Arms	Marian-Glas, Benllech, Isle of Anglesey	64
Penbont Inn	Llanrug, Gwynedd	65
The Red Lion Hotel	Llansannan, Denbigh, Conwy	68
The Swan Inn	Llanfair Talhaiarn, Conwy	71
The White Eagle	Rhoscolyn, Isle of Anglesey	73

POWYS

The Green Inn	Llangedwyn, Oswestry, Powys	101
Lowfield Inn	Marton, Welshpool, Powys	102
The New Inn	Llanbadarn Fynydd, Llandrindod Wells, Powys	103
The Oak	Guilsfield, Welshpool, Powys	104
The Old Ford Inn	Llanhamlach, Brecon, Powys	105
Stonecroft Inn	Llanwrtyd Wells, Powys	109
Triangle Inn	Cwmdauddwr, Rhayader, Powys	110
The White Swan Inn	Llanfrynach, Brecon, Powys	111

SOUTH WEST WALES

The Angel Inn	Narberth, Pembrokeshire	134
The Begelly Arms	Begelly, Kilgetty, Pembrokeshire	135
Black Lion Hotel	Llanybydder, Carmarthenshire	137
The Black Ox	Abergwili, Carmarthenshire	138
The Boncath Inn	Boncath, Pembrokeshire	139
The Bridge Inn	Narberth, Pembrokeshire	140
The Bunch of Grapes	Newcastle Emlyn, Carmarthenshire	141
The Carpenters Arms	Llechryd, Cardigan, Ceredigion	142
Caulfield's Hotel	Burry Port, Carmarthenshire	143
The Cross Inn	Penally, Tenby, Pembrokeshire	145
The Crown Inn	Tenby, Pembrokeshire	146
The Dragon Inn	Narberth, Pembrokeshire	147
The Ffynone Arms	New Chapel, Boncath, Pembrokeshire	149

Special Interest Lists

SOUTH WEST WALES (Cont.)

SOUTH WALES

SPECIAL INTEREST LISTS

Live Entertainment

SPECIAL INTEREST LISTS

Restaurant or Dining Area

NORTH WALES BORDERLANDS

The Bridge	Caergwrle, Wrexham, Clwyd	22
The Crown Inn	Pant-y-Mwyn, Mold, Flintshire	24
The Eagle & Child Inn	Gwaenysgor, Rhyl, Flintshire	26
Tyn-Y-Capel Inn	Minera, Wrexham, Denbighshire	29
The White Horse Inn	Bagillt, Flintshire	30
Wynnstay Arms Hotel	Ruthin, Denbighshire	31

NORTH WEST WALES

Ael-Y-Bryn Hotel	Dyffryn Ardudwy, Gwynedd	54
The Bridge Inn Conwy	Conwy, Conwy	55
The Douglas Inn	Tregele, Caemes Bay, Isle of Anglesey	56
Gaerwen Arms	Gaerwen, Isle of Anglesey	57
The Giler Arms Hotel	Rhydlydan, Pentrefoelas, Conwy	58
The Gwydyr Hotel	Betws -y-Coed, Conwy	59
Penrhyn Old Hall	Penrhyn Bay, Llandudno, Conwy	66
Plas Coch Hotel & Restaurant	Bala, Gwynedd	67
The Red Lion Hotel	Llansannan, Denbigh, Conwy	68
The Swan Inn	Llanfair Talhaiarn, Conwy	71
The Town House Café:Bar	Llandudno, Conwy	72

POWYS

The Angel	Llanidloes, Powys	94
The Bull Hotel	Presteigne, Powys	95
The Corn Exchange	Crickhowell, Powys	97
The George & Dragon	Knighton, Powys	99
The Glansevern Arms	Pantmawr, Llangurig, Powys	100
The Green Inn	Llangedwyn, Oswestry, Powys	101
Lowfield Inn	Marton, Welshpool, Powys	102
The Oak	Guilsfield, Welshpool, Powys	104
The Railway Inn	Forden, Welshpool, Powys	106
The Star Inn	Dylife, Llanbrynmair, Powys	108

SOUTH WEST WALES

The Begelly Arms	Begelly, Kilgetty, Pembrokeshire	135
The Black Ox	Abergwili, Carmarthenshire	138
The Bridge Inn	Narberth, Pembrokeshire	140
The Bunch of Grapes	Newcastle Emlyn, Carmarthenshire	141
The Carpenters Arms	Llechryd, Cardigan, Ceredigion	142

Restaurant or Dining Area

SOUTH WEST WALES (Cont.)

SOUTH WALES

PLACES OF INTEREST

ORDER FORM

To order any of our publications just fill in the payment details below and complete the order form. For orders of less than 4 copies please add £1 per book for postage and packing. Orders over 4 copies are P & P free.

Please Complete Either:

I enclose a cheque for £ [   ] made payable to Travel Publishing Ltd

Or:

Card No: [   ] Expiry Date: [   ]

Signature: [   ]

Name: [   ]

Address: [   ]

Tel no: [   ]

Please either send, telephone, fax or e-mail your order to:

Travel Publishing Ltd, 7a Apollo House, Calleva Park, Aldermaston, Berkshire RG7 8TN Tel: 0118 981 7777 Fax: 0118 982 0077
e-mail: karen@travelpublishing.co.uk

Hidden Places Regional Titles	Price	Quantity
Cambs & Lincolnshire	£7.99	
Chilterns	£7.99	
Cornwall	£8.99	
Derbyshire	£8.99	
Devon	£8.99	
Dorset, Hants & Isle of Wight	£8.99	
East Anglia	£8.99	
Gloucs, Wiltshire & Somerset	£8.99	
Heart of England	£7.99	
Hereford, Worcs & Shropshire	£7.99	
Highlands & Islands	£7.99	
Kent	£8.99	
Lake District & Cumbria	£8.99	
Lancashire & Cheshire	£8.99	
Lincolnshire & Notts	£8.99	
Northumberland & Durham	£8.99	
Sussex	£8.99	
Yorkshire	£8.99	

Hidden Places National Titles	Price	Quantity
England	£10.99	
Ireland	£10.99	
Scotland	£10.99	
Wales	£9.99	

Hidden Inns Titles	Price	Quantity
East Anglia	£5.99	
Heart of England	£5.99	
Lancashire & Cheshire	£5.99	
North of England	£5.99	
South	£5.99	
South East	£7.99	
South and Central Scotland	£5.99	
Wales	£7.99	
Welsh Borders	£5.99	
West Country	£7.99	
Yorkshire	£5.99	

Country Living Rural Guides	Price	Quantity
East Anglia	£9.99	
Heart of England	£9.99	
Ireland	£10.99	
Scotland	£10.99	
South of England	£9.99	
South East of England	£9.99	
Wales	£10.99	
West Country	£9.99	

Total Quantity [   ]

Post & Packing [   ] **Total Value** [   ]

READER REACTION FORM

The *Travel Publishing* research team would like to receive reader's comments on any visitor attractions or places reviewed in the book and also recommendations for suitable entries to be included in the next edition. This will help ensure that the *Hidden Inns Series* continues to provide its readers with useful information on the more interesting, unusual or unique features of each inn or place ensuring that their visit to the local area is an enjoyable and stimulating experience. To provide your comments or recommendations would you please complete the forms below and overleaf as indicated and send to:

**The Research Department, Travel Publishing Ltd,
7a Apollo House, Calleva Park, Aldermaston, Reading, RG7 8TN.**

Your Name:

Your Address:

Your Telephone Number:

Please tick as appropriate:

Comments ☐   Recommendation ☐

Name of Establishment:

Address:

Telephone Number:

Name of Contact:

READER REACTION FORM

Comment or Reason for Recommendation: